LIONS
&
TIGERS
&
BEARS
∞
OR I?

A Once Private Journal

SINCLAIR

Copyright © 2024 by Sinclair

All Rights Reserved.

No portion of this book may be reproduced or used in any manner without prior written permission from the author, except for the use of brief quotations in a book review.

Cover design: Sinclair

ISBN: 979-8-9915730-1-6

Published by Orchid Breath Press

This Is My Private Journal

The Names Are Different

Any Other Changes Are In Italics

PART 1

Or I?

INTRODUCTION

∞ 11-16-23 ♡

Thank you thank you thank you thank you thank you thank you. Thank you. Thank you. Thank you.

It's all real. All of it. Wow.

My Higher Self is always watching over me. Always has been. Always will be.

You made it through the test. Non resistance. Listen to your intuition.

ALWAYS BE ON THE LOOKOUT.

INSTINCT.

∞

(Journaling was what I was supposed to be doing after the experience. I'm realizing this using the intuition I was told to employ.)

We are at one with the Universe. Everything. Everything has Happened for a Reason. Everything that's been going on here has been real. This has been the journey. There is nothing to worry about. "Look up?"

Talked to Dad. Journaled about it. Was sitting there trying to finish writing the description of the INFJ Door Slam starting to kind of space out.

Was feeling a little anxious. Wasn't feeling that same feeling I'd had. Was starting to doubt. Wondering if I'd just been manic. Questioning whether it was the right thing to call Dad having just had so many realizations and wondering if it was going to affect my progress. I was worried.

I went to my room. Sitting on my bed thinking I'm going to journal when I hear a "voice" tell me to *meditate*. The suggestion rang true somehow? Kind of *a* semi-conscious understanding that was exactly what I needed to do then.

Was drawn to the idea of a Higher Self meditation. Why did I choose that particular one? Destiny. The Universe. My Higher Self. God.

AND THANK YOU.

Meditation starts as normal. In and out breaths begin to start the meditation. I'm feeling the need to really hum the darker energy out of my body. It's clearly working. I can feel the energy come out with the breath.

My body starts adjusting naturally. I'm in tune with what my body wants to do and where it wants to go. I follow without resisting. Body slouching. Head down. Slight adjustments. Deep breaths. Back of head feels pressure.

Bell dings at some point. Can't say for sure when.

The one thing I remember for sure is that at some point it felt like my head was moving outside my control. It was scanning around the room with my eyes closed and at some point locked into a very specific place with my now specifically relaxed posture in place.

Head looking straight ahead.

The meditation is ongoing. My eyes are closed and I feel the sensation of them kind of press more closely against my shut eyelids. I see a light but think it's just shadows in the room. It may have been.

The meditation begins talking about a bright sun (or something like that) coming towards me. Shapes start to move around. Not in an unusual way. Have seen this before when I close my eyes. I begin to get a sense though that I'm deep in the Universe. I do see some brighter spots but nothing clear. A bright ball forms. It's still somewhat obscured and not clearly anything. I wonder if it's the sun that's being discussed *in the guided meditation*. I'm unsure. The ball disappears. Three rings emanate from where it was towards me. The meditation is saying that the Higher Self is about to appear at that moment.

I see what I could only describe *as* looking deep into some sort of Universal abyss with "clouds" and "shapes" moving around. But in a way that could be confused for and which I was consciously interpreting as just shadows of the room. Somehow though I knew to be expecting more.

Or I?

The following series of events is very fuzzy. There's no way to tell for sure what was going on and it was so abstract it's hard to recount properly or explain. It's also quickly fading. I'm not sure exactly the order of things or really even what was going on but the only thing I know for sure that happened first is the first paragraph below. But this is my best retelling.

I started to see more concrete shapes but was questioning what I was seeing. At some point I see the lights in the room go out. Things started moving quicker. The faint shape of what looked like the side profile of a single eyeball with perfect beautiful eyelashes looking up at around a 45 degree angle appeared here and there. Shapes are popping in and out. It's all a little fuzzy. Then it kind of goes back to normal and I'm left questioning if these were just random images or something.

The meditation is continuing and what I'd experienced so far was absolutely the most intense meditation I'd ever had but you'd be hard pressed to say anything definitive happened. There's a "ding" or something signaling that the connection is going to be made and at that very second I get enveloped with the most intense body sensations. Hair on the back of my neck stands up. Flashing electricity type waves through my body. All sorts of things I can't describe. All I can say is that I was overcome with certainty that it was real. I let myself completely go to this.

I can feel that there are places my head wants to go. It was almost as if it was tuning a radio. All the while my head is moving around and this "tuning" is going on, I can see definitive shapes and shadow type patterns taking shape in my field of view. Some are moving themselves. Some are static and stay in place as my head moves.

My head would move around "on its own." Again, it felt that it was very clearly tuning to find the right frequency or something. I remember my head going back on the headboard and moving side to side kind of like it was trying to find the right pressure point. At this point I'm kind of questioning the validity of this *again* but as my head is moving side to side, it's like I could feel it was getting close to its spot when all of a sudden – BOOM – there is like a Rorschach inkblot test type explosion in my field of vision. Everything goes dark, and it's very clear that something else is going on.

At some point it's clear that my head is supposed to go straight down into my chest. Then right as it touches a fantastical series of images begin flashing and moving in my mind's eye. The Eye I saw earlier starts flashing around in different places. It's flashing mostly in side profile but every once in a while it would flash looking directly at me which connoted a very powerful feeling. I am transfixed, astonished, awestruck. Dumbfounded, grateful, shocked, and *now* certain this is real without a doubt in my very traditionally eager to question mind.

I was so in the moment that I'm not sure exactly the series of events that follow but this is my best attempt at putting them together.

I am put through a series of what I can only describe as a combination of energy clearings and "tests." They came in waves and there would be moments of respite in-between. I'm not sure who was testing who or what was testing what. There were times throughout where this "voice" would give me *guidance*. I can't remember if the meditation was even still talking at this point because I was so invested in what was going on. These "tests" would alternate between eyes closed and eyes opened. My eyes were closed in the beginning of this, I believe, at which point there were all sorts of things moving and changing in my field of view. This was always mostly blacks, greys, and whites of various shades and specificity of shape.

The first one was with my eyes closed and I don't remember much about that one. I don't know. I'm feeling like that was some sort of energy clearing or something. Don't remember specifically enough to comment on it. But I do remember continuing to see the Eye looking up like that's what it wanted me to do. At this point I start actively thinking. I notice that doing so causes all the images to slowly fade. I'm intuiting that the head needs to stay completely clear and no resistance or active thought is necessary or I will lose all of this.

I'm clearly not understanding what I'm supposed to do and am stuck. Luckily I didn't get frustrated and knew I just had to wait. I can feel the homeostasis of the whole thing starting to go off. I didn't "decide" to do anything but with eyes closed…

∞

INTUITION. And LIVE IN CONSCIOUSNESS.

DONT RESIST.

Or I?

EVERYTHING HAS HAPPENED FOR A REASON. YOU'RE ON THE RIGHT PATH.

GOLF BALL. (GOLF BALL SHREDDED PIECE?). MANY MANY LAYERS. Consciousness believes this is all responsible for poor performance in golf. Ohhhh that fucked up golf ball situation in that tournament is a core shame wound. Cheating.

LAYERS. THOUGHT GOLF RELATED AT FIRST BUT DIDN'T RING TRUE AS TIME WENT ON. CROSS SECTION CUT OUT AND HOLE DOWN IT. But not in the middle, on the side.

Eye throughout.

Triggers

GOLF CHEATING – Putting myself back in that same dissociative state to feel like it's ok.

EYE – The beautiful Eye is my Higher Self.

THERE WERE MANY OTHER EYES.

YELLOW SCARY EYES – Something about really being seen. Think actually really being seen. Because this person is so flawed.

GOBSTOPPER HOLE – Think this was maybe FMRI.

WEIRD ROUND BALL.

IS IVY THE EYE?

THE EYE WAS THERE THROUGHOUT THE ENTIRE THING – Is that her?

∞

RESONANT FREQUENCY – Is the consciousness. The whole thing yesterday was about getting in it.

DISSOCIATIVE IDENTITY DISORDER – This is what I have. Fuck I always knew it. I can be a totally different person with different people.

The house analogy – with the rooms. I'm always playing a role. That's why I'm so good at acting.

THE LIE – I think this whole thing may have been an elaborate lie to myself to absolve Ivy from guilt. I slipped into mania when I realized about attachment styles because I knew I had found the answer. Although I'm not sure.

MANIPULATIVE – I can be so manipulative.

VISION – Was it God OR mental break.

RELAXXXX INTO CONSCIOUSNESS.

THINK BRAIN IS STRUGGLING TO ADJUST TO NEW NORMAL RIGHT NOW AND IS VERY MUCH FIGHTING THE IDEA OF UNCERTAINTY. IT FEELS UNMOORED LIKE IT DOESN'T KNOW WHAT'S GOING ON.

THINK EVERY TIME I TOOK ACID I INTEGRATED. THINK *DURING* THE LAST TRIP *I* REALIZED I WAS FUCKED. BOTH *ON* SHROOMS & ACID.

ON ACID FELT HOW MY BRAIN WAS FUCKED UP. BUT DON'T KNOW IF OCD OR SOMETHING ELSE.

11-22-23

Flawed Perception

We all come from the same thing. We all are the same thing. Atoms. Stardust. Mystery. Magic. All of it. The creation. The destruction. The murder. The mayhem. The funerals. The births. The deaths. The worst. How can we live this way. What is it all for? It's for the mind.

It's for the body. It's for the spirit to become one. Those who have seen this know. Those who have not will question. Those who will not will never know. But just like any institution there is strength in numbers and the strength for us lies in this. This realization. This revelation. Is

Or I?

one that can't be undone and will never die. And just like any great empire, hubris eventually takes hold. When it does overexpansion is all but guaranteed to catalyze its demise. It's the greed of the whole enterprise – that insatiable need for more more more. Now now now. All. All. All. Mine, Mine. Mine. That undoes the false divine.

What does one do when fate meets its match – when we hide and hide and hide from the path. We see what we want and hate what we see. But all is lost through perception when the gaze is unkempt.

Watered seeds in the garden of our own discontent. This garden is your life! I know you didn't plant the seeds. None of us did. We all want a different garden. No one thinks their garden is perfect. What the fuck is wrong with us. If everyone likes everyone else's garden better and if no one likes their own garden, then who's garden is really the best. No one is fucking right. But worst of all is that whether we like our gardens or not, we all know deep down that we didn't grow them at all. That we're sitting here blaming it on the fucking seeds we didn't plant. Or the fact that the crops were already grown. And some of the ones you like didn't grow as much. And some of the ones you hate grew too much. And how some people keep killing some of your plants when you're not watching but you can't remember which ones. And now you don't even recognize the garden that was your whole fucking life…. Yea. That is sad. And it IS tough…

…

…

…

Start caring for one plant you love. Slowly. Little by little…

…

…

The best gardens come when all the plants get the same amount of water.

…

Then prune.

11-23-23

I've always been scared to be seen for who I am. That's my attachment style. My personality is what you see on top of that, which is the unknowable combination of the environment I grew up in and my genetic predisposition. It's the neurological phenotype. But I've always wanted more than anything to be known.

This is everything there is to know about me. No one else is at fault for anything in here. See my perception about everything was flawed so I was completely complicit in everything that happened. I created the situation with everyone else.

I'm approaching my biggest fear in writing this. But finally, for once and for all, I'm ready to be loved OR hated. But only so long as I'm being judged while being me.

So here I am.

Do your worst…

Or I?

CODE EDITOR

2-2-23

Firing Recap

My Last Boss' Justification
- Bad attitude (raised questions re: office return)
- Work suffered (simply untrue, no examples given when asked)
- Kept telling me I am unhappy (I've never said this, I told her it's unfair to make assumptions about my feelings)
- Complained about going to office (I never did, went every day with no complaint but when I asked questions they were met with extreme responses) 1 week notice as well
- Company going in a different direction & that I will thrive elsewhere
- She just wants me to be happy…
- Mentioned "setting boundary" with *Co-Worker* so I was obviously ratted on – I responded that situation with *Co-Worker* was not right – she then became concerned that I would talk to *Co-Worker*
- *Big Boss Actress* on board with this…

My Responses (very confused & shocked)
- How did work suffer? Mentioned *TV show* submission log (*she* could not provide examples)
- It's problematic that I was unable to ask questions without being attacked
- She's putting words in my mouth about not going to office – I went every day without complaint
- She can't know about mental state and I disagree about attitude – she just didn't like my questions
- I don't understand what I did wrong – no response/reason
- Thanked her for opportunity
- Not mentioned – there was no warning – this came out of nowhere

Totally Blindsided & Gaslit

2-18-23

Or I?

Well it happened, I told Ivy I have feelings for her. This was the Monday after the Superbowl *(2-13-23)* at *Her BFF's*. She said some things that really stung and that I wanted to confront her about but I couldn't do so without telling her the reason it hurt, the bigger issue, which is that I like her. I was hopeful going into it. I felt like we'd had such a great time in Park City and were connected more than ever before. When I told her, her first words were a shocked "OH NO." I was obviously wrong. It was a tough conversation after that. The past week has been rough. I keep feeling that I don't know that she told me everything. She said she thinks of me as a brother. I feel that there has to be more but maybe that's just hope and Ego talking. I need to accept this at face value and move on. That's the only way. Jump to today. Obviously things have been awkward in the apartment. I feel bad for making it so. Each day has been less awkward than the last but for some reason the normalcy bothers me. Maybe it's because the more normal things are, the further away the possibility of anything materializing becomes. There were some strange vibes today.

She wasn't here for most of the day. When I got back from the gym she was back and immediately started telling me about her problems, but there was something different about her tone. Some sort of wall was up. I engaged as normal as possible and the conversation flowed. Then she asked me to watch Fido while she's with *Boy Toy*… Fuck. I didn't realize what she was asking at first – that she'd be with him. She said it's so Fido isn't away for too long given her upcoming trip, but still. How heartless. I can't help but feel used with that. We didn't really talk much – barely at all – for the rest of the night sitting on opposite sides of the room. She seemed upset by the end. I don't know why. When going to bed I told her I would wake up to say goodbye. I don't know if that was a mistake… I'm just trying to be a good friend.

2-20-23

Crazy shitty travel day going on right now. Started with gratitude though. For some reason my alarm was set for the wrong time. Luckily Fido's barking woke me up. First and last time I will say that with gratitude. Anyways, made it on time, boarded the plane, and eventually had to deboard because the problems with the plane are too significant.

Started to think about my situation at home with some new flavors right now/yesterday. I feel like the situation is showing me some of Ivy's true colors, which I may have been blind to. On top of the fact that I was asked to watch Fido while she was with *Boy Toy* (IDK if saying yes was a mistake or not), she posted a very "I'm single and looking" post on Instagram. I don't expect her to act differently or anything, but that shit just strikes me as so insensitive to the situation. Like just take a fucking minute off from going out of your way to say that. The literal post was "I may come with the house… Depends on the buyer." This whole thing and the way she's handling it really makes me feel like she doesn't really give a shit about me or my feelings. And that may be the truth.

Through everything that's happening/with the whole picture, I very well may have dodged a serious bullet in life with this rejection.

2-24-23

Yesterday I hurt my butt in the gym. While doing the most basic core exercise there was a sharp pain. I think I pinched the sciatic nerve. It's hard to walk or do much of anything but I'll manage. The biggest bummer of all is that it keeps me from being able to ski with *An Old Friend*, who I haven't seen in forever.

Reflections
Yesterday – and over the past couple of days really – I've been in a highly avoidant place. Honestly it's understandable with everything that's been going on. But if I'm being critical of my behavior, I could be more engaged. Re: Ivy – I have not been dealing with this. What to do to move forward? Cannot have expectations of her. Cannot be acting in a way that's a reaction to rejection. But at the same time, you need to act in a way that's true to yourself. What are the boundaries to put in place? Are there any? The biggest perspective shift is centered around the reality that it doesn't make sense to be in to someone who isn't in to you. In your life you are the prize. That is the mentality that needs to inform everything. NOW. There is no waiting.

Career
I signed the release today. I'm free. I'm happy to be getting a month severance when they only offered me a week originally. That was really

Or I?

made possible through my privilege/Mom & Dad covering if things went wrong. But the most important thing is that I'm free... Now it's time to move forward. What to do? Over the past 3 weeks you've done very little. The best change you can make is to start taking baby steps each day. Happiness comes from solving problems – if you can solve this problem it will make you very happy. The best thing right now is that I can do anything I could possibly conceive of. The world is my oyster. Let's figure out how to crack it.

2-25-23

I feel better waking up today than I did yesterday. I think a lot of it has to do with keeping a journal and satisfying the goals I set out for myself. What could I have done better yesterday? I keep thinking about the guy that I didn't bitch out at the grocery store. I wish I'd have said something, but why? Would that have just been Ego? Me taking out my frustrations on someone else? It could have been those things for sure. I certainly didn't feel scared, I actually couldn't believe what I was seeing. He looked like an innocent, normal looking guy. The lesson in that is that anyone could be the bad apple. Don't judge a book by its cover. I love what I read in "Living Untethered" last night. It was talking about living in the moment and enjoying every moment to the fullest. It really is a miracle that we're even here. Stop trying to get the world to bend to your will and preferences, and instead make the most out of what's in front of you.

<u>Today</u>
Keep on the positive train as much as possible. Enjoy the day and time off. Fit a meditation in there somewhere. Eat a bit more disciplined – the bad eating has been weighing you down. And let's get on the track of reducing the caffeine consumption a bit as that's been weighing heavy on you for a while now. Enjoy the dogs, they're hilarious...

•

1. I am grateful for the principles I'm learning about in "Living Untethered" because they have the power to change my life.
2. I am grateful for the trials I am going through at the moment because they are providing me the opportunity to gain strength & to pass the life tests.

3. I am grateful to have had this time alone to have the chance to reflect & heal.
4. I am grateful for the miracle of this life – no matter how bad things get to be alive is the luckiest opportunity possible.

2-26-23

Today was a fucking crazy ski day. After being out of commission the last couple of days because of the pinched nerve, I really let it rip today. I set the fastest time of the year on various runs I went down today. On 2 of the runs I was top 10 fastest all time (Strava). Despite this, what I am most proud of today is actually a fall I had. Today was my first time ever skiing Chute 4. The cornice was huge and standing at the entrance of the run is scary as shit. The first 2 times down the run I dominated pretty hard. On the 3rd time down I took a massive and very scary spill. I was still at the very top of the run when I took a bad turn which ended up turning me around. I'm now skiing backwards down the hardest run on the mountain – a run that is elevator shaft narrow – with no idea whether I'm about to run into a tree or fall off a cliff. Knowing the danger I'm in, I thought it was hilarious that while still skiing backwards I calmly said "Uh Oh..." out loud. Luckily all's well that ends well as I fell without injury. After sliding halfway down the mountain to retrieve the ski that had ejected, I was both relieved & terrified about what had just happened. Using "Living Untethered" as inspiration, I knew that I had to face the fear head on so I made myself redo the run immediately. While acknowledging and embracing the fear – which was very real – I crushed the chute again. I was proud.

2-28-23

I'm struggling with how to deal right now. Ivy just got home and I'm freaking out a bit. I have nothing to say to bridge this gap. What would the books say? "Living Untethered" *by Michael Singer* – Watch the emotions. Anxious, fearful, lost. Accept them for what they are. Things may never be the same. That's OK! Use this to make sure no samskaras take hold. Let the emotions pass. "The Subtle Art of Not Giving a Fuck" *by Mark Manson* – Care about the right things. I care about this relationship.

Don't let it die. Be who you are right now. *"The Power of Now" by Eckhart Tolle* – There is only now. Take advantage of it. Don't get caught up in Ego. I am caught up in the Ego right now. Unconditional love. *"The Tools" by Phil Stutz & Barry Michels* – The Mother. The Tower. Only those who die can truly live. *"A Manual for Manifesting Your Dream Life" by Eric John Campbell* – We are best friends. We are cool. Everything is going to be alright. Pure love.

The now can be found in the space between silence. The now can be found in the space in the Universe.

Time heals all wounds.

The real job search starts tomorrow.

3-2-23

The situation with Ivy is killing me right now. I oscillate between being ok and being consumed by it. Yesterday I spent the day at Miramar *(parents' vacation home)* and felt relief while away. I didn't want to see her. But why? It seems fine when out of sight out of mind, but being in her presence is difficult. Today we sat in silence for a while and it was definitely awkward. When I said I was going to the gym she seemed to soften a bit. Then awkward silence when I got back. Then she got ready to go out and just before leaving was talkative again. I can't make sense of the pattern. I thought she was going on a date, which hurt. But I made myself sit in the living room. The only thing that seems to help is the mindset of enjoying when things are uncomfortable and the sense of pushing through that. I think the hardest part of this is realizing just how one sided our relationship has been. It's always been me supporting her. Always talking about her. There is no space for me. Not once since my firing has she asked how I've been doing. And while bringing my feelings up was obviously my choice, there has been no acknowledgment of how difficult this must be for me. I feel like I'm being as cool about this as possible. But there is no awareness of that. I notice she presents every situation as the victim and I'm sure that's how it's been with everyone she's told about this. In reality *I* don't lose much with the loss of our friendship, and whether she realizes it or not, I think she loses a lot.

•

1. I am grateful today for the feeling of being comfortable with and seeking out uncomfortability.
2. I am grateful for Brutus *(my neighbor)* agreeing to go to dinner on Saturday – esp. when I've been distant.
3. I am grateful for this free time.
4. I am grateful everything is working out with health insurance.
5. I am grateful to have completed my unemployment application.
6. I am grateful for my conversation with Gilly *(a lifelong friend on the other side of the country)*.

3-3-23

I spent most of the day at the parents' house today trying to avoid Ivy. Little did I know she wasn't here the whole day. When I got back she said she'd just gotten home from LA. I didn't want to see her. She was definitely looking to talk normally when I came in as she told me about the trials & tribulations of her day with *listing Her BFF's* house. I listened and I gave some feedback to be normal but quickly said I was going to watch a movie. She got pretty quiet after that. I wonder what she was upset about/why the change in desire to talk initially. I wonder what *Her BFF* has to say about the whole thing. What could *Her BFF* have said to make her want to be chatting? I grow more resentful of Ivy the more I think about the situation. Of course she didn't ask me about my day. Regardless of her feelings and the consequence of my decision, I think I did the right thing going to my room right away. I need to show her and myself that I'm not going to default to being her whipping post sounding board. I hope she doesn't start to resent me but it's possible. I guess my ultimate hope is that distance makes the heart grow fonder. But knowing that our relationship is not healthy for me, I don't know to what end that hope is. Responded to some job stuff today which felt good. The Universe definitely responded to some of my prayers. I need to keep following its lead... Thank you for that God.

3-4-23

Or I?

Hurting bad... Ivy's on a date right now... Why dating immediately after my admission? Why so conversative with me before leaving for it? I can only surmise that's the offshoot of some guilt. I want to get over this but for some reason I'm holding on. One thing that helps is to consciously avoid a victim mentality. Something I am prone to for sure.

How can I stop taking this personally? Were I to go on a date I would hide it but would also want her to know. But I know that for me that would be with the desire for her to change her mind. I just want to feel wanted. I don't. The difference between my actions and hers is that she's the one who rejected me. I know she doesn't owe it to me to not date because of what I said, but she also wasn't dating at all before so it feels like my actions were a catalyst – it sucks. She may be dating to move on herself. I hate that and the sense of loss I'm feeling. For a potential relationship and for our friendship.

There are many reasons she's not right for me – especially in light of everything that has gone on. She doesn't ask about me or my day & doesn't seem to care. I'm insecure about feeling that's because she justifiably thinks I have nothing going on. But knowing everything I'm dealing with I can't help but feel insulted for her lack of concern/inquiry. I need someone who I think cares about me. She only wants to talk about herself. She never wants to include me in her life and treats me like an accessory. Everyone I see her with receives such affection which is something I never receive from her. I know my distance has played a part in that. She is still partying in a way that wouldn't be good for me.

I just feel like something to be hidden away. It's a horrible feeling. Is there some part of this that is Freudian? Yes. So many things she does are similar to the ways in which I was neglected as a child. I need to make steps to break out of this pattern. Please help me God. I need help and want to maximize my potential. I just need help getting that jump start.

•

Looking back, what could I do now to deal with this situation that would make future me the most proud?

•

My heart is breaking & I don't know how to deal. Ivy went out at 5 for what was clearly a date. It's now 1:30am and she still isn't back. She doesn't owe me anything but I'm gutted and my mind is wandering to the worst places. I am so sad. I am so devastated. I am feeling so much. I just want to get my mind off of her and to focus on myself. I have to. But I don't want to be rude or appear bitter. I guess it just comes down to a matter of my intentions. If my intentions are pure in terms of self-focus rather than on vindication then that's what's important. She clearly doesn't really consider my feelings as much as I would have hoped, so why should I consider hers to the degree that I am. It has to stop.

•

- There's been for too much focus and agonizing over Ivy. The vaping is something that is pretty much a pure negative as well.
- Working out was great. The note left on my car with the girl's phone # was a much needed pick me up.
- Tomorrow I will quit the vaping. Will work out. Will wake up earlier.

3-5-23

I'm done. I can feel the attachment to Ivy going away because of her actions. She spent the night with whatever dude she was with last night and, as much as it hurts, a part of me is grateful for it because the pain/reality of it has gotten me to place of apathy with her. I simply refuse to give her so much of my energy at this point, I'm saving it for myself. The biggest goal for me right now is to be powerful in my rejection. But I think what the apathy results from is that I have fully realized and accepted just how one-sided our relationship has been. I'm sure I could come up with something if I really thought about it, but at the moment I can't really think about anything of significance that she's done for me.

The interesting thing is that when I got back from the gym she tried to have an overly friendly tone. I took a shower & am making it a point to watch TV in the living room so as to not give her the satisfaction of having me hide away in my room. I also don't want her to be able to say that I hid away when she gossips about this. Interestingly she's the one who's been doing the hiding away. She just came out and tried to goad

Or I?

me into responding to her saying "let's sell a house today." I didn't respond, which is unusual for me. She then tries to bait me saying that "Fido is so soft right now." So annoying. When leaving she continued saying she was "going to sell this house today." I wished her luck. In a weird tone she told me to have a great day, I told her "see ya." I'm sure she feels conflicted about what to do. I see that she's trying to maintain the status quo. I respect and appreciate that but also feel like "of course she does." Things were perfect for her. 100% in her favor. My mistake is for contributing to the dynamic. But I'm also hurt and insulted by the reality – one that I've always known, at least implicitly – that she will do whatever the fuck she wants regardless of how it makes me feel. I simply can't accept that from a self-respect standpoint. You go and fuck someone else, leave Fido here all night to do it, we both know it. How can I just sit here not being affected by that. My speculation is that her conflicting emotions are knowing that she's doing whatever the fuck she wants and that it hurts me, but being unwilling to act any differently. If I react in certain ways I know she's going to victimize herself. But at this point it's probably true that this simply can't be of any concern to me. The attachment is toxic and needs to be addressed. Nothing good is going to come from my maintaining it, as hard as it may be to address. I can't continue to care about what she's thinking, it's about what's best for me at this point.

3-6-23

Purgatory

The last I saw her it was "see ya." At dinner tonight, Auntie thought her behavior was totally disrespectful. Everyone does. It is. Didn't want to come home again, of course. Will I ever be comfortable here again? When I got back Ivy was extra eager to engage. Asking me how I was doing. Told her I went to dinner. She's asking about it. I was a little off. Should I have been more so? Make it clear I was at the car mechanic today so she doesn't think I was running away. She brings it back to herself. Starts telling me about her listing she just locked in. I engaged but not as much as usual. Tell her I don't feel well & am going to bed. What's up with her trying to talk?

There's really only 2 things that could be going on. 1. She's oblivious. This may be somewhat true. 2. She's testing the waters after the fucking. This is more likely. She obviously knows what she did. Knows it was wrong to some degree. If that's the case how did I do? I could have just been very cold, which I wasn't. That is a nuclear option & just would make everything weird. I definitely wasn't super engaged, but I did give her something. The question is does she feel vindicated? I hope not. I need to work on continuing to be more detached. She clearly is worried about really losing me. She needs to know that she did to some degree. Continue to spend less time here. Talk to people enthusiastically. Get support elsewhere. Move on. There is still too much of a pull. The only way is to eliminate her from your head. Apathy is the name of the game. "See ya!"

•

Does she know what she's done and how uncool she's been? Definitely not to the full degree. You need to start enjoying distancing yourself. I think what hurt today is the presumption that she could just get everything back right away and the feeling that I was slipping back into being there. Like with *My Last Boss*, I preserve the relationship out of some sort of fear. But what's the worst that could happen? Tomorrow be cold. Change the relationship. You lose nothing. She loses you. Fuck her and her shitty fucking treatment of you. You deserve better. Don't be passive. Don't lie down. Take control. You are in control now. Do what's best for you. And right now that's owning the situation. Never let her get to you or use you again!

3-7-23

Fighting For Life

Fuck I'm struggling. Feel like it's been beaten out of me. Hate where things are at. Yearning for positivity but feeling so stuck. Woke up today overhearing Ivy talking about her one night stand with someone from the office. Essentially says "I'm not going to date him, I just needed to get back in the game." Somehow the fact that the whole thing is so blasé for her made me feel worse. She really did just fuck some random guy with no care in the world. Fuck. I essentially snuck out of the apartment

Or I?

after that to go to Miramar so I didn't have to see her. I don't know what to do or how to act now. A part of me hates her at this point and knows that things will never be back to the way they were. I mourn our relationship and the image of her I'd created in my mind. It's time to move on now. It really is. Time for a plan between her and the job situation.

Why do I feel so stuck? I'm overwhelmed by the amount of effort I perceive that this is all going to take. But everything I've been reading talks about the importance of taking baby steps/momentum. I got to get to steppin. I've been engaging with/repressing my emotions too much. Observe them. These are big problems to overcome, but solving them is the way out.

•

So What's The Plan?

<u>Ivy</u>
- No more active hiding but do what you want.
- Emotional detachment.
- Observe thoughts & let them pass through. Be the observer.
- The relationship would not be a good one. Close that door.
- She's used & abused you. Be who you are but know that.

<u>Job</u>
- 2 hours a day.
- Eat the frog.
- Baby steps.
- Action comes before motivation.

•

The End Of An Era

Tonight was pretty much the fucking worst. I decided to stop running away & went back to the apartment. I stuck to the plan and detached and it was awful. We literally sat in silence all night. I feel horrible. I could see she was feeling some kind of way – I want to know what she was thinking. While sitting there I was so anxious. One part of me was sticking to my detachment script, stubbornly, the other part of me wanted to reach out but was drawing complete blanks. All I could think was that this is the end of our relationship, and it very well may be. Again, I just want to know what's on her mind. Things have deteriorated so much so fast. It all starts with her night out. Yesterday she was seriously trying to engage, today, nothing. I'm sure it's because I didn't stick around last night and now she's getting frustrated. I honestly feel sick about this whole thing. I'm shutting down. But I'm also trying to avoid falling back into old habits. I can't talk to her about her problems 24/7 and she's not asking about me or mine. This is so sad and so fucked. Please help me God, I need guidance and strength. Please help me find my way. I want to do the right thing for me and for the situation. I don't know what to do ☹. Things are getting worse and it's taking a big toll on me. The gap is widening and I'm starting to not see a way back. But I also feel like this has been a massively one-way street. Please help me.

•

1. I am grateful for Aston *(a lifelong friend on the other side of the country)* to be there for me when I'm down.
2. I am grateful I was able to make it to the gym despite how I'm feeling.
3. I am grateful for my new TV to watch shows when I'm down.
4. I am grateful to be going through this so I can grow.
5. I am grateful to be experiencing these emotions because this is how you know you're alive.
6. I am grateful to be realizing that you can't change people because that's the only way to move on.

3-8-23

With how awful yesterday was I worried about our relationship and what was best to do all day. I didn't even wake up until like 3:30pm. Yea, that kind of depressed. Last night made it clear to me just how bad and uncomfortable things could get. Talking to Rose *(my sister)* today helped. She also feels like Ivy is being immature in her response to all this. She felt like I should have a conversation with her, but I just don't want to have another serious talk. I know Ivy doesn't either. I don't think it would go well. In order to salvage our relationship I decided to offer an olive branch by talking to Ivy about the car she's about to buy. A sense of normalcy returned, which was a relief. I could tell she was yearning for

Or I?

it too. Of course I wonder if I did the right thing, but the awkwardness that was brewing as well as the loss of friendship that was coming was too much to bear. I just hope she's reflected on some of her actions. But I guess I'll never know. I still went to my room earlier than usual, which I had to. I do feel like I let her off the hook but also know that the alternative wouldn't have been good for anyone and was largely being driven by a bruised Ego. The one big positive is that I didn't go down the path of the silent treatment which I've done before and is ultimately immature. I know I'm being the bigger man here, but it's hard. I'm really not looking forward to her dating, but we'll cross that bridge when it comes. For now it's important to shift my focus to the job hunt to really move forward once and for all.

3-9-23

Today was OK. Ivy wasn't here in the morning so I chilled. When I saw her for the first time things were more normal than they've been in a while. Went out to dinner with Mom, which I'm sure Ivy thought was a date. She didn't try to talk when I got back and was watching TV. Tomorrow will likely reveal what she thinks about that. I wonder. Really need to stop the vaping, I feel much better without it. Tomorrow is the day. Stopping will provide me with some serious positive momentum. Also talked to Sally *(a friend & Harry's fiancé)* / Harry *(a lifelong friend on the other side of the country)* today. Sally was probably right that Ivy's moves were to remove any shadow of a doubt about her feelings for me. I accept that. Need to remember the truth, which is that I likely dodged a bullet here. Onwards & upwards.

3-11-23

Recovering

Today was a pretty good day. First I've had in a while. Things are getting to me less. I think I'm starting to move on. It's currently 2:45am, Ivy's out partying and at the moment I really don't care.

Great dinner with Brutus today. He's an awesome guy. Will definitely be kicking it with him more. I'm excited to build more of a relationship with him & it's a great reminder that there are so many people out there for you.

Good run today. Weak because of the vaping but a great reminder of why that needs to stop. Also proud of not pushing too hard and for listening to my body more. It's ok to take a step back. Fitness, like everything, ebbs & flows. Let's just make the next peak bigger than the last. Keep pushing.

•

(The Next Morning)

Off

Slept like absolute shit last night, it was awful. Don't think it really had to do with the fact that I know Ivy was out getting fucked either. I woke up to the sound of her getting back home at 9:30am. The realization doesn't feel great but doesn't sting nearly like last time. Great progress. But why does it still sting this morning? Some of it has to be general irritation and tiredness for sure. There's an unknown dark quality to this feeling too. I think it has to be some mix of FOMO with feeling like I'm *not* being chosen over some random dude which makes our relationship feel meaningless and me worthless. But I need to focus on the fact that none of this is personal. It has nothing to do with you. Although the timing is curious – can't be purely a coincidence that this comes just one day after she would clearly have thought I was on a date. The other part of this that I came to realize which is a tough pill is that this shit just can't help but make me feel like Ivy just kind of sucks in a way that I didn't realize. Of course a part of that is Ego projection and a part of you would love to do what she is doing, but that's the dark part of you. And if the roles were reversed in this situation, I would feel extremely bad in her shoes. Again & again the refrain is that you dodged a bullet. I'm envisioning and reacting to the idealized version of her, not reality. The real version is hugely flawed. Dodged a bullet motherfucker! Remember that and keep trucking.

•

Or I?

Exhausted

Absolutely exhausted today and totally on edge. The lack of sleep was brutal on me. This morning with Ivy was fine. I'm just not looking at her in the same light. Her behavior does suck. It feels good seeing her differently, but I struggle to act differently for some reason. For instance, after dinner with Mom I was so tired & didn't want to see her at all and felt so much pressure about doing so. Immediately went to my room but felt bad about it. I don't know why. I'm just sick of it always being about her & don't want to put up with it anymore. Hopefully I feel better tomorrow because right now I'm straight up worked.

3-12-23

Conflicted

Still exhausted but feeling very conflicted today on top of it all. Struggling with how to deal with Ivy. Went out to nails/lunch with Mom. Did not want to see Ivy so thought about going back to their place but also thought Ivy might not come back after her open house. I was wrong. She came back and we watched The Oscars together. The whole time I was freaking out internally with angst. Fight/flight type response. My exhaustion really hurt on top of it. Was really struggling with how to act and was stuck between being short in my responses or being friendly. Just really difficult time figuring out now to be myself. I focused on depersonalizing everything which helped. I also focused on centering myself & being present, which helped. We watched "The Last of Us" finale afterwards and then I went to my room. I had a bad feeling at the end of it all for some reason. I think I'm still holding out hope and felt like things weren't looking good? Maybe? I also was feeling distance. When she's texting I'm still feeling jealous & thinking the worst. But I was worried about continuing to be short, as I was at times, because it makes me look bad. It all comes down to me not liking feeling like I can't be myself. She tagged *Mom's Company* in some posts today, which I couldn't help but feel had something to do with me, but that could just be wishful thinking. Then I think would it have been better if I continued to ignore her. But that's just gameplaying, which I don't want to do. Oh and the *Mom's Company* posts were of the vest we picked out together. I didn't say anything about it. I'm glad I didn't take that bait. Ugh I hate all of this.

It's time to move on. How? Accept once and for all it's not going to happen. She's not good for you. You know that. You have a great opportunity here to practice some really hard shit. The hardest shit for you, which is to prioritize yourself. Don't be mean, be yourself, engage, but don't give yourself up. Focus on you & making improvements to yourself. If you need space take it. Take up space here. Build yourself up. Being tense/silent/resentful is taking energy away from yourself. Be who you are!

Is it just in my head or did she get more distant when I started giving energy back? Is this all just about attention to her? You're never going to have answers to these questions. Acceptance is the name of the game.

Vaping sucks. *Getting* off of this stuff is the first step forward. Everything will fall in place afterwards. The shit clouds your brain, as does the associated shame. You got this. Let's do it tomorrow. I believe in you, I really do.

If she doesn't want you it's not meant to be. So let it be. Also just realizing that she just pulled that shit yesterday so that may play into everything today. But who knows. Onwards & upwards.

3-13-23

Normalcy

Today was a pretty good day. Applying to jobs made me feel much better. Running made me feel much better. The biggest return to normalcy so far with Ivy. Glad we're getting back there. Did not stop the vaping but came close. It makes me feel terrible. Needs to stop. It will. It's always a yearning for instant relief that keeps me going back.

The keys to today were working on being my pure self & connecting with dopamine. Both eliciting it in myself and in others. It's a key to connection with others and I believe it's what's released when I venture outside my comfort zone and into my authenticity. The false dopamine that comes from vaping is horrible energetically & the associated shame is even worse psychologically. Let's be done once and for all tomorrow!

Or I?

3-14-23

Travis Matthew

Hey *Employee*!

File this under the category of a shot in the dark but I recently applied to the Director, Creative Services role at Travis Matthew. I'm so excited by the possibility of it and hope that reaching out might help me get on the radar.

I've spent the last 10 years working in TV show development. This involved identifying, creatively developing (overseeing the show creator, showrunner, and writing staff), producing (overseeing the entire production), casting, show/talent PR, and marketing shows, but am wholeheartedly focused on transitioning into the retail space, which if I'm being honest, is where my heart has always truly been.

Most recently I was a VP at *Big Boss Actress'* production company, *Last Company's Name*.

I know my experience is a little out of the box, but it seems to perfectly align with this role, and I think the perspective I have gained in the TV world is exactly what would make me stand out in this role.

I've attached my resume, hope to hear from you, and thank you so much.

3-15-23

IDK

Definitely feeling stuck and lost. Woke up ~10:30 because Aston called about his job offers. Still focused on the idea of dopamine which was good for the conversation. Ivy was filming. Got back later and we chatted for a bit but not long. Getting the dryer fixed was a pain in the ass. Was losing my mind in frustration thinking I was going to be late to dinner with *A Friend*. Hitting the vape like crazy to deal with anxiety but it

1. I am grateful for Aston's kind words about me today because they make me feel of value.
2. I am grateful to have been able to go on a bike ride today because it helps clear the head.
3. I am grateful to be able to escape to Mom/Dad's house because it gives me some much needed space.
4. I am grateful for my new pants.

3-19-23

Vaping No More

I just took my last puff of the vape. I'm ready to be done. It's killing me literally and mentally. Using it as a crutch to avoid feeling worse for sure. It's affecting my skin. It's affecting my sleep. It's affecting my workouts. It's affecting my relationships. It's affecting my job search. It's affecting my wallet. What isn't it affecting? What are the benefits of continuing? Nothing! Make this one of the most important days of your life by stopping.

Things to remember/that help. You are now not a smoker. You don't do it. The bad feelings are the nicotine leaving your body. It's fighting for its life. Manifest this. This really isn't that hard. Remember that. Remember all that you're getting by stopping. Don't let the nicotine trick you. You are in control. Don't buy into the negative thoughts. Observe them. You got this. Think about how good you will feel & how proud you will be tonight. This pain is a small price to pay for the rest of your life. This is the way forward. When cravings come, ride them out. They will pass. Watch the clock. Let's go start the rest of your life. This feels good. I love this pain.

3-20-23

Take A Break

Or I?

I think today is the day for a break from the gym. I'm feeling very run down. Part of it has got to be the nicotine withdrawal, but I've also been going hard for a while and it may be catching up with me. What are the challenges that I need to overcome right now/how can I fill myself up/build my self-esteem.
- Go to bed at a reasonable hour
- No more caffeine today
- Ivy doesn't get to you anymore
- Maybe work out?

Frustration & a negative general energy courses through my body. I don't know how to account for it. Realized that at least a part of the jealousy I get is from feeling left out and not chosen. There's power in that realization. There's also no reason not to be yourself. You have to be. There is no other way. Be grateful you are young. Act a fool. Have as much fun as you can.

•

Looking through my past entries and self-compassion is key right now. This is so hard. You're going through a lot and this is very hard. What can you do? Please please please help me. I release myself to you. Resist no more. Use your brain. Be who you are. Stop hiding. Embrace the discomfort. It is right now. There are no problems because it's right now. Detach from Ego. Love. Love. Love. Love. Love! I am all yours. Please show me the way.

•

★

Everything's Easy! The brain is totally malleable. What's extremely hard for some is extremely easy for others. Being kind, being mean, having discipline, being lazy. Cold calling, emailing. It's just about changing the hardwiring. The thing is that everyone finds either virtue or Ego in what they're doing, which is what keeps these behaviors so firmly etched in place and their opposites/alternatives so seemingly out of reach. It's a threat to the Ego/status quo which makes them seem hard. But there is no virtue in being stubborn and no true consequence to changing. If you can just realize how easy change & the other way is, it becomes so. Everything is easy!

If you think about it, many of your problems come from trying too hard. From a young age my response to adverse situations was to drill down & go full effort. In reality, the best solution is to think about the easiest way something might be done. It's often the most natural & right thing to do of all.

3-22-23

I'm doing what I can to feel fulfilled from the inside out. I'm definitely struggling with a feeling of frustration stemming from many attempts to quit vaping. But I do think that today is finally the day. Was so disappointed when I caved in yesterday and smoked. The truth of the matter is that I always feel worse afterwards.

Focusing on trying to be more free and not trying so hard. The trying is a major form of internal resistance for me. Going with the flow is my way of connecting with the Universe.

Dopamine – Helps me in my interactions when I think about them in terms of dopamine hits. But what helps even more than thinking about this concept in general is to think about trying to elicit dopamine hits for myself. I've stifled my self-expression for so long and in so doing have been avoiding those hits. I think I developed a sense that if I enjoy it, it must be wrong. To compensate I turned to the false hits of weed/alcohol/nicotine. NO! Have fun on your own terms.

There's no solution – Things are going to be hard forever. Always got to keep working through. Happiness comes from pushing through despite it all. There's no perfect time. But everything's easy at the same time. It is such a relief to give myself permission to do whatever I want, come what may. That's what I've always wanted and it's yours. You're young and you have the here & now. Enjoy everything as much as possible. The biggest hits are for you.

3-28-23

Good Vibrations

Or I?

Realizing how low my vibration is and has been and really wanting to focus on raising it. It's important to realize that the vibration, like life, is all about the journey. Don't forget that. My highest & best vibration is always felt when I'm centered and acting most like myself & in my truth. I've not been feeling that much lately. Have been feeling really jammed up. Applying to jobs helps because it gives me a sense of forward momentum. Working out helps for the same reason – a sense of momentum. Clearly forward progress is important to me.

Vaping is something that's really holding me back. I feel worse pretty much every time I do it. Immediately. But my brain convinces me that I will feel better if I do it. Not quitting is providing me with the opposite sense of momentum. It's making me feel stuck. Only 5% of people can quit cold turkey. Be one of those people.

Gratitude is something that comes up repeatedly in vibrational discussions. I think I need to tap into this more. When I'm feeling grateful I really can appreciate life. That appreciation is of paramount importance.

Focusing on making things easy is an unlock for me. I've been trying too hard for too long and it's creating resistance. That has to be a big reason things haven't been coming into my life. Stop trying & start living.

3-29-23

Beginning Again

I felt pretty good today. A big part of it was likely sleeping pretty well. But I think the biggest contributor was yesterday's realization that the biggest thing worth struggling for is to live as authentically as possible. This is a battle I'm going to have to fight daily. I'm ready & excited for that fight. I'm simultaneously reconnecting with my mojo, which I haven't felt in years.

Another big unlock for me is paying attention to my emotions/fears/anxieties and trying to understand the lessons each of those things is trying to impart upon me. I.E. my anxiety often comes when I'm subconsciously abandoning myself.

Knocked out a 7 mile run today @ 8 min/mile avg. Very happy to still be able to do that. A big relief that not all has been lost with all the vaping. I'm starting from a good place physically and am eager to kick the habit once and for all.

1. I'm grateful for my run today.
2. I'm grateful to be included in Ivy's party.
3. I'm grateful to be finding myself again.

3-30-23

Let's Get Unstuck

Feeling on edge & anxious. Just jammed up. Vaping fucking sucks. Still caught up thinking too much about Ivy. I know she has a date on Friday and find myself thinking about that more than I'd like. It's not like before. The feeling reminds me of not wanting to quit cigarettes or move on with my life. But like both of those things, I know I will feel better when I do. You know she's not right for you. Best to enjoy the friendship while using this experience to push through the resistance and hurt. Remember that finding yourself is worth fighting for and that it's all in the journey. Yesterday – Successes were going on that run. Focusing on finding/being yourself. Settling into your version of cool. To work on – Vaping! Creating momentum. Spending money. Not giving into urges and knowing success is on the other side.

How can I make a difference in my life today? Quit vaping you fucking idiot! ☺ This will create the greatest sense of satisfaction possible.

I just took the last hit of the vape. You are not a smoker You're gaining your health. Get hard.

•

Rumination

Why do I find myself so fixated on Ivy despite everything. The relationship is one-sided. She excludes me. She disrespects me. There is no spark. The relationship would not be good for me. I get jealous when she's out. Think about and get jealous thinking about her sleeping with other guys. But at the same time cringe when she tries to be overly sexual on Instagram. What the fuck is going on with me? I can only surmise it comes down to a matter of a lack of self-esteem & a scarcity mindset. She's really the only woman I have a relationship with. My mind doesn't want to lose it. Childhood issues are also obviously at play here. She ignores me like I was ignored in childhood. Everything was about Mom like everything is about Ivy.

What is my problem with women? Why am so scared of them. A great partner and a great career is all I've ever really wanted so those are the two things I've avoided the most. WTF. How can I change this? Like quitting addiction, I just need to go for it. Why am holding back? I want to fucking explode in frustration. How can I get my fucking life back? What will fulfill me? I simply have to start putting in real effort with my authentic self. Shit is too hard with Ivy, it will never work. Drill that through your fucking skull and lose the hope. I don't even know what I'm hoping for. Because ultimately a relationship with her would be a disaster for you. Phoenix from the ashes time motherfucker. Reveal your true self. He's hidden down there.

3-31-23

Ok I'm so fucking over it. At this point the tables have turned. She needs to prove herself to me. I can no longer be there for her in the same way. She goes out last night, doesn't come back and doesn't feed Fido dinner or breakfast so I did. It's simple she doesn't really give a fuck about me & doesn't respect me. Keep fighting for that new perspective.

Of course trying to be all buddy buddy. Definitely shame driving that.

Keep the vibration right though. Don't be a little bitch. Everything's for you now. It's easy to change and that was the last straw.

Allow yourself to be happy. Have fun. Be who you want to be and don't worry about anyone else.

GOAL – Be over it but be cool.
GOAL – No one can affect you.

GOAL – Realize everything is in your power & how you look at things.
GOAL – To be a leader.
NEW PERSPECTIVE – I'm free.

No matter what has happened in your life up until now, it should have no bearing on how you live your life from now on.

Focus on self but be cool while doing it. Find the right vibration.

•

L For The Good Guys

Fuck man. I'm in a bad spot. Ivy doesn't genuinely care about me and I need to deal. The attachment needs to be dealt with. No more doormat. Self-esteem will only rise the more you distance yourself. Realizing that my sense of inferiority is costing me everything. No more. That shit is bullshit. You've given too much. Dial it back. I hate where I am but take accountability for it. Time to make a change. Maybe that means leaving tomorrow's party early. No one will even know. Just watch. But don't go in manifesting a bad time. Kick it with *Her Show BFF*. That will be fun. Maybe you can find someone for yourself. Remember the importance of manifestation/visualization. Thinking back to childhood, that was a major key to success for you, you just didn't know the practice you were employing.

4-1-23

Processing

Just back from Ivy's birthday party and I am in shock. Don't even know what to say. It was simultaneously one of the most eye opening and confusing experiences of my life. The fakeness of everything was unlike anything I've ever seen. I was disgusted. And Ivy was right in the center of it. Everyone was straight up performing for the cameras. I'm proud of the way I carried myself by not getting dragged in. While everyone went to dance in the fake club I could not bring myself to be that fake. Ivy

Or I?

took her clothes off to get in the hot tub, but the whole thing was staged. Watching her wait there with all the cameras trained on her until someone told her to take off her pants was honestly horrible. Then she's in the hot tub clearly all over *Cast Member's* brother (I think his gf was there?) was too much to bear. I can't believe that whole thing happened. Looking around the party and seeing how vain everyone seemed and how eager for attention was crazy. I don't think the ever felt more out of place or like how the fuck did I end up here in my life. This has completely changed my perception of Ivy. I feel like such a fool for my feelings for her. The people who are her so called friends are almost like caricatures of people. So different than who I want to be around. I can't believe I've given her so much. I can't believe I've been so blind. While in the "dance party" which I avoided, multiple people told me Ivy was asking about me. I'm honestly surprised but am also convinced she was just worried I left with her clothes. I can't believe I was jealous of *That One Guy*. Or of her hanging out with those guys at all. They are so not my type of people. When Ivy asked where I'd been I just said "chillin." She didn't ask more questions. A bit later, I don't know exactly what prefaced this, but she said something along the lines of "you good" which I just brushed off. Right before I went to get her clothes from the car, she asked if I was going to go out. I said "no I'm super beat." She gave a pouty face but didn't seem to care that much. When I came back with the clothes, she asked again if I was going out. I'm assuming she forgot because she was drunk and doesn't care that much. I said "no" straight up. She had no response. Next I saw her I took the bag from her. She gave me a hug. I said "Happy Birthday." She tried to act like she didn't want to go out. I just said "you'll have fun" and left.

Ultimately the take away was to always make sure to act how you want and would be proud of. I didn't acquiesce tonight and am proud of that. I glamorized and glorified her whole world and life. It's a horrible environment. Ivy really had no friends at this thing which says so much. I'm glad I didn't go out with them afterwards. I would have in the past so that was a big step not following. I don't care what those people think of me. I'm sick to my stomach *over* how much I gave Ivy and then seeing this side of her. The mask fell for me tonight.

4-2-23

Fuck

Really spent a lot of time ruminating over last night today. I'm spent. Very much mourning. The silver living in it all is the realization that I must act in accordance with who I am and according to how I feel. What that means now is that I'm done. I have given so much. I have put it all out there. Clearly I am not right for Ivy and she's clearly not right for me. Attention front and center on yourself.

This is such a tough pill to swallow. I'm not sure why I'm having such trouble moving on and accepting Ivy for who she is. The pedestal I've put her on is not reality and her flaws are massive.

Another major silver living is that I think yesterday will go a long way towards alleviating my jealousy long term. I really didn't like what I saw. That's how she really acts. The real show she's putting on is the one with you.

It's time to be strong. It's time to be a man. It's time to stop allowing people to mistreat you. You deserve so much more than this.

I'm so sorry this is happening to you. This is so hard and you've been trying your best. That's all you can do. But this clearly isn't working. Something's got to change and it's not going to be Ivy's behavior. It's got to be yours. I know it's scary, I'm here for you.

4-4-23

Trying To Move On

Yesterday was a day of ignoring. Very much trying to detach from Ivy. But trying also to stay true to my nature in doing so. Really trying to avoid being manipulative and instead just trying to focus on myself. Because of my lack of engagement, we spent much of the time in each other's presence not speaking. This is obviously very uncomfortable. REMEMBER – She is not someone who's worth suffering for. You must learn to love yourself first. And have the courage to be disliked. That is freedom.

Or I?

Today, focus on being detached but positive. Don't forget what's happened, but also don't take it out on Ivy. Use that knowledge to stay your course. Self-improvement must begin. Work out. Meditate. Less caffeine. Less nicotine. Life tasks.

4-5-23

Getting Fucked

I've been largely ignoring Ivy over the last couple of days trying to deal. She hurt me so bad at her party. She's kept my b-day card next to her computer. Brought me jerky yesterday after I ignored her. She was coming back from *Reiki*. Obviously trying to get me to bite. I didn't. We didn't really talk. I was short with my responses. Didn't see her all day today until tonight. We said "hi" then nothing else. Silent treatment on both sides. She goes to her room to "organize her closet." Puts headphones on to do it. Never done that before. I pack. At one point I see her sitting in her dark closet just listening. I'm feeling fucked up by it all. Don't want to leave in silence. When I tell her I'm leaving tomorrow she acts all good. "Oh fun!" "Tell parents hi" "What time's your flight?" "I don't have anything going on this weekend." I'm so confused. Feel so jammed up. Don't know if I should have just left. I just don't want to be manipulative. Don't want to have the conversation I know we need. I'm so tired of hurting. Obviously I got to tell her but I don't know how. I don't know how to move forward or what the right thing to do is. It feels like our friendship is over and I don't know if she cares. I'm so hurt. Please help me God/Universe. I need strength and clarity more than ever right now.

4-15-23

B-day

The b-day was a pretty tough one today. No job and things falling apart at home is a hard pill to swallow on this day. Can't stop thinking about the situation with Ivy. She tried engaging hard after The Masters. We talked for a minute then silence. I went to bed pretty shortly thereafter. Before that I actually spent a couple days (Mon/Tues) @ Mom & Dad's because I just couldn't go home to face her.

The next day we pretty much ignored each other. It wasn't until later that night I told her I was going to San Fran *to visit Rose & Fischer (my brother-in-law)*. She acted all positive about it like she didn't care. In my room I could hear her on the phone with people (other dudes) until like 1am. She left a present out for me that morning but purposely didn't come out to say goodbye. I felt like good riddance leaving but have since been ruminating hard. She texted me happy birthday at like 2pm. No way she forgot until then. She didn't respond to my response. I was upset. I texted her later thanking her for her present – thanking her for her thoughtfulness – which I regret saying.

She was thoughtful about this but hasn't been thoughtful about anything else. Look at all the evidence. This is over. I don't even know what I'm trying to salvage. Moving on is a must. This is another drug you have to quit. Looking at her Instagram was a mistake. This has become too much. Please help me accept and move forward. I need your help.

•

Book

Unwinding Anxiety

by Dr. Judson Brewer

•

Unwinding Anxiety **Habit Loops** *Exercise*

- Going Home -

<u>Trigger</u>: Anxiety about going home
<u>Behavior</u>: Avoid/Stay at parent's place
<u>Response</u>: Don't have to deal
↳ More anxiety about going home

- Caffeine -

<u>Trigger</u>: Wake up/feel tired

Or I?

<u>Behavior</u>: Drink caffeine
<u>Response</u>: Feel less tired/get a buzz
↳ Anxiety increase/crash

- Tense in Conversation -

<u>Trigger</u>: Think "what if I go blank/don't have anything to say/look like a fool"
<u>Behavior</u>: Worry/tense up/get distracted in conversation
<u>Response</u>: Not engaged in conversation & forget
↳ Validates concern & proves point

OR

<u>Trigger</u>: Conversation
<u>Behavior</u>: Worry I'm dumb
<u>Response</u>: Anxiety/hard to engage
↳ Proves I'm dumb

- Sleeping In -

<u>Trigger</u>: Worries/anxious about what tomorrow will bring
<u>Behavior</u>: Stay up late
<u>Response</u>: Get up late/shame and feel behind on the day

- Job Search Procrastination -

<u>Trigger</u>: Anxiety about career/future
<u>Behavior</u>: Workout, watch TV, etc. to avoid
<u>Response</u>: Don't have to deal
↳ Increases anxiety about career

4-26-23

Coming Back Online

I have come a long way towards processing everything. The more I detach from Ivy, the more I feel like myself. It all came down to the difference in her behavior after my admittance. Then acting like everything was fine & above board really hurt. Moving forward cordially but very much on my own terms.

Positives from today – Hot yoga in the morning. Very hard but always good. Proud of myself for taking a break when I needed to. Listening to the body is so important and I was about to pass out. Keeping the image in mind of who I want to be and acting that way is key. I love when I can tap into that. Also tapping back into the Philly in me and not trying to be so technical and smart is where I really feel at home. Finally, remembering that everything is hard is a game changer. I've been looking for something that would make everything easy. A guarantee that my emails and thoughts are "right." That's never coming. Mistakes will be made and that's a good thing. Did some job searching but need to do more. Let's get after it tomorrow.

4-27-23

What To Say

At somewhat of a loss for what to say. Trying to figure the Ivy of it all and need to rehash in order to digest because she's obviously upset with me. Going back in time. Back from Rose & Fischer's and she's standoffish but somewhat talking. I'd actually spent a couple days @ Miramar not ready to come home. I quickly tell her I'm going to take care of Auntie. End up staying there almost a week. Come back and things were OK. Talked a bit then she goes into *her* room for a while. Shuts the door so I don't see her when I leave for dinner. Don't see her when I get back. Next day don't see her in the morning. I go to yoga where I get very frustrated with myself and everything. Backing up, I did not feel good being around her and listening to her blab about her nails before going to dinner. She's not there when I get back from yoga & I go back to Miramar. Spend the night because I can. When I get back today she's distant. When I go to the gym her tone is weird. "Have a good time." I'm on zoom when she leaves for yoga. When she gets back I say "yo" she sadly says "hi" and goes to her room. When she comes out one last time before bed she shuts her door without saying goodnight even though we looked at each other as she was walking in. She knows & doesn't like the distance I've created. She doesn't realize, or maybe she does, that I just don't really give a fuck anymore.

Or I?

4-28-23

A Revelation

Was listening to Bill Burr when he hit the nail on the head for one of my biggest problems. He was a people pleaser too. He said that growing up in a time where people were aggressive with each other and much more gruff in general made him feel that if he ever disagreed with anyone he was subconsciously worried he was going to get his ass beat. THIS! THIS! THIS!

This is one of my biggest fucking problems. I feel the exact same way. I'm consumed by fear that I'm always on the verge of getting in a fight. That disagreements put me in harm's way physically. If I can train my brain to realize that this isn't the case – that it's not in danger & doesn't need to be in fight or flight – that will go a long way towards solving my problems. This realization brings me great relief.

4-29-23

Is This Fuckery?

Ivy & I slowly began talking again over the past couple days. The day after she went to her room without saying anything she obviously regretted it because she tried to be conversative in the morning. Still weird silence here and there because I'm not asking her questions about herself. She doesn't ask anything about me really. Last night I bit the bullet & engaged with her a bit before she went out. This morning I go to the gym while she's still asleep. When I get back and after I shower we're sitting there and slowly start talking again – but only because I start asking questions about her. She says she's staying at *A Hotel* tomorrow. That *Her Show BFF* is there with a new boyfriend. I'm like cool and suspect she's going with a guy but she doesn't say anything about it. Then she takes a call. I can hear it's a dude – she goes to her room but doesn't close the door and is talking about what they're going to do at the hotel together! Then she calls the hotel and makes reservations for them! Hahahaha. Shit is ridiculous. Again, just as things are cool she rubs another guy in my face. This has to be on purpose. Right? Either way it's laughable. Either inconsiderate or cruel. Childish way of letting me know. Clearly new supply since I dipped out. What hurts me is just hearing her talk to him and being cool. That's what I wanted to do together. At this point it's been long enough that I'm not upset with her about other guys, just the passive aggressive communication. I knew shit was going to happen like this. She has every right to be dating, but again it's just when things become cool that she does this. I've approached the pit in my stomach with curiosity. I can't exactly figure the feeling out. But when she was talking with the dude I was laughing and eye rolling. Because fuck her. I really was just like wow she is such a bitch. Feeling like good riddance she's this guy's problem now. But think I was jealous hearing her talk like normal and cool with him. You knew she was going to get a new supply. Intuitively you knew how this was all going to play out. But hurts to see it come true. Honestly I thought she was going to hook up with someone blatantly last night. You were just one day off and the rubbing in the face transpired differently than you thought. If she was hoping for a response & for hurt from me she didn't get it. I was just like whatever. Because again fuck her, she sucks. You can't be friends with girls. Getting away from Mr. Nice Guy feels good. Ultimately the hurt comes from being hurt – again. But also again whether she's doing it on purpose or is unaware, fuck her! You're growing and becoming stronger from this, I can feel it. Prepare to continue to be nonplussed.

•

No talking when I got home. Ivy to her room until she went to the gym. Completely different attitude when she left. Overall her mood is just all over the place. So fucking annoying. Got to be like a duck's back.

5-3-23

Job Experience From Spotify Application

I'm a Hollywood creative executive looking to make the transition into the music space. I have experience working at major Networks (USA, Syfy, Bravo, E!), Studios (Lionsgate, New Regency), and Production Companies (*Last Company's Name* Entertainment – *Big Boss Actress'* Production Company). In these roles I have successfully identified, developed, and produced TV shows. This involved overseeing the entire

Or I?

creative process, hiring and managing all those employed on a show, and dealing with marketing, PR, legal, business affairs, etc. There is nothing I use more than Spotify and nowhere else I would rather be so I hope to hear from you.

5-4-23

Rehashing

Reading over the past journal entries & wow have I been dealing with a lot of pain. So much so that it speaks to how strong you are. I'm so proud of you. And I'm so sorry you're going through this.

- A pattern has emerged with Ivy. When things get good again she throws a guy in my face. Is nice to me before/after she does it. Regardless of *whether* my response *is* positive or negative quickly changes behavior to more distance.
- She has extreme & constant shifts in engagement and behavior. When she hoovers me back she quickly becomes distant again. For example, yesterday she opened up to me about struggles (*Sister's* father in law died, show bullshit, lost *Her BFF's* listing), I engaged which temporary smoothed things over, then detachment/distance from her again today.
- Detachment when she gets what she wants.
- Will never ask about me unless it's to get back in somewhat good graces. Once back in good graces, completely one-sided again.
- Always the victim.
- Re: *Sister's* father in law – used that to get sympathy, then when talking about all other problems, they were about the show & losing a listing. Didn't really seem to care about it.

I'm grateful to have kept a journal because it memorializes what I've been going through and provides evidence for the bad behavior. Focus needs to shift now, this has been going on for long enough.

(feel much better after journaling)

•

Book

Codependent No More

by Melody Beattie

•

Codependent No More Activities

Chapter 11

1.

I have a very bifurcated view of myself. Intellectually I understand that I have good qualities but they're buried under a fog of self-doubt and lack of self-worth/belief. It's hard for me to come up with things I like about myself. I know I can be dedicated – like with exercise. I know I care about people. But I'm sitting here trying to think about other things and nothing is coming which is not good. I know I must be strong though to have dealt with all the self-hate/self-doubt and to still keep going. Things I don't like about myself. How much I hide away. I avoid confrontation and standing up for myself. I let people walk all over me. I constantly worry and put myself down. I constantly tell myself I'm stupid and have allowed that to hobble me. I don't go far what I want. I'm scared of other people. I constantly put myself in situations that are bad for me and stay in them thus forcing myself to suffer. I have allowed myself to believe that I am not enough. I avoid growing up. I avoid taking steps to improve my life – i.e. nicotine, job search, sleep – even though I know I need to. I have let myself stay stuck. I have surrendered to fear. I don't stand up for myself. The list goes on and on and unlike the positives, this just flowed.

2.

Obviously there is a clear disparity between the positives & negatives. I vow to talk to myself more positively. To not get caught up in the negative. I will work on accepting myself. On honoring my emotions. On truly living my life. I will work most on detachment from others & from the fear/fight/flight I have been living under for so long. And most of all I will not judge myself while on this journey.

•

Or I?

Visualization

On the importance of visualization. Visualization & manifestation combined are a key for you. Given your understanding of the brain this makes sense. This will unlock the potential that neuroplasticity allows. Essentially, visualizing that you have already achieved the mindset you're striving for makes that mindset so. The more this is done, the more the brain will adjust to make that mindset the status quo. It will take some repetition, but this is one of the best ways to rewire the brain.

5-5-23

Article

16 Questions That Will Show You Who You Are (And What You're Meant To Do)

by Brianna Wiest

5-6-25

Staying Sane

Memorializing because things have gotten weird again. This is important to stay sane.

5/3 – Wake up/make an effort to talk. Because I reached out she engaged and told me about her problems. Of course nothing about me. Convo cooled off. I went on a run. Talked to Harry. Watched Sixers. Nothing particularly memorable.

5/4 – Distant before interview. She's gone most of the day. Here when I get back from gym. I ask if interview went well then go to my room to watch Lakers. Pass out. She's gone when I go out again.

5/5 – No talking. I do work in living room. We sit there in silence. When I say I'm leaving to parents she acts nice. "Tell them I say hi! Have fun!" Not there when I get back for the night.

5/6 – Not awake when I leave for golf. Besides "hi" when I get back, hard silent treatment.

•

From "16 Questions" Article On 5-5-23

What And Who Is Worth Suffering For?

What
Becoming my authentic self
My health
My career
Love
True connection
My future
My intellect
My wants & needs
Focusing on myself

Who
Rose
Tulip *(my sister)*
Fischer
Whitman *(a friend from college on the other side of the country)*
Aston

What Would You Stand For If You Knew Nobody Would Judge You?
- Myself.
- Asking for what I want.
- I would use my brain more to analyze situations & to act accordingly instead of people pleasing just to fit in and get people to like me.

What Would You Do If You Knew That Nobody Would Judge You?
- Reach out to everyone I could think of to network for a new job.

Or I?

- Move out of my apartment.

Based On Your Daily Routines, Where Will You Be In 5 Years? 10? 20?
- I will be nowhere if I continue this level of procrastination.
- This is an emergency situation.
- Keep visualizing. Keep focusing on people like is presented in "Meditations" *by Marcus Aurelius*.

Who Do You Admire Most & Why?
Marcus Aurelius – Because MEDITATIONS is quickly becoming a life changing work for me. His ideologies are a true north to follow (Book 2, 1 & 13).

What Do You Not Want Anybody Else To Know About You?
- How scared I am.
- How insecure I am about my intellect.
- How unwanted I feel.
- The cam shit.

What Are A Few Things You Thought You Would Never Get Over While You Were Going Through Them? Why Did They Seem So Insurmountable? How Did You?
- *High School Girlfriend*. I thought I would love her forever. Time healed that wound.
- Unemployment #1 & 2 – It felt like I had no one & nothing. It felt like I was never going to get another job & was totally helpless. Other people eventually helped me out. I just had to connect with them & put myself out there.
- Skin Issues – Felt like it was never going to go away. That I was never going to be the same. Time healed in one instance, taking action in another.
- Exams/School – The amount of work felt daunting. Pressure mounted due to lack of preparation. But I always made it through and none of it matters now. It was always better when I did prepare and what I remember are the triumphs.
- *Last Company Name/ 2nd to Last Company Name* – Felt so stuck but wasn't doing anything about it. But when they ended the issues quickly resolved.

★
<u>Understanding the importance of time, making changes, and effort</u>
★

What Are Your Greatest Accomplishments So Far?
- Being acknowledged in *Radio Personality's* book.
- Getting into Vanderbilt.
- Graduating Vanderbilt.
- Getting into the Page Program.
- Winning tour *guide* awards.
- Getting job @ E!

★
<u>All things where my effort is what made me proud</u>
★

What Would Be Too Good To Believe If Someone Were To Sit Down And Tell You What's Coming Next In Your Life?
- You're going to begin living the rest of your life on your terms free from concern over outside judgement or influence.
- You're forever more going to begin using your brain to solve problems that are meaningful to you in the moment and which provide a sense of purpose.
- You're going to get a job you love, with people you love working with and which keeps you from having to worry about money. It will be the true beginning of what will be a very successful career & life.
- You're going to meet the love of your life who will compliment you & support you & make life better than you could ever have imagined.
- You're going to become someone you're truly proud of.
- Your anxiety will melt away.

5-8-23

Didn't see Ivy yesterday. She was gone when I went to give Mom and Dad a ride to the airport, and in her room by the time I got back late. Went to Miramar again today. Ivy & I got back around the same time. Talked for a minute or two then she walked Fido & went to her room early ~9. I struggle with how to act around her. Heightened fight/flight response, which I need to get under control. Trouble speaking. I'm working on understanding the underlying trigger/trauma. What am I worried about and why is it so hard to speak? What is it that makes the silent treatment so triggering for me? If someone is giving me the silent treatment and it hurts me so much is it because it makes me feel that I'm unlovable? It has to play into the same sort of mechanism as the people pleasing. A desire to be liked. And fear that people won't like the real me. But I'm not being the real me so what does it matter. A fear of rejection as well. Why am I finding it so hard to have faith in myself? To move forward? I'm so scared of something. I'm so scared that if I try and don't succeed then I really will be worthless. But why am I so convinced that I bring nothing to the table? You do. But need to be completely authentic. Need to be trying as you deep down. That's the only way. Must stand up for yourself. Must face fears. That is how you're going to build confidence. Approach your fears. You can and you must. Stand tall. Stop trying to please anyone but yourself. It's time to become a bad motherfucker. But a good one. Let's meet our fate. Let's become someone. I am READY.

•

Recurring Themes

1. **Mindfulness**
Become aware of emotion and/or sensation and become curious about it.

2. **The Present Moment**

3. **Feel**
Feel, don't repress. This allows emotions to be processed and to move on. Feelings are what let you know you're alive.

4. **There Is No Answer**
Things are always going to be difficult. Expecting an answer is looking for fool's gold. Continuing to try your best in the moment regardless of difficulty is the key.

5. **Act & Think According To Who You Want To Be**
That will become who you are.

6. **Fear & Fight**
   There's no such thing as fear. There's nothing to be afraid of. The state of fight/flight you've been living in is made up.

7. **Acceptance**
   Accept what is to avoid resistance. This is fundamental.

8. **You Are What You Visualize**
   You can put yourself into whatever mindset you want.

•

Become Unstoppable
Forward Progress Everyday
Build the Life You Want
All You – That's the Ideal
Be the 1%
Manifest it All
Make Mistakes
It's All Easy!

Keep it Simple!

•

Be

Your

Cool

5-12-23

Time For A Talk

Or I?

About to have the talk with Ivy. Feeling nervous worrying about how she's going to react. But that does nothing to help. Deep breaths & curiosity are key.

My Goal – To make things better around here. Keep it light. Good tone. Authenticity. Quick on toes.

Points:
- Healing
- I dropped *feelings* bomb
- Change in behavior – didn't know what to do – withdrew
- Needed some space
- What are you feeling?
- Macro level – over it and moving forward

5-14-23

Ivy & I talked it out on the 12th. The conversation went realistically as well as it could have. She admitted to being resentful about my telling her I had feelings. That was her big thing. This was after I told her how bad I felt about doing it in the first place. I told her that her change in behavior and how one-sided I realized the relationship was ultimately led me to withdrawal and that I eventually ended up getting pissed. This is the one place I wish I'd been a little clearer. She essentially admitted to acting in a way that tried to make it clear that she wasn't interested. Instead of bringing up her dates, staying out, and Fido as things that made me feel like she didn't give a fuck (as well as her silence) – she kind of denied the dates – I wish I'd emphasized that what it really was was her efforts to make her lack of interest clear. I told her I'm over the feelings and don't think dating would have been a good idea anyway – that we aren't compatible. She admitted to not handling this well. Was pissed about not feeling comfortable at home and not knowing where the line was. I get that. We both admitted to being fucked up by the whole thing. I'm glad she said I am one of her best friends/family and wants me in her life forever. I emphasized that this is all about clearing the air and moving forward to heal. We both were relieved and admitted to being nervous about this. An overarching fear the whole time was about how things just couldn't get worse. We both were very relieved afterwards. We'll see what happens next as at some point she talked about not being fully ready to move on. Got to take things slow. We both talked about how huge/serious of a conversation it was. She said only confronting her ex-husband was more so. I emphasized I was there for her and doing this was trying to show that. I talked about not wanting to run away *and* being careful not wanting to hurt or abandon her.

I'm very proud about having the conversation and initiating it. Big time & big learning. Organizing my thoughts in writing was very helpful. As was adopting the mentality that I am someone who approaches fear. Another huge unlock was having an air of curiosity. This helps with everything.

I'm excited to move forward now. Let's see what the future holds.

●

Book

Think and Grow Rich

by Napoleon Hill

●

Desire (*Think and Grow Rich* Chapter 2)
(A series of steps to get what you desire)

1. $100 Million dollars

2. Free time – Lean into fear – Good sleep schedule – Wake up early – Full focus – The Philly in you

3. 5 years (by 39)

4. Plan:
- Brainstorm idea
- Determine how it will work (merchants/logistics/etc.)
- Determine resources needed
- Acquire resources
- Execute

Or I?

5. I will have $100 million by the age of 39. For this I will dedicate my free time to its acquisition, will attack fear. A good sleep schedule is necessary as is waking up early to get on it. This will require full focus. The plan. I must first determine the idea. Next comes figuring out all the logistics & the amount of capital required. Get start up capital. Execute like a Man on Fire.

Read *this* 2X/day & Believe You Already Have the $

5-23-23

Desire & Faith

What do you want most in life? $100 million and to achieve my destiny in all its authenticity. This needs to become an obsession for you. It is. I am that guy. I truly truly am. Everything that has happened up to this point has Happened for a Reason. I will achieve my destiny. I am the guy who approaches fear. I handle all difficult situations well. I am the realest me. I have it all. Let's fucking go. Satisfaction will come from effort & overcoming struggle. I am not a bitch. You've been trying to manifest failure & stupidity & you couldn't even make that come to fruition. This is major evidence of your inherent value. You are hard. You are fair. You do what you want. You don't avoid. Let's seek out the difficult. Use your brain. No more energy focused on the negative, redirect to problem solving. No more expectations of others. Accept where you are and dig out. I'm proud of you. Make your child self proud of you too. This is just the beginning.

5-24-23

The Plan

Things need to change for your mental health. No one's going to save you. No one cares and that's ok.

1. Caffeine consumption – this will stop. One more today. One more tomorrow. Then none.
2. Nicotine – Begin to taper to none.
3. Sleep – Lights off by 12.
4. Career – At least 2 hours a day.
5. Belief – You have been through a lot and you have it all.
6. Fear & Discomfort – You are a person who runs towards it.

This is a hard time and you will get through it. You are ready. I am open to life. I release myself to the Universe. I am grateful.

5-29-23

Perseverance

The best part of today was making the decision to strive to only do things that will build you up. That will make your life better. This is the commitment.

It all started with going to the gym when you didn't want to. It was so clear how much better you felt afterwards when you had been in such a low place before. These are the decisions.

Ivy & I had our first real normal interaction today since our conversation. She then went to meet up with whoever she's seeing. It still hurts me. I'm trying to figure out why. I guess this is all part of the process. I'm sorry this is so hard. You will get through this. I acknowledge and accept these feelings.

Gratitude:
1. I am grateful I went to the gym today when I was feeling my lowest.
2. I am grateful for getting a glimpse into the mindset that the world is full of possibilities for me right now.
3. I am grateful for my health.

The world is your oyster right now.

Or I?

5-30-23

Digging Out

The goal is to do those things that build you up. You have the opportunity to do anything you want. You will take advantage. Your mind creates the reality around it. THIS IS THE SUPERPOWER.

1. I am grateful to be here today.
2. I am grateful for the opportunity to determine my path. What an opportunity.
3. I am grateful for this challenge in life which will allow me to grow.

•

Career Realms

- Fashion
- Startup
- Creative Advertising
- Media Related Investing
- Media Related AI

5-31-23

Keep Going

Repeating old patterns of stagnation. Went to sleep & woke up late again today. Haven't done anything productive. But actually, talking to Aston & Gilly was good. Remember, everything to build you up. Gym next. Then job stuff in earnest. Watching TV has not been & is not helpful.

Create the mindset you want. Everything else follows.

6-1-23

Creating The Mindset

- Always keep in mind that you create your reality.
- Constantly do those things that improve you.
- Envision who you want to be and act accordingly.

•

A Winner Never Quits & A Quitter Never Wins!

A Quitter Never Wins & A Winner Never Quits!

6-5-23

Keep Trying

Feeling very off today. Anxious & headache. Woke up late again. Need to get back on track. I want to. Big hurdles are the pills, caffeine, & nicotine, in that order. Why do I keep doing them? It's immediate gratification which takes away from the investment in the future.

Work on focusing on what you want, putting yourself in that mindset, and then acting accordingly. Nothing is going to change if you don't change it.

What was good yesterday. Left in a good place with Mom. Watching TV with Ivy. Getting into the right frame of mind with both of them.

What was bad yesterday. Too much caffeine. Modafinil. Bed late.

What can you do today? Run. Think forward. Get in the right mindset. Find the frequency. Action.

•

I am the Universe. We all are. We are made from it, we exist in it, and we constitute it. Who is to say our collective consciousness isn't God experiencing his own creation. Or the Universe being able to experience

Or I?

itself. This would make sense from a manifestation standpoint. The urgency here becomes to connect with the right frequency. The right wavelength. All efforts must be put towards this task. You can live any life your heart desires. You must attack this realization with urgency. All the power is in your hands. Time and time again your power to create the reality around you has been demonstrated. Use that realization to create the life of your dreams. It is all in your control. Be the magnet to those things you so desire. I love you. Please help me. Please be with me. I am so grateful to you. I am forever yours.

6-6-23

Tough Work

Today was tough. Woke up extremely late ~2pm after staying up until 3:30am. Felt off. Depressed. Anxious. Battled with the demons all day. Constantly trying to get in the right frame of mind. I wasn't really able to achieve it but I'm proud of the fight. Also proud that I went to the gym and worked out hard. A good battle today.

Texted *A Connection* after much procrastination. The fact that I had been putting it off was really weighing on me. Immediately felt better after texting. She never got back to me and I don't even care. A lesson here. You're not really concerned about other people's opinions of you. So what's with the anxiety? Very strange. But also recognize the reality that you don't really care what other people think. What you care about is failing yourself. Make doing your best your purpose.

Was helpful to read yesterday's passage about being the Universe. More of those realizations when they're needed.

Meditation helped as well.

Sleep is improving. Keep on this train. A lot of answers are in better sleep.

I love you. I am here for you. Things will get better. Keep going.

6-7-23

Fully Jammed

Feeling so jammed up. Can't get my energy right. Very depressed this morning. Did wake up earlier ~10:00am. That was good. But I don't know where the low mood is coming from. Took Modafinil again and got fully anxious. Very all over the place thereafter.

Had the interview with the recruiter regarding the job at *NFL Star's* production company. I was initially very excited to hear about it. As time went on in the day, I started to get more negative on it like it might not be the right thing to do. I'm concerned about going back into the Hollywood fold. I'm concerned about my ability to succeed in the position. Is there an opportunity here? Yes, but I think success will be hard to come by. It will depend largely on their programming strategy & what they want to accomplish. Who has had success in this arena? LeBron. Success seems to come in the same arena as the sport they played & is easier in the unscripted space. It's possible but not something to bet on. So assuming all goes well here, what's the play? Do you take the job for a paycheck? Do you really commit to making a change? My gut is telling me this is a bad idea… But need to sleep on it and really consider what's good. I'm not sure how clearly I'm thinking right now.

One thing's for sure. Sleep needs to be sorted out. Modafinil fucks me up. Move on to tomorrow. It's a new day.

•

Fashion Meeting Prep

What Do I Do?
- Identify and purchase content (based consumer and market trends and according to the brand you work for)
- Lead the development of that content (alongside show creator and anyone else on the creative team)
- Sell show to network
- Collaborate with network to develop the show further to specifically fit their brand

Or I?

- Build out leadership team and continue overseeing them over course the show's lifecycle
- Oversee creative over the course of the show's lifecycle

***Media* Industry**
Crap shoot & integrity problems

Weakness
I've been willing to take on too much at times

Strength
I really care

6-10-23

Text

The important thing is to have a goal in mind while trying to get into that wavelength. You can't get into the right wavelength if you don't have aim.

6-12-23

Despite anxiety & depression still being present, have been feeling pretty good the past couple of days.

Big reasons for this:
1. Unleashing my personality
2. Better sleep
3. Affirmation sleep meditation

1. *Unleashing my personality*
This has been a huge unlock. So much of my pent-up energy has been due to muzzling myself & trying to act a certain way. I can literally feel the energy dissipating properly when I am letting my personality flow. It's amazing. Fear subsides. I'm more courageous. It feels good.

Focus on action. Let's make moves. Let's build a life. I'm ready.

6-13-23

All Over The Place

Why do I feel the way that I do? I am losing my mind anxious right now. I am also hyper focused on things with Ivy. Feeling very anxious about our relationship. We had a great couple of days together yesterday and the day before. Stayed up late talking both days. Today I went to her open house, which was filmed. I took Modafinil halfway through & I guess that must have really contributed to this because things have been very anxious ever since. I did feel some kind of way about the whole thing, which I can't figure out. I think part of it is being treated kind of like a stranger. Ivy found out she closed on her house at the end. When I gave her a hug, it was the quickest most sterile hug in the world. Then she hugged *Her Co-Worker* in a normal way. I clearly clocked this. I definitely felt awkward standing around. When I was leaving, one of the producers said "I'm sure we'll be seeing a lot more of you this season," which I thought was curious. But maybe something she says to everyone. Ivy & I got home at the same time. Of course she sits as far away from me as possible. I may have gotten a little too intimate in my congratulations of her. I don't know though. She went to the beach with Fido and said she was going alone but left her car here so I suspect went with someone, but why lie? She got back right after I got back from the gym. I was shirtless and I felt like she was avoiding looking at me. She immediately went to *Her Co-Worker's house*. When she got back she had good energy – joking about my ID pic – but pretty much immediately went to her room. What's going on here? Is she avoiding me? Is she worried I'm catching feelings again? Am I just reading into all of this too much? Ahhhh! I just want to cry. I feel so left out. So like we're not close. So used. Is she sick of me? What do I do? Why am I so concerned about this? She obviously doesn't really feel comfortable around me. I need to get over that because it's affecting my self-confidence. The whole thing is making me feel less than. It's making me feel so undesirable. So unlovable. So alone. I am going to Auntie's the next two days so it will be good to get away. My brain goes to worry that Ivy will have someone over here. This needs to be dealt with emotionally. She's not into you. It's never going to happen. Get over it. Anything else is a disservice to

Or I?

you. The worrying about her dating & who she's with out of fear over losing her needs to stop. Accept the situation for what it is & move on with your life. No one's thinking about you. No one cares about you. You need to do that for yourself.

I love you. Keep going.

6-18-23

Book

No More Mr. Nice Guy

by Dr. Robert Glover

•

NMMNG Activities

Breaking Free Activity 1
People to support – Aston, Brutus, Whitman

Breaking Free Activity 2
It's not rational to try to hide parts of yourself. My attempt at hiding obviously has something to do with feeling like I'm not good enough. What is it that I think is wrong? Always felt like my personality was too much for Mom & Dad. Topline it's all about trying to get people to like me & that they won't like who I am. But it doesn't make sense to not be yourself. Then people aren't really liking you, they're liking a persona. People try to change who they are to fit in. I hide my annoyance. My fear. My masculinity. My overwhelm. My resentment. My desires. My wishes. My dreams. My power. Hiding to seem cool which is not cool at all. Being yourself is.

6-19-23

NMMNG Activities

Breaking Free Activity 3

This is a hard one for me. There are similarities to all 3 of the stories presented *in the prompt about Alan, Jason, & Jose*. Like Alan I did well in school and sports and felt that was something that set me apart but it was never enough. I always felt like I could never do good enough. When I did well the message was that that was just how it should be. Like Alan I also developed a problem/compulsion believing I was a sinner. Whenever I felt like I sinned I would say a little prayer of "forgive me lord, Amen." Also like Alan I believed that my parents could do no wrong, despite the controlling, critical, and emotionally invalidating treatment of me. This put all the power in their hands and made me beholden to their opinion of me. I also made a decision to be nothing like my parents. To be nowhere near as strict, controlling, emotionless, and distant as them.

Like Jason I believed the family was perfect. This was reinforced by family friends who would tell me how great Mom & Dad were as parents. But of course they had no idea what was actually going on. But it gaslit me. Mom & Dad were both very controlling – especially Mom. I don't feel like I was ever really given a choice about what I wanted to do. I "had" to do all the sports, plays, extracurriculars, etc. for college. Mom still tells me what to do and treats me like a kid. I also don't remember Mom & Dad ever really showing affection to each other. And constantly worried about them getting divorced. They never vacationed by themselves. I still try to be perfect like they told me I had to be.

Like Jose I try to repress my anger and never show or do anything that I think will upset anyone. I also very much seek out recognition & don't want to show any flaws.

Ways it was implied that it wasn't ok to be myself:
- Grades/performance – Would get punished for bad grades. Tons of pressure was placed on me to succeed. I only felt accepted if I did. This created a ton of performance anxiety and worse performance. I started to think "what if I mess up" or "what if concussions have made me dumb" which would affect my performance. The focus on grades & lack of recognition even when they were good made me feel both like I was only ok if I did well but also like I was never good enough.

Or I?

- Focus on intellect – There was an extreme focus on the fact that I am smart. It made me feel like this is where my worth comes from. When I got a couple of concussions, it ripped me to my core because I worried that I was now defective. I became obsessed with the fear that I might now be dumb and the anxiety that resulted affected my performance and caused me to procrastinate out of fear that I would be proven right. I felt my identity & acceptance was tied to how smart I am. I still do. But also find ways to still worry that I'm not and so am worthless.
- Focus on appeasing others/questioning my behavior/the importance of being high status people – It was always so important to appease the high status people my parents seemed to seek out to be friends with – who were often my friends' parents. The more high status, the more the pressure to "behave." Whenever I would get home from someone's house it was always "did you behave/have good manners." This always drove me crazy because I always did. But it made me both feel like the most important thing was to appease other people and that my behavior was not seen as "good" enough. This left me with extreme anxiety and pressure to be seen as a "good kid" at all times. It also made me feel like everyone was better than me & that I should always be deferent to status/authority & eager to please both.
- Punishment for minor trouble – It was always such a huge deal when I got in any amount of minor trouble at school which made me terrified of showing any edge to my personality.
- Being called a hypochondriac – Dad always called me a hypochondriac whenever I said I had any problems which totally invalidated my feelings & made me feel like it wasn't ok for me to have any. There were times when I was legit hurt and it was brushed off.
- Not acknowledging OCD/Mental Health – No one believed me when I said my stomach hurt for months after moving to San Fran. This ultimately led to the development of my OCD. When I finally opened up about it, I wasn't believed.
- Ostracized for liking baths & implication that I was gay – This made me feel horrible and also made me so worried I was gay, which I knew would not be accepted.
- Self-deprecating comments by Dad drove home body issues. Also making fun of me for not wanting to be naked in front of other people made me extremely shameful.
- Body/looks comments – Was made to feel that it is unacceptable to be fat. Looks were made to be so important. Mom would make

comments about body hair that ultimately left me to believe it was unattractive and gave me a ton of shame about it.
- Dad freaking out over losing – Made me anxious about beating him and like that was not ok. This translated to beating others. Would dull myself so as to avoid making people upset.
- Forced to sing at parties when I didn't want to – Made me feel like I had to perform and appease. They were definitely drunk when they made me do this.
- Moving for Mom's job – Made it feel like my life didn't matter. No stability, raised by multiple different babysitters.
- Criticism of friends – Made me feel like a POS for my friends. Highly critical of me for standing up for them. Made me feel flawed & hide my real personality from them.
- Rules around sex/girls made me so anxious to ever bring anyone over & that my sexuality should never be seen & wasn't ok.
- I don't remember there ever really being much support, only pressure, which signaled I wasn't valuable to them.
- Dinner conversations always revolved around Mom & work. I don't really remember them asking about us or our day. Signaled we don't matter.
- Punished for arguing with Rose – Signaled I was always at fault & arguments were not ok.
- Dad always used to ask me why I looked mad/sad when I was just chillin, which made me feel like it wasn't ok to just have my natural face.

6-20-23

NMMNG Activities

Breaking Free Activity 4

Having hair *just right*: Do this. Not to an obsessive degree but I do seek approval through & spend time on my hair (constant haircuts).

Being smart: Absolutely. This is fundamental to me. It seems everything is about being smart and I experience great anxiety & shame about appearing dumb (Emails, texts, conversations).

Or I?

<u>Having a non-threatening voice</u>: Yes I modulate my voice for approval. Both appearing more masculine. More feminine. More Philly. I'm not even sure exactly what my real voice is at times. This needs to change.

<u>Appearing unselfish</u>: Yes. Scared to have any demands of my own. Don't want to upset others.

<u>Being different from other men</u>: Yes. Pride myself on this even though it clearly isn't working for me and gets me nowhere. Need to embrace my masculinity.

<u>Staying sober</u>: Yes. Much of my sobriety now is centered around what other people will think if I drink. But this needs to be considered carefully.

<u>Being in good shape</u>: Yes. There is absolutely a vanity part of this which is ok. But I was raised to believe that being in good shape is the only acceptable thing.

<u>Being a great dancer</u>: Yes to the point that I am always thinking what other people think when I'm dancing instead of just enjoying myself.

<u>Being a good lover</u>: Yes. Definitely have self-worth & anxiety about being accepted in this way. Although I do believe I'm good at sex. But certainly more focused on partner's experience rather than my own.

<u>Never getting angry</u>: Yes. I hide my anger so as to not upset others and gain their acceptance. Ex. Don't tell people how I feel when they upset me.

<u>Voice example</u>: Different voice when talking to different people. Different voice when trying to show toughness.

<u>Unselfish example</u>: Don't ask for help when it's needed. Don't take up space.

<u>Being different example</u>: Never showing masculinity. Never pursuing sexual desires. Being non-threatening.

<u>Making other people happy</u>: All the time. Afraid to upset anyone or show my true feelings. Afraid to dominate even when I can.

Being a good worker: Everything with work. Afraid to make mistakes. Going above & beyond.

Clean car: That one's for me

Dressing well: Approval seeking but also personal pride.

Being nice: Always. Does nothing for me.

Respecting women: Always. Does not attract them.

Never offending anyone: Yes. Always.

Appearing to be good: Yes. Always.

Other Issues
Rarely showing needs or wants
Body hair
Nose
Not singing
Not being excited/celebrating

★ Fucking all of these things ★

Breaking Free Activity 5
(A prompt on the impact of not caring what other people think)
I would be free. I would talk to anyone I wanted to and not talk when I didn't. I wouldn't care if I clammed up in conversation. I would reach out to anyone & everyone to find a job. I would go up to any girl I thought was attractive. I would do whatever I wanted. I would be sexual when I wanted. I would not worry about upsetting people. I would act exactly as I feel. I wouldn't feel nearly as much stress. I would say what I feel & feel what I say. Honesty.

I would be more demanding. I would be more upfront about things that bother me. I would date a lot. I would cut things off when it wasn't right for me. I would be more assertive. I would be more relaxed. I would be a better version of me. Conversation would flow more smoothly. Everything would be better. I would be more dominant & take on more of the male gender role. I wouldn't simp. There would be no fake bs.

Or I?

I would be more discerning about who was in my life with less stress around everything. I care too much what people think about me & it's causing me stress & to be less authentic than I'd like.

6-21-23

NMMNG

Breaking Free Activity 6
I hide (to gain approval/avoid disappointment)
- Anytime I lose/misplace something I don't tell anyone about it because I'm afraid of making mistakes/asking for help.
- Hate being late and feel like a complete failure if I am.
- Terrified of breaking things – remember being petrified when I broke windows on the garage when practicing sports. Was super punished for that. Hid issues with the Subaru. Will hide things to avoid taking accountability for things if I can.
- Never want to admit I don't know things (interviews/conversations). Talking to Ivy/Mom/Dad/anyone. Good at hiding this but it's extremely taxing. Not worth it.
- Will own up to it if I very obviously do something wrong.
- Hide my depression from everyone. Feel like people won't like me if they know. Don't feel like I'm entitled to it. Parents never accepted it was real. Feel like I'm good at hiding it.
- Hide my pain. Was told I am a hypochondriac so I don't know how to properly deal. Very good at hiding my physical & emotional pain.
- Really do whatever I can to hide the fact that I have messed up. But I'm also terrified of messing up so I rarely do. But I spend way too much time worrying about it. It would be better to just own up to it.
- Hide that I'm sexual all day, every day. Writing this makes me want to cry.
- Completely hide bodily functions. Good at this.
- IDK about getting older although I am ashamed of my age.
- Not losing my hair but try to hide just how hairy I am. Not good at this hahah.
- Good at hiding my needs for sure. You'd think I didn't have any. FUCK.
- Try to be perfect at ALL TIMES. Embracing imperfections now.

Boy am I good at hiding.
Fuck Me.

6-24-25

Oy Vey

Welp, got into it with Ivy today over Fido. She goes out to a beach filming day yesterday at like 2:30pm. Doesn't come home until like 10:00am the next day. I wake up knowing she's been out all night. Had some lingering FOMO pangs of jealousy weird feelings but managed. When I woke up I knew Fido had been left alone all night. Didn't want to walk him but felt so bad for him that I did. She's here looking totally worked when I get back. She's acting totally blasé about the whole thing like "oh I've been a bad dog mom" but in such a bs way. I tell her "you can't do that to him" and she gives me such a fucking bitch shrug back. I'm so heated I go to my room to compose myself. Eventually I go outside and confront her. She takes basically no accountability saying she feels no guilt or shame. My messaging was basically I'm willing to help you but you need to ask for it. I feel used if not. And don't expect me to just clean up your mess. Things resolved basically because I made it so. The convo was tense at times and she was being honestly fucked saying "Fido is fine" and just taking no ownership over the badness of her actions. Despite the convo being handled, I'm disgusted & disappointed in her. She kept saying "this only happens once in a blue moon" as if that makes a difference. I'm like "well I love this dog and have lived with it for years so I feel responsibility for it even if it's not my dog." Lost a lot of respect for her today. Gained respect for myself confronting the situation. I am good at this shit. NMMNG, channeling energy, embracing fear were all big factors. Also the idea of focusing on your essence/personal power & impressing yourself all played a role. Think today was very helpful in detaching. I am grateful for that. Don't really want to see her (drove around for ~1hr instead of going home to make sure she was in bed). You will deal though, you always do. She is not your person & never will be. Fuck her for today & for the selfishness & neglect she displayed. Good riddance.

Or I?

6-25-23

NMMNG

Breaking Free Activity 7
I intellectually understand this to be the case but for some reason still struggle to show my imperfections. In thinking about it I realize that it's when I show who I really am, warts & all, that people like me the most. How I'd be different? It would fire me up to really speak my mind. To feel comfortable raising whatever issues I have. To freely express my emotions. I wouldn't feel pressure to put on a mask.

Breaking Free Activity 8
Go on a moratorium from:
- Trying to be smart
- Appearing unselfish

Breaking Free Activity 9
Importance of doing things for yourself (p. 69 list). This is something that I've actually been pretty good at.

•

Journal

Felt really good hanging out with *NYC Roommate* the past couple days. I felt valued. I felt appreciated. I felt accepted. And I was really my full self the whole time. It was great. I really tapped into my authenticity. It was so validating to hear *His Wife* say she thought I was a great storyteller. She repeated this multiple times. It was also great to hear her say that I must have disappointed a lot of girls, & that it was ridiculous for me to have been so worried about molluscum *in college*. The whole thing reminded me of my value. It also emphasized the importance of being around people who lift you up. Felt great to make people laugh again. Felt great to enjoy life. Remember this and the feeling of being in touch with yourself.

6-26-23

Dialing In

What is contributing to negative emotions in your life & what can you do about it? Bad sleep. Getting a better sleep schedule will pay massive dividends. Caffeine. Reduction will be beneficial. Ivy. Obsessing over our relationship is causing major mental strain. Lack of momentum. Got to get the ball rolling.

The thing that helps me the most is when I can put myself first. You've realized that doing what you want & being who you want to be is about being able to maintain a mindset that is focused on yourself rather than on external validation. This requires focus & constant effort. Train the brain like a muscle.

The big line from today is **"what would the ideal man do in this situation?"** The answer to that is the action to take.

Another line is **"If you weren't afraid, what would you do?"** This provides great framework for the right way to behave in any situation.

•

Text

Feel the fear and do it anyway

6-27-23

NMMNG

Breaking Free Activity 12

Intellectually I know it's ok to have needs but subconsciously I don't think this is the case. Of course having needs is ok. But why don't I believe that my needs are important? This is very curious. I've been putting myself last for a long time. My needs are important. I think it comes from moving a lot. This made me feel like my needs weren't important at all. Also not being given the chance to develop my own interests. But none of this matters anymore. It's time to focus on myself and what I need.

Or I?

I don't really feel that people want to help me meet my needs but that's probably a consequence of the people I've surrounded myself with which makes that a self-fulfilling prophecy. I know that people like Brutus, Whitman, Aston, & to some degree, Gilly, want to see me happy, but I do get down feeling like for the most part the people around me are not very supportive.

I know that the world is a place full of abundance, but for some reason it feels very scarce to me. The world is full of abundance though, and I see the most when I put myself out there in it.

A change in mindset is needed.

Find the people who support you!

6-27-23

NMMNG

Breaking Free Activity 13

I give all my time & attention to Ivy (caretake) with the covert contract hope that it will get her to like me. This is unfair to both of us. My fear is that if I don't caretake (to her & to other people) that they won't like me. This is inauthentic as there are so many times that I don't want to be doing the caretaking but do so in hopes of being liked and accepted. But if people don't like you for who you really are then the friendship isn't real regardless.

•

Journal

I've been feeling so off. So uncomfortable at home around Ivy. The energy is off and I don't know what to do about it. I am so on edge around her. I am so focused on making things good between us again but she doesn't seem to care. I don't feel like myself around her. I'm struggling to connect with her. I pine for her and think about her when she's away, but in her presence don't feel a longing. I just want to feel loved and valued but don't. I want to be the best for her as a friend. But now it's best if I focus on myself and my needs. I deserve to feel loved and connected. I've sacrificed so much of myself. Get curious about the feelings you have around her. Remember to focus on your life force. Those who get what they want are those that can focus on themselves and their needs longer than others. I'm sorry this time is so hard. You deserve someone who loves you. Be 100% you.

6-28-23

Alter Ego

★ Sinclair ★

Sinclair is everything you want to be.

Sin is the man
Sin loves fear
Sin is poised
Sin doesn't give a fuck what other people think
Sin does what he wants
Sin goes for what he wants
Sin is calm
Sin is hard
Sin doesn't suffer fools
Sin is love
Sin doesn't take things too seriously
Sin is funny
Sin is fun
Sin is sexual/gets all the girls/isn't a simp
Sin is attractive
Sin is an animal
Sin stays in the zone
Sin uses his power
Sin focuses on himself
Sin has edge
Sin has *IT*
Sinclair is detached
Sinclair knows best

Or I?

Sinclair doesn't give a shit
Sinclair gets what he wants
Sinclair is the leader & never follows
Sinclair is a self-promoter

6-29-23

Abundance

Great things are coming your way. Everything is Happening for a Reason. Everything you're going through is teaching you the lessons you need to learn. Belief is the underlying factor. It doesn't matter what people think about you. AT ALL. Abundance mindset. Abundance mindset. Abundance mindset. Great things are coming. Authenticity is key. Right now is an opportunity. The body is a VR Suit to your consciousness. Get the Suit to operate at the right frequency. Get to the right frequency and then let it flow. Figure out what you want, figure out what that feels like, and then live in that frequency. What does it feel like to be the person you want to be? Live in that mindset. It all comes down to the atomic level. Align the atoms with the frequency of who you want to be and what you want. This is where your success came from as a kid. This is where your success came from with women. Remember these moments. The unshakeable faith you had in yourself is what determined your success. Tripping on shrooms & acid aligned you right and you always slept with people afterwards. It was about the alignment on a quantum level. You've been doing your best to undermine your intelligence. This reprogramming has worked to your disadvantage. But you've been given a good Suit. So despite your best efforts to undermine yourself, it hasn't worked. Focus on yourself & being the best you can be. Find the magic frequency & live in it. You're so close. Keep progressing. Anything is possible!

6-30-23

Mindset Foundation

★
You can't get into the right mindset without a destination/purpose/goal in mind
★

I.E. "I don't care what other people think." The goal of that and that thought allows you to find the frequency that aligns with that mindset. This still isn't the best example though because it's too broad. The more specific the mindset the better.

7-6-23

Maintenance

I feel ok today. Lots of 4th activities definitely drained me a bit. Got back very late after talking to Tulip on the 4th and slept late yesterday. Felt very depressed most of the day. Felt good to have people be so complimentary of me over the weekend. I think having that go away was tough in the aftermath. The fact that I'm so stuck while everyone is being so complimentary also makes me feel like something is wrong with me & that I'm wasting my life away.

When I was able to tap into my emotions & to be my unapologetic self is when I was doing my best & when I was best received. Thinking back to when I first started having issues @ college & at work, what I was doing was being fully focused on what I thought other people wanted & acting accordingly. This put so much stress on the brain. This also leads to a constant state of uncertainty because you can never know what other people want. You will never know. The only way is to be constantly looking inward. It always feels the best to be yourself. If you do that there is nothing to feel bad about. This is authenticity.

I am ready to move forward in life. I really am. Better sleep. Ween off caffeine. Ween off nicotine.

SET GOALS. PURSUE THEM.

Or I?

7-7-23

NMMNG

Breaking Free Activity 16

I am making the decision to put myself & my needs first. I am grateful for this guidance. Thank you. Thank you. Thank you.

•

Journal

I am feeling so down. I want to cry. I have no idea where to go from here. I have sacrificed so much of myself. I don't know who I am. What can I do to get where I want to go. It does begin with making the commitment to putting myself first.

•

Today I asked Ivy if she wanted to grab dinner with Mom & I in an attempt to do something together outside of the apartment to strengthen getting back to normal. She said she just wanted to take it easy/didn't want to get dressed/put makeup on. When I got back she was out. Still not back @ 1am. Clearly the truth is that she just doesn't want to hang with me. This one hurts. I'd said we need to celebrate the closing of a house she sold recently. She agreed but when I waited for her to bring it up so as to not force the issue, she never did. I won't ask her to do anything again. She has moved on & doesn't want to.

I also had a rough dinner with Mom. I told her I wasn't doing well & she went in to her usual schtick on getting a job. But this time it hit me hard. I'm alone. I felt like I wanted to kill myself. She is trying to be helpful, I know, but the approach hurts so bad. I was feeling numb during the conversation. Can hardly remember what she was saying. I do remember her saying no one was going to come to help & that I need to go out in the world. I know this is true but it made me feel so alone. I left the night feeling like all I have are enemies. Like it's just me. It is.

7-8-23

NMMNG

Breaking Free Activity 17
<u>Doing It Right</u>
In childhood: Feels like everything was about trying to do it right to appease Mom & Dad. School would be the big example. Always trying to get good grades. Or else... Lots of anxiety resulted. Feels like I loved drinking so much because it was an escape from that.
Adult: Now it's in work. Feels like I won't be accepted if I'm not perfectly executing. Also in social interactions. Trying to always do it right. Whatever that means. But always trying to guess makes me stiff & boring. Also anxiety. Remember when you realized that the more you were your crazy self, the more people liked you? Come to think of it, I'm always trying to "do it right." There is no right way, all ways were created by other people just like you. Keeps me from fun.

<u>Playing It Safe</u>
Childhood: Singing – Wish I'd taken the risk. Golf – Wish I'd taken the risk. Acting – Wish I'd taken the risk. Was worried I'd be shown I wasn't as good as I thought I was.
Adulthood: Right fucking now. Not going for anything out of fear. I also play it safe by not showing who I really am. Don't speak up when I want to (for the most part). Don't date. Don't do anything that may rock the boat. Fuck me that's bad. Makes me feel powerless to do what I really want.

<u>Anticipating & Fixing</u>
Childhood – Mom & Dad with their arguments. Played therapist multiple times so things would be smooth. Felt beholden to their moods.
Adulthood – With Ivy. Anticipate what the problem might be or what might cause problems and adjust myself accordingly. Makes me feel powerless to behave how I want while she does whatever she wants.

<u>Trying To Not Rock The Boat</u>
Childhood: Afraid to get in trouble. Afraid to ask for what I wanted. Afraid to be myself – felt rejected. Made me feel completely powerless.
Adulthood: All the same plus @ work. Still completely afraid to ask for what I want. Afraid to upset people or make them feel bad. Makes me feel totally caged in.

Or I?

Being Charming & Helpful

Childhood: Parent's parties/whenever their friends were around. Remember developing anxiety around this and wouldn't want to socialize knowing I had to be a certain way.

Adulthood: Everywhere. Feel very responsible for being the fun, entertaining one wherever *I go*. Again, both make me feel powerless to be how I want & to act in a way that is authentic in the moment.

•

★ Eliminating The Pedestal ★

Mom said something that really resonated yesterday. I was talking about my fear of authority when I noted that I wasn't afraid of my teachers growing up. She replied "well bosses are just the teachers of business." Really reframes things in a good way for me that eliminates the pedestal.

7-9-23

An Opportunity

Today was a strange one. I'm trying to reprogram my brain/subconscious. But in doing so it feels like I'm getting some major pushback. Woke up realizing just how much Ivy is on my mind. It's an obsessive thought pattern that is engrained & reinforced through automatic repetition. Working on acknowledging the thoughts and then letting them pass like in meditation. Also refocusing & replacing the thoughts with positive ones.

I'm doing good & focusing on myself when she gets back from wherever she was. At that point my brain goes into overdrive. She's in a good mood/engaging with me. Things are good. She brings up my sobriety & asks about dinner with Mom. Breadcrumbs I realize. At that point it's like I vomit out all sorts of stuff about myself trying to connect. Completely reverting to old behaviors & basking in the light. I was able to focus on myself more. And most importantly was able to focus on not trying so hard, but I still regret some of the vomit. I was able to be my charismatic self, and she was engaged in the conversation until she went to her room to "clean." She shuts the door and is out. Whenever I saw her for the rest of the day there was distance. She spent much of the rest of her day in her room. Immediate discard? Was she just trying to make up for the other day?

The remainder of the day I had the familiar anxiety around her & preoccupation on her mood. Basically not knowing how to be myself. Waiting for the other shoe to drop & wanting connection. These are attachment issues for sure.

Herein lies the opportunity. These next 6 months are the perfect opportunity to work on your issues. There is no riper situation to work on detaching & self focus than this. There is no future so it's a great dress rehearsal. This is what the Universe is trying to teach me through this experience. It's perfect. It all makes sense. This will benefit me for the rest of my life. Thank you Universe. I'm excited to get curious, get started, and get to work. THANK YOU! I AM SO GRATEFUL!

7-13-23

Email To G/Fore

File this under the category of a shot in the dark (or maybe more appropriately in this context, a blind tee shot), but I'm reaching out in hopes of getting on your radar because there is no place that I would rather work than at G/Fore.

I'm a lifelong golfer and a fashion enthusiast who's trying to transition into retail after 10+ years working in Entertainment at places such as USA, Syfy, Bravo, E!, New Regency, and Lionsgate. With this comes experience in creative project management, marketing, creative concept development, PR, and production.

I absolutely love golf, love clothes/shoes, and love your brand. I don't think anyone's doing it better. With that said and with the understanding that your company represents the culmination of all the things I love, I would be so grateful for the opportunity to speak with someone further about my passion for G/Fore and why I think I would be a great addition to your team.

Or I?

Thank you!

7-14-23

★ The Parasite ★

The feelings of insecurity/self-doubt/anxiety/procrastination are a Parasite that feeds off of you. It wants you to be a bitch. It feeds off of that & belief that it's right. It wants you to be small. Fight it. Talk back to it. Ignore it. Fuck that Parasite. Starve that motherfucker & laugh at its demise.

This is the final boss. Beat this Bitch & The Real You Emerges.

★ Phoenix From The Ashes ★

•

★ Article ★

Facing Your Parasite

by Mitch Y Artman

7-15-23

MINDSET *YouTube Video*

From Jay Shetty YouTube Interview With Dr. Joe Dispenza: "Dr. Joe Dispenza ON: How To Brainwash Yourself For Success & Destroy NEGATIVE THOUGHTS!"

90% of thoughts are the same as the day before – if you don't think differently then everything will be the same.

Life is the following experiment:

Personality *is* how you think, act, and feel. If you think *the* same way life is going to be the same.

Remind yourself how you're going to think, how you want to act, how you want to feel (and how you don't want to be in each of these things). Changing this is how you reprogram.

The experiment is changing these things and seeing what changes in your life.

This is going to be uncomfortable. Embrace the uncomfortable because that means the change is happening.

•

Look at how you don't want to think anymore and fuck that. That is really really working right now. No more fucking worrying about Ivy and I don't want to care what anyone thinks anymore. FUCK THAT.

7-16-23

Battling

I've been working on controlling my thoughts & not feeding the Parasite. It's working but it's brutal. The biggest thing that's helped is to focus on the mindset that I don't want to be in – one that I'm currently in – and then getting out of that. This is as opposed to striving for a specific "good" mindset, which is so much more of an amorphous target.

The mindset I don't want to be in is 1. Preoccupied & anxious over Ivy. 2. Concerned about what anyone thinks. 3. A victim of my circumstances.

The preoccupation with Ivy is the toughest. I'm able to get out of it but my brain constantly wants to revert back. This morning I was short with her as far as attention goes & immediately was anxious about it. Now that I'm home (which I avoided after dinner with Auntie) and she's not

Or I?

here I have the familiar FOMO/pre-occupation/jealousy. It's the Parasite. It's also the continued reminder that she's always chillin with other people & doesn't ever want to do anything with me outside of here. You want her to like you & she doesn't. Remember, you are wasting your attention on her. She's gone. You must be too. How many times are you going to repeat the same thoughts. No more. She's not worth it. It's interesting how this very behavior which should be off putting keeps you interested.

7-19-23

Text

Basically with all the things that go on in life love is the counterbalance (thing) that keeps us alive.

And makes it all worth it.

7-20-23

Tired As Fuck

I am so fucking tired. Bad sleep the last 2 nights. Causing me to revert to old thought patterns. This is when focus on mindset is most important. Stress causes you to revert to familiar states due to Amygdala activation. The biggest thing is I don't want to be concerned with how other people think about me anymore. I want to feel free. What does that feel like? Imagine that & stay in it. Feels very good when you can get there. The key is the feeling. The other key is to acknowledge when you're feeling some other kind of negative way & not to judge that. One final thought that's been helpful today is to really live every day like it's the last.

I'm continuing to feel so boxed in by this feeling that I have to do what other people want. I feel enslaved by it. But you're the slave driver *so* who's doing the shackling. Time to unshackle this motherfucker. It is uncomfortable but learn to appreciate that as the sign that things are changing. You are no one's slave. Fuck that!

7-22-23

A Realization

Pretty interesting day today. Struggled psychologically for much of it. Struggled to break out of the loop with Ivy this morning. But the first interactions with her I was able to adopt a more detached mindset, which was good. Then fell back into attachment before she left for filming. Struggled to figure out why it is so hard for me to be myself around her. But then I had a general realization. That realization is that with her & with everything else I've simply been trying too hard. This is the form of resistance that has been holding me back. When she got back I focused on really not trying & everything was better.

She also divulged some of her thought process as her day played out on set. Basically she was super manipulative & passive aggressive to her producer. The look in her eyes as she was telling me was straight scary. It proved just how manipulative & conniving she is. I was busting her balls & laughing about it. She talked about how she uses her passive aggression in a way that the other person could never say anything was wrong & that in a week *Her Producer* will think everything was back to normal. I was giving her shit & saying this shit was crazy. Obviously this is major Red Flag shit but the strange thing is that it made me want her more. This is a major indicator of your trauma. The worse she is the more you're attracted. What is going on here? Notice that when you're mistreated, you like it. This shows it's not love but trauma shit. Dig deeper on this.

I did focus on leaning into making her uncomfortable and not being a yes man but leaning into my wits & power. This felt amazing. Need more of this.

Stop trying & start making people uncomfortable.

Or I?

7-29-23

★

Officiated Harry & Sally's Wedding in Park City

★

8-14-23

Notes For Job Interview

REMINDERS

- Stay in the Feeling
- Don't Try Too Hard
- You Are a Serious Person
- You are qualified and they would be lucky to have you
- I don't want to care what anyone thinks anymore. FUCK THAT.
- No Expectations

8-22-23

Stuck But Trying

I'm stuck. What else is new. Feel so jammed up & don't feel momentum. Want to get it back. Been smoking weed for a week & it really doesn't help. Remembering what it's like to be stuck in this cycle & it fucking sucks. Reminds me why I don't want to drink. Big positive. Reminds me also why I want to eliminate the caffeine.

Been interviewing with *A Company* but found out yesterday they're doing a *hiring* freeze. Only good part about that is that there's still a chance & that I didn't bomb the last interview, which was a legitimate concern. Interestingly, what this showed me is that I don't actually mind getting rejected. But I am totally scared of approaching getting rejected. Have I just been forcing myself to care too much? Clearly I don't actually care what other people think. So why do I feel like I do? Very strange but clearly an opportunity to retrain the brain.

In general need to work on accepting fear/emotions/thoughts instead of repressing them as a means for the energy to dissipate. This resistance is going to result in health problems if allowed to persist.

8-24-23

Text

You can only be brave when you're afraid

8-25-23

Next Steps

High right now. Just saw Ivy for the first time since I left about a month ago. I avoided coming home & seeing her for so long. She had to have noticed. No doubt. I've been dreading it so much. Part fear of falling back into old routines. Part scared of how much I suspect she doesn't care. Part because I don't miss her but know how much I'm going to get hurt just by being around her. She hurts me. And I know that, because of & after this avoidance on my part, I'm going to get her best shot right now. Get ready.

When we saw each other – she knew I was here because I was making noise – she walks out and kind of acts like she doesn't know I'm here. Very casual hellos & how are you doings. Definitely seemingly not really caring. Of course I reciprocate this vibe. She tells me she's hungover from going out in PHX & is watching S2 *of her show*. She goes to watch in her room & at that point I hug her and tell her it's good to see her. She gives me another terribly cold hug. No warmth. No missing to it.

What comes next? We'll see.

Or I?

Find your Resonant Frequency & operate in it. I want to break free from the shackles. All of them. I want the frequency of freedom. I'm open to it.

•

Feeling immediately overthinking and emotionally all over the place after talking to Ivy for real for the first time. She comes out after finishing watching S2. She's like "we're like passing ships in the night." Tells me she's going "to *New Guy's*." I'm like "is that the food guy?" hah. She then goes on to tell me about how she "called it off but got roped back in. It's going to end in tears…" I'm like "welp." I'm like "well we can catch up tomorrow" "I've got an open house" "Well maybe not then" "What are you doing" "Um I don't know trying to figure it out" "Ok well then maybe Sunday if you're around?" "…"

I then ask her how she's doing and we catch up a bit. She asks about the "wedding job interview." I tell her it *was* good & was partially why I stayed. And that it's on hold. And that it's in NY and I thought I was going to move there. She seemed excited for me saying it's not over yet. I suspect & fear that she was excited to hear about the NY part too. That could just be the overthinking part of me talking.

We talked for a minute or two more about the show. Then she left. Then I felt immediately triggered & smoked & wrote this.

I am happy with being able to identify my proper frequency though. Definitely helps with perspective in conversation.

9-1-23

ADHD Symptoms

SEND BLOOD WORK

Impulsiveness
Disorganization and poor prioritizing
Poor time management skills
Restlessness

Mood swings
Distractibility

•

At all times – Extreme difficulty concentrating despite a desire to do *so*.

Very very hard time organizing thoughts or taking action – thoughts all over the place and feels like thoughts are hidden by a cloud of fog.

Very into whatever I'm into at the time but it's constantly shifting and most of the time I sit there feeling like I'm not interested in anything/that nothing can get me excited enough.

Repeat the same thing every day to avoid having to make choices.

Only feel good about myself when I'm productive but can't bring myself to do anything out of a lack of interest.

Perfectionism run rampant.

Constant burnout (constant pressure, constantly trying to use all my energy to focus, constantly feeling like there's something I'm not doing, disorganization) – never ending cycle.

INATTENTIVE SYMPTOMS

Attention to detail – Forgetfulness – constantly losing the little things but can remember very specific details at times. Knowing that I can be careless causes me to overthink and take too long on everything trying to make sure I didn't miss anything important.

Difficulty staying on task – With everything until the situation becomes dire and things must get done NOW.

Trouble listening – Conversation/Interactions – spend all my energy trying to concentrate on a conversation or task at hand – little energy to focus on the actual thoughts. Often say/do whatever the first thing that comes to mind is rather than what I actually want to say in conversation out of fear of forgetting.

Lack of follow through – Avoiding things like important work. Speeches. Etc.

Or I?

Disorganization – Disorganization and problems prioritizing – if I don't clean things up right away or organize things right away they will get very messy. Very hard time organizing thoughts.

Procrastination – Defining feature of all aspects of life. Mail. Bills. Work. Job search. Problems following through/completing tasks – procrastinate until things become absolutely dire and then I push through usually finishing at the very last minute.

Loses things often – Constantly losing the small things.

Easily distracted – Intrusive thoughts or other people around – constantly distracted. Once I'm distracted by something it becomes an obsession even when I know it's irrational. Going blank – constantly going blank in the middle of conversations as I forget what I'm talking about – too many potential thoughts or ways to say something. Makes me feel like an idiot. Thoughts feel inaccessible like through a cloud of fog. Flow comes very rarely. Anxiety & depression stems from this. Stress and avoidance stems from this as well.

Forgetfulness – Forget important dates/responsibilities/etc. Might remember them for a second then they're gone again until I realize I didn't do something.

HYPERACTIVITY SYMPTOMS

Fidgeting – Playing with hair/compulsions.

Getting out of your seat often – Always at work.

Chronic restlessness – Can never relax even when I should be. Always feels like there's something I should be doing. Procrastinate on sleeping as a result. Late night is the only time I can be sure that there's not something I should be doing.

Difficulty engaging in quiet activities – Definitely get very bored reading or *during* meditation. I have trained the meditation though. If I'm really into a book I'll crush it, if not it will take forever.

Always on the go – Always trying to fill my days. If there is nothing I go crazy. I do the best when my days are jam packed and I don't have time to think.

Talking excessively – Constantly over explaining. I know I do and have swung far *in* the other direction to go out of my way to not say anything out of a fear that I'm talking too much.

Blurting out or finishing sentences – Yes do this for sure. Often times do not give people the chance to finish what they're saying if I know what they're trying to say and they're going too slow.

Difficulty waiting in lines – Hate lines.

Interrupting or intruding on others – Unintentionally interrupt people all the time even though I hate doing it. But it's like I have to share my thought when it comes to mind and my brain short circuits and I interrupt.

All over the place – Things like packing. Leaving my apartment.

Hyperfocus – Whatever I'm into at the moment becomes the most important thing. Go overboard with the things that I'm into at the time. If I start cleaning I'm going to go way overboard. If I start doing a task I might forsake doing a more important one feeling like this one must get done right now. Contributes to poor time management/task prioritization.

Impulsiveness – Interrupting during conversation. Reckless driving, skiing, thrill seeking behavior.

Trouble multitasking – I really can't. It's whatever I'm doing at the time. I'll get distracted if I don't give full focus.

Constantly on edge – Feel constantly irritable. Constantly like I'm not getting anything done. Constantly overwhelmed by thoughts. So many thoughts at once it becomes overwhelming and I become almost catatonic.

Low frustration tolerance – With everything.

Frequent mood swings – Go through all the emotions all day every day.

Hot temper – Definitely get super frustrated super easily.

Or I?

Overthinking – On EVERYTHING.

Emails/texts/papers – Can take me hours to write a single line. Will see texts and not respond to them to avoid the angst of responding.

9-3-23

Resonant Frequency

★ 2 Massive Realizations I've Had Recently ★

1. Finding the Resonant Frequency. Navigate the bullshit thoughts, feelings, & emotions to find the Resonant Frequency within you that consists of how you really feel/think/want to behave in any given situation. This is finding your true authenticity through the noise & living unapologetically in it. The key feature of the Resonant Frequency is that it is the easiest mode to exist in and requires the least amount of effort & is associated with no thought. It's a state of being.

2. Re-parenting. It is completely my responsibility to look after myself. Visualize and take care of the younger, hurt you. Reassure him when he's upset & recognize when actions/emotions/thoughts are the result of the child being wounded.

> P.S. – If having trouble finding the frequency, a cheat/hack can be to think "how would I ideally want to be/feel" and then tap into holding onto & embodying that feeling.

9-11-23

What's Next?

Ivy's show came out. Ivy's been in Palm Springs since. The whole situation is weird. My change in feelings has led to an improved situation with Ivy, but there are still some strange feelings. I think a part of that is the brain resisting & being slow to change. Other parts of it are continuing to deal with exclusionary behavior that causes me to question the friendship. Such as not inviting me to Palm Springs, which makes me feel left out. There is also the emotions resulting from delivering the news that I'm moving out & feeling like she doesn't really care. I know this can't be true but do question this.

One big indicator as to the toxic/unhealthy nature of the relationship, which I don't like, is the fact that I like seeing the criticisms of her in the show. People hate her. I think for me it's the validation that her behavior sucks. It's the reinforcement that this isn't good behavior & *is* not desirable. There's still weird jealousy there, probably always will be, but that's irrational. This shit is a joke, she's quickly becoming a serious joke, and this is embarrassing stuff. One thing is very clear, she is not better than you. Just think – as a thought exercise – what people would say if they knew about our relationship. She doesn't deserve him. Lots of versions of that. Also this guy's being a simp bitch. What does he see in her? He needs to escape. Etc.

Been stuck in weed purgatory, which has been fucking me up. Know I'm going to stop & that it is doing me no good, but stuck & taking comfort down in the hole that I'm in. Definitely has reminded me that I don't want to drink & don't like feeling trapped by substances. Think this will go a long way towards me not glamorizing or missing this shit in the future.

Feelings of hopelessness have been coming up – a lot of it having to do with feeling completely stuck & purposeless. Remember the frequency & battling through. It's all about mindset & changing yours. It's all in your control.

Remember: No one's going to help or save you. It's all on you. But you have literally everything going for you. Let's get it. Let's attack this life. You can do it. I'm here for you. I believe in you. I'm the captain now.

9-12-23

Gaining Control

Or I?

I'm in the process of trying to make improvements. Of trying to live in the right frequency. My brain/body feels jammed up, per usual, but I'm aware that this is my brain resisting a new default state and wanting to maintain the status quo.

Despite the feeling of complete overwhelm/uncertainty about life, I'm feeling hopeful. I now know the importance of training my brain. I love the relief that comes from the moments when I'm not overthinking. I feel great when I can turn inside & detach from the external.

All the negative in my head are just thoughts that I'm buying in to & latching on to. They can be just passing clouds. All that's required is to be the observer of them rather than a participant buying into them. Even anger/frustration/anxiety, recognize & acknowledge these feelings, feel them, then go back to identifying with & becoming the observer.

Take care of that child within you. You are the parent now. I will be a great one – the one I needed & deserve.

9-14-23

Re-Birth

★

Our journey is about being deeply involved in life and yet, less attached to it. – Ram Dass

★

★

What would a disciplined person do?

★

★

What would the ideal version of me do?

★

★

What would you do if fear wasn't a factor?

★

•

Self-Discipline Is Key

It all comes down to self-discipline. You can have all the knowledge in the world but nothing will happen without discipline. Therefore, discipline is foundational. This applies to behaviors & thoughts. Discipline to behave the right way & discipline to control thoughts & emotions. Discipline will allow you to stay in control. You have demonstrated the ability for extreme discipline in the past. You can apply that globally. You are clearly happiest when you are the most disciplined. The choice and the path are clear. Let's eat.

•

Article

You Are Good Enough, How To Stop Trying So Hard and Simply Be Yourself

by Adam Murauskas

9-15-23

BDOML

The realization that everything is under my control is setting in. I read something today talking about how any & every day can be the best day of your life – you just have to decide that's how it's going to be. You're seeing evidence as to how you're able to manipulate your state of mind & what an impact that can have on your overall experience. This is the process of getting your brain under control. This is the ultimate pursuit. This control is what opens the Universe's limitless possibilities.

The things that *are* currently fucking me up and holding me back: Sleep, Weed, Believing Thoughts, Lack of Job Search Discipline. I would like

Or I?

to and can address these things. What's holding me back? Folding to a desire for immediate pleasure & instant gratification over long term goals.

9-17-23

Day 1

Feeling a sense of hopefulness this morning that isn't usually there. Excited to be starting day 1 of a 30 day meditation/journal commitment.

Have made some real progress mentally DESPITE the weed, which is a big deal. Inner Child, frequency, discipline are the three main things right now.

Big step throwing those joints away. I forewent immediate gratification for the right choice. Feels good. Also feels good to wake up earlier today. Would love to really dial the sleep in.

Misc. thoughts – I'm deciding right now that today is going to be a great day. Want to focus on having fun & being focused on internal satisfaction. Don't allow the thoughts to catch on. Remember to tap into the space in the brain which is expansive enough to hold onto all human experience.

Good yesterday – Running. Chillin with Brutus. Diet. Staying at house because I wanted to.

Could improve – Weed. Immediate thought after smoking – extreme anxiety & "man I hate this."

9-18-23

Inner Child

Great Inner Child meditation today. A reminder that the child is always with me & we are one.

Head is buzzing today. Could really feel it during my meditation. Could not identify emotions associated with the sensation. Just feels like an annoying pressure/blanket on my brain that is distracting & which keeps me from accessing my whole brain. Caffeine/nicotine/weed/sleep all likely contributors.

Honestly, you should never be too surprised that you feel off every day considering these negative influences on your brain.

Money is a big stressor right now. I would like to get the spending under control. The feeling of financial insecurity but continuing to spend somewhat frivolously is giving me a lot of anxiety.

The idea of impermanence is very relevant to me right now. It always helps to remember that nothing lasts forever & everything changes in these moments of struggle. You will be free one day. You will be comfortable. You will be proud. Just be a pro as you push through.

I've decided I'm going to be happy & have fun.

SOS: <u>S</u>top – <u>O</u>bserve Thought – <u>S</u>witch to a Better Thought

9-19-23

Getting Off The Sauce

Trying to stop smoking weed today. Know what I'm in for. Know it's going to suck. But not as bad as you think. Just remember, you want to do this & you actually don't like being high.

Detaching from Ivy. Been spending as much time outside of the apt as possible. I'm not sure exactly why but my body is having an extreme aversion to being at my apartment & around Ivy. It's largely subconscious. The feeling in my body is anxiety & frustration. I think – it's hard to pin down. I think a part of it is not wanting to force myself into the mindset/frequency of being receptive to her/engaged in conversation.

Or I?

But then there's also the latent desire for her approval, which makes no sense given how much she's been a bad friend. Want to continue doing whatever I want. Want to not care about the affect I'm having on her. She doesn't come close to deserving your attention.

Great talking to Whitman today.

Great meditation today. Very helpful.

1st Psychological testing meeting today. Helpful. Says they think I have ADHD/OCD pretty bad.

9-20-23

Inner Child

Just completed a very interesting Inner Child work meditation.

I recalled upon a series of memories from younger versions of myself where I was feeling similar to how I'm feeling now. The memories were: Sitting at the dinner table listening to Mom recap her day to Dad (complaining) while Rose & I (for some reason no Tulip) sit there quietly. Sitting in the car with Mom @ Pennstone *(childhood home)* after I'd hurt my back but then was called a hypochondriac *by Dad*. She didn't seem to believe me or do anything about it either. And then finally, getting in trouble @ Carden Hall *(kindergarten)* and being forced into that weird time-out room where I felt all alone. This felt like the core memory intuitively. While writing this others have come up. The theme they share is feeling completely alone, unseen, abandoned, feeling neglected, feeling angry, feeling unloved, feeling hurt, feeling flawed, feeling not good enough, feeling wrongly punished, feeling like it's not ok to be me. I visualized my younger self and connected with them by looking in their eyes & feeling their emotions. I validated them & told them I'll always be there. Interestingly, there was also hope in my child's eyes, he just wants someone to love him. I told him I love him & will always be there to support him.

Profound experience.

9-22-23

New Beginnings

Definitely improving with my mental state. Detachment is key. So is getting into the right frequency. And the right frequency is one of detachment & acting in the Resonant Frequency (typified by no thoughts and minimal effort).

Eliminating expectations has also been a major key. I have had far too high of expectations of those around me, which only leads to disappointment.

On jealousy – I still get pangs of jealousy when I hear about Ivy dating. But it's only with new people. I want to get to the bottom of that. Pursue Inner Child work to get to the root of this emotion. My guess is that it has to do with abandonment wounds.

1. I am grateful today that I'm getting control of my mind.
2. I am grateful that we've gotten to a good place @ the apt.
3. I am grateful to be getting exposed to and to come to realize what detachment & managing expectations means.

•

A Realization

★ You just don't operate as well around some people ★

There are people you are your best self around and where you feel the best. Then there are people where things are slightly off & you don't feel like yourself. That's OK & that's natural. There's nothing wrong with you nor is it your responsibility to fix the vibe if it's off. The main responsibility in these situations is to maintain contact with yourself & to act how you want with the playfulness & chill that defines you. Don't judge the bad feeling, act how you want to despite it.

★

<u>Anxiety Realization</u> – It's possible that my anxiety/tension around certain people relates to the way I was meant to feel beholden to/to people

Or I?

please those people/parents around me growing up who were deemed to be more "important" than us or who carried a certain social benefit. It feels like the same emotional signature. This happens, I notice, when I'm around people I like and want a good relationship with. This should be the focus of the next reparenting.

★

•

Article

Escape the Hamster Wheel Already: The Surprising Path to Sustained Happiness

by Alex Miguel Meyer

"Awareness is about learning how to let everything go and connect to your true self. That's all it is. Some refer to it as **Enlightenment**."

9-23-23

★★★
★ Realizations Abound ★

Major revelation & unlock over the past couple days relating to frequency. The key element is not trying so hard. It's not that you don't care, it's that amping yourself up only increases tension/resistance/anxiety. This makes it harder to operate. You've always been naturally relaxed and this is reverting to your natural state. Mistakenly you've been believing that your issues are born of a lack of effort when in reality the opposite is true and I've been pressing so hard that it's been making it more difficult to think.

The key feature of "not trying so hard" is an empty mind. It's not apathy or lack of caring, it's relaxing into the empty space in the mind. This is the Source from which knowledge springs eternal. It has its own intelligence that supersedes and is additive to your own.

This tendency to press absolutely comes from childhood conditioning. The emotional signature reminds me of when people would come over to the house. I didn't want to see them & I'd force myself into the right frequency with great effort. I was performing and not being natural because that would not have been acceptable. More generally, I can see how I was constantly taught that everything could be fixed by more effort, which implies that every issue or failure was fundamentally my fault. This combined with the sense that I had to please others & act accordingly told me that other people's comfort/opinions were more important than my own. This told me I had to care what other people think. To always look for external validation. This is why I always think everything is my fault & I press to impress.

The thing is that there is no reason to be anything other than relaxed. To be detached. Getting hyped, trying to perform, worrying about what you're saying does absolutely nothing but drain energy.

You're either going to know the answer or not, have something to say, or not. Whatever it is is ok. But you only have the space to do what you really want when you're detached. When there are no expectations & you go with the flow.

•

Article

This Powerful Question Helps Me Silence Toxic Thoughts Immediately

by Moreno Zugaro

Great article: When stuck in a negative spiral, ask "what's my next thought going to be?"

★

Another thing was the visualization of elevating above the plane of everyone else & operating from there.

★

9-24-23

Or I?

Journey On

Feeling much better after meditating just now. Was spiraling before & mentally all over the place. I find myself shifting constantly between frequencies in my brain, seemingly as a means to find one that feels "right" or to avoid feeling what I'm feeling, but this only leads me to feel anxious, on-edge, & out of control. The big problem is that I'm not focused on being mindful & re-centering myself, instead I'm aimlessly searching for a frequency to solve my problems in the same way you'd look to anything external to escape/avoid your problems. The key is to reconnect to the watcher & to delicately & actively settle into the blank space in the mind.

So much of your habit that is most detrimental is the unconscious behavior of automatically trying to rev the brain up into a higher or more hyped state rather than settling into how you actually feel.

Inner Child meditation continues to be revelatory. Connected with the Inner Child today to remind him that I'm here. He seems satisfied but almost needing a minute to adjust to the new reality. I felt his & my shared desire to be making moves. I continue to see how my people pleasing & feeling beholden to people was engrained but no longer serves me.

★

What worked the best yesterday was when I was able to detach & settle fully into my autonomous, self-satisfied, independent, confident self. This quiet, knowing without trying frequency carries confidence with it at its core. The Ego goes away as does the need for external approval in behavior & speech. I know I've got it no matter what & it's so relaxing. The brain operates so much more efficiently only focusing on itself & with room to breathe when not spending so much bandwidth trying to perform the impossible task of reading other people's minds or trying to bend the world to my will.

9-25-23

Feelings

Feeling uncomfortable today & feel like I'm buying into my feelings/trying to rev up into a frequency that is unnatural to me as a means of solving the problem. Shifting into mindfulness now.

The anxiety is really trying to grab a hold of me. I'm accepting it. I also feel dehydrated. Fixing that now.

The goal today – Continue battling for mindfulness but without resisting. Drive towards your authentic self. Full detachment. No expectations. No trying to prove yourself. Just be. Melt into the empty space in the mind. Take the higher position that gives you a view of the whole field in front of you. Jocko Willink describes this in a YouTube video *(with Andrew Huberman)* of a battle simulation you've watched. This is natural to you.

Goals:
Mindfulness
Meditate
Gym
Job
Connect w/ Child
EAGLES

Gratitude – I'm grateful for Ivy. I'm grateful for Fido. I'm grateful for growth.

9-26-23

Autonomy

Today & everyday it's all about autonomy. All previous concepts & theories pertaining to frequency & mental state are driving towards allowing you to exist autonomously with everyone else as extras rather than as masters. Throughout life things have always been best internally & with external relationships when you're acting fully as yourself. This is detachment from the world around you.

Or I?

Mindfulness is the key to getting back into the autonomous state. *S.O.A.R.S.* Stop • Observe • Accept • Replace • Sink into blankness.

Yesterday – Detachment. Mindfulness. No expectations worked the best. Spent lots of time in my frazzled/stuck state. Started to feel old attachments. Continue to observe and dissolve them. Caffeine: Immediately feel worse after consuming. Caught in delusional habit loop. Felt I could have focused more on job stuff.

Today – Focus on mindfulness & improving/supporting the child. Stay in the higher plane of detachment.
Meditate
Gym/Yoga

I am grateful to be making progress with the work.

•

Autonomy & Mindfulness

For everyone the true purpose of your life before anything else – or maybe fundamental responsibility rather than purpose – is to operate autonomously as oneself outside the influence of others. This is your natural state. This is where you are engaged with the world but detached from it. This is where self-esteem springs eternal because every action you undertake is what you want to do. This is where focus on satisfying the self above all else both makes you immune to outside opinions, and, ironically, allows you to show up in the world better for everyone else around you through pure presence.

Most concepts & theories pertaining to frequency & mental state are driving towards allowing you to exist autonomously with everyone else as equals & fellow humans rather than as the masters to your people-pleasing tendencies.

Autonomy is your natural resting state. It is your Resonant Frequency.

9-27-23

The Adult

Success in mindset over the past couple of days has come when I've assumed the role of the parent. This puts me in the frame of mind where I realize it's my right & responsibility to act autonomously as myself. Most importantly it makes me feel calm & in control.

★

I know it's time to be the parent when bad frequencies take hold

★

Yesterday's good: Waking up earlier. Controlling weed consumption. Being the parent. Adopting the role of strength. 5 hours.
Could improve: Caffeine. Sleep. Networking.

Today's focus: Staying in the parent frequency. Being the strength. Discipline.

Today's meditation asked "what do I need to become my ideal self?" The answer is a change in habit towards the disciplined. This includes mental & physical health. Eating healthier. Sleeping better. Solid schedule.

I'm grateful to be alive today & to have more time. I'm grateful to realize that it is my choice to be happy – my choice to have the life I want.

9-28-23

Maintenance

On the flight to Austin right now. Don't feel good physically. Feel very worked & dry. Possibly dehydrated. Also has something to do with weed/nicotine. Sleep has been off.

Continuing on the mindfulness/work journey. Felt like I was really able to settle into being myself talking with Ivy yesterday. Settling in is the key word too. I realized while running yesterday that a trick of the body/mind is to relax into the vibe/Resonant Frequency instead of trying to force anything. This requires the conscious meditative practice of observing anxieties/thoughts/emotions that are occurring but not latching onto them or trying to push them away, *and* letting them dissipate naturally *instead*. Combine this with being the parent when bad wavelengths take hold & you have a winning formula.

Things are great with Ivy. We'd been in a good place before everything went down with Fido *(cancer diagnoses)*, but that all really has re-bonded us. She drove me to the airport today. I know she's a narcissist and that I will be discarded. I am being mindful not to get too attached & of my feelings. The more detached I am, the better things are. It does feel great having things be good again at home.

9-29-23

Governor's Mansion

Currently staying @ the Governor's mansion in Texas and what a trip it is. This is a very special experience. Rolling up you have to go through serious security complete with a metal detector. The home itself is an active museum. ~25 Texas Rangers guard the property at all times. I'm staying in the Sam Houston room. Aka Houston Texas.

It was a special moment last night reading "Leaves of Grass" by Walt Whitman in the Sam Houston room at the Governor's Mansion of Texas. What a sentence to write...

I don't feel great. Stomach is weird & body feels like a raisin. Could not go to sleep until ~3am. Surely most of this has to do with weed withdrawal combined with horrible sleep hygiene.

Today's focus remains on the parent, mindfulness, & settling into the real you. I'm going to go walk around UT, get a local bite, meditate, & read. Focus on the Source & yourself. Remember the highest version of yourself & take all action that fits that bill.

Only 1 more caffeine drink today. Mind + body discipline. Meditation last night showed just how malleable the mind is.

9-30-23

Austin

Bucket list trip complete.

Stayed up until 5:30am talking to *A Family Friend* last night. She's awesome. Felt great really being able to settle into myself around someone like her. I was really happy with my mentality during the trip. The work is paying off.

Loved kicking it with *some new friends*. Really connected with *one*. Feels great to be around other girls/people who actually like me.

Went to the UT/Kansas game today. Rode to the stadium in the motorcade, which was amazing. The suite at the game was incredible. The stadium was incredible. The love for Texas was incredible. Austin is amazing.

Told *A Family Friend* about Ivy. She could not believe the feelings weren't reciprocated. Realize that people saying that is implying your worthiness. Excited to go back to continue my journey of personal growth around disconnecting from her & changing the dynamic of our relationship.

10-2-23

Ellipses

Traveled back from Austin yesterday. Trip was great and I'm absolutely exhausted.

Some reflections – I stand out in every crowd. This is not a matter of Ego, this is simply a fact of the matter. You are good enough. Someone like *A Family Friend* wants to stay up until 5:30am talking to you. *Mom's friend* was telling you how easy you are to talk to. Everyone having confidence in you. I've been denying the reality of myself this whole time. I'm not sad but am grateful for the realization.

Or I?

Another reflection – I am at my best when I settle into the "who cares" self-confidence state. I can feel the difference in energy in my body. My voice is less strained. My brain works better.

A hack that is working – remembering my Higher Self – identifying, encapsulating, and becoming that feeling/person & then acting accordingly frees you up. It's like the opposite end of the spectrum of the Inner Child work where I am the child now & a better, future me is parenting me now. So while I guide the child, the Higher Self guides me.

Today is the last day of weed. The last day of 5 hour. The first day of the acceleration. The continuation of you.

10-3-23

Feeling Pretty Good

Woke up feeling pretty good today relative to the past couple weeks, which is great considering I passed out on top of my sheets again.

★ Yesterdays' realization – The Resonant Frequency IS the frequency of authenticity ★ If you're struggling to find it through re-parenting, detachment, or other strategies, focus on being wholeheartedly yourself and let that drive your mental alignment.

Psych test today. Going to be as truthful as possible to get the real deal results.

Discipline – Let this be a focus today. Woke up @ 8:30 so off to a great start. Let's pursue only those things that are good for your body & mind (Zyn gets a free pass right now).

I am so grateful to have woken up earlier today. I am so grateful to see the work beginning to pay off. I am so grateful to have hung around people who value me last weekend. I am grateful to have paid rent today.

•

Article

Finding The Space Between Your Thoughts Is Simpler Than You Think

by JB Hollows

10-4-23

Over & Out

Yesterday I was really feeling stuck in weed purgatory. Felt out of control after smoking it. Wanted to be off. Ate like shit. Slept on top of sheets. All bad habits. Remember to be gentle with yourself & to not trust your thoughts.

Had the realization yesterday that at any moment you can choose to be your best self. I can choose to only do those things which are beneficial to me & can start that immediately.

Funny & great seeing Ivy's video with Fido yesterday. So corny. Love those reminders which eliminate the pedestal.

Sleep hygiene – this is something that comes up repeatedly & which is clearly dragging me down. I want to work on this.

Existential anxiety yesterday around life. Had to do with being stuck. Accept, don't resist, 1% better every day. That's going through to get out.

•

Feeling really fucking anxious right now. I'm in the losing my mind weed spiral. I forgot what this feels like. It's horrible.

The never-ending shame/anxiety cycle begins with anxiety causing you to smoke. Whether you enjoy the high or not, eventually you have shame over smoking. Then you vow that "this is the last day." The next day you have more anxiety than before, because you smoked, which leads you to be ineffective in life & pre-occupied, which leads to more anxiety. To escape the now existential level of dread you're feeling, you smoke.

Or I?

This time, the dread you were experiencing mixes with the high to lead to psychosis level anxiety. "I'm never smoking again, today's the last day." Rinse & repeat. Mental state continues to deteriorate which is further reinforced by the sense of failing yourself each day combined with the nicotine addiction, which has now taken hold.

Look at the cycle & be kind to yourself. You're now caught in a vicious cycle. It doesn't help to shame yourself. You've done this before. You have the tools & it's never as bad as you think. This is a lesson.

10-5-23

Mr. Brightside

Make the decision to be happy. Make the decision to make every day one of the best of your life.

Feeling good today, despite the latent anxiety that is ever-present. Feeling in the ideal zone where I am sitting above the conversation & not consumed by it. This is a part of detachment. This is where I feel not offended or stressed by the conversation & having something to say, rather I'm operating as my carefree self. Let's see how much you can stay in & come back to this state of mind.

As far as weed is concerned, remember that the discomfort is actually the goal & the indicator that the brain is changing back to its natural state.

Combine forces with & become one with the child. Remember that little kid *and that* you want to do whatever he wants. You still are that kid. There are no rules. You can do whatever you want. That is actually the point. Move forward with the child and meet your destiny.

> The winds blow the sails, move the clouds, cool the
> seas, and shake the trees. The winds bring change.
> The change is the present. The present shifts to past
> never to be felt again. The winds continue to blow perpetually.

10-6-23

On Caffeine

Fully coming to understand just how detrimental caffeine is to my mental health. The past couple days I've felt great waking up despite horrible sleep. All that changes the minute you drink caffeine. Immediately irritable, anxious, on-edge, fight or flight type response. Had two 5 hours today and have been spiraling until now, now that the caffeine is wearing off.

Battling nicotine/weed too. My brain keeps telling me to smoke it despite the fact that I want to stop. My brain is looking for the temporary relief. The issue is that I'm going to find myself in the same place tomorrow if I delay. TBD what happens but staying strong right now.

Have effectively found myself in the detached mindset today. It's the best when I'm in it. Remember that feeling from high school & settle into yourself. It's in this state that you're able to think most clearly & when you're most yourself. You're able to see the playing field more clearly & to determine how you really want to act/respond.

> We come from stardust. We're borne of the Universe.
> Waves are to ocean as we are to all that is. Each wave
> is perfect as we are. The wave's only responsibility is
> to be exactly what it is. This is the responsibility we share.

10-7-23

Spin Cycle

Really spiraling right now. Massive amounts of anxiety & inner turmoil. Very very irritable. Definitely has to do a lot with weed. Not stopping is very much deteriorating my mental health. Find it very hard to be able to focus on anything. I wonder if weed exacerbates ADHD symptoms. I'm sure it does.

Or I?

I had dinner with Mom & Auntie tonight & feel bad about the energy I brought to dinner. I was battling my mind to stay cool, but my body & emotions were fighting back big time. I tweaked out on Mom because she asked me when the World Series is. It sounds so ridiculous writing it out. It's all part of a larger annoyance about constantly being put on the spot with these questions. But I feel bad because I know it's not helpful to our relationship. There is just so much resentment there. I hate that there is and hate that I'm having such trouble with our relationship. I am really going to have to either learn to accept her completely, or to really distance myself because the current situation isn't good for anyone.

> Oh melancholy. The nagging ache of existential despair. What function do you serve except to erode my *resolve*. The moment is now. The solution is now. The Choice is now. Choose now.

10-9-23

Psych

About to get the results back from the psych testing. Suspect I'll be given Adderall.

I ended up getting to a good place psychologically yesterday. Ultimately my favorite mindset is when I'm able to seriously minimize the importance of the people around me to the point that I legitimately don't care what they think about how I'm acting or what I'm doing. This is freedom.

An effective way that I've been getting in this mindset even when I'm struggling consists of 2 steps. <u>First</u>, recognize the bad wavelength & realize that changing it is your INTERNAL responsibility. It needs to be changed from within. <u>Second</u>, begin to settle into the detached, careless state. The major key is the understanding that my mental state is totally up to me & is under my control. Acting like some external circumstances are the culprit or thinking that a mental state is unchangeable are mental fallacies that keep you stuck. All that said, intellectualization & psychological understanding are also limiting. It's all about embodying feelings

& wavelength. It's all about training this VR Suit. Excited & grateful to be in the training arena.

10-10-23

Agency

Feeling pretty good today despite continuing to smoke weed, do caffeine, and sleeping horribly last night. Woke up on top of my sheets in my clothes @ 7am. Smoked a J and then decided to stay awake. Happy I did. There are so many more hours in the day that way.

Have continued reminding myself that it is fully my responsibility to get out of whatever bad mind state I'm in. Using this change in perspective I then focus on finding that mind state of self & ease – the varsity high school state of mind. These two steps are leading to great success. This is how detachment is achieved right now.

My confidence is coming back in a major way as I realize just how much I bring to the table. Harry told me what the girls in NYC have been saying. Compliments from *A Family Friend & others* driving things home. Wedding speech. ADHD/OCD diagnosis. Everything is contributing to the current breakthroughs. Feel like Everything is Happening for a Reason & everything right now is setting me up for life. OCD/ADHD really taking the pressure/shame off my shoulders & keeping me from so much resistance.

10-12-23

Fighting

Realizing that my attachment to Ivy is strengthening again. Time to focus on detachment. This is a constant battle. The refrain is that this is all under your control. It's your responsibility to manipulate your brain. There is resentment in there and that's something that doesn't do anything for anyone.

Or I?

What would you be most proud of for doing today? Something that moves your life forward. What could that be? Getting control of your brain and doing what you want to do.

Arggg. So battling internally. Feel so unsettled. So irritable. Yes it's the irritability that is really bothering me and that I want to escape from. But all escapes just push the consequences back for my future self to deal with. Make the current you the strongest you.

All healing needs to be internal. Nothing from outside will lead to permanent change for the better. This is your struggle. And boy do you know how to do that.

Live untethered. Find that freedom. Recognize the thoughts. Accept them. Replace with something better.

•

Really struggled all day. Clearly all withdrawal induced. Constant ruminating over Ivy which was horrible. Things are very weird to me about our relationship right now and I'm struggling to cope. I'm feeling triggered in some kind of way. Kicking it constantly. It all changed when I'd been super distant and was at my breaking point. I don't even remember what that was about. That's very telling with how unmemorable this all clearly is. Regardless, we were having fun again & then Fido got sick which really made us close. I hate to admit it but a part of me felt sad that would go away now that Fido is doing better. I can feel myself getting more attached again. Jealous when she's out. Jealous right now that she's out. Yesterday when I got back from yoga & she was in her room, I was sad. Sad about the distance this morning, which I helped create. But also concerned that I am making this a self-fulfilling prophecy. Awareness about this. Remember she is going to discard you again. This is all coming to an end. It would be a real shame to waste any more time fretting over her. I mean really, on a night like tonight, what did you hope for in a dream scenario. For her to wait around for you to come home? For her to ask to watch a movie? To have some sort of drastic change of heart? I don't know. You know she cares for you. My big fear is that she is just using me. Yes, that is it. Oh my God dude you guys never do anything together. This is not a thing. Really I think a lot of this is a strategy by my brain to torture me back into smoking.

Detachment is key here. She can't be having this kind of an impact on you. It's not her, it's you. She's literally done nothing wrong. Right now she's out having fun. You're over here worried about her meeting dudes when you're never going to be with her. So that's absurd and a waste of energy. You're also jealous when you don't even like that version of her. There's something very toxic about that.

You keep trying to figure out what she's thinking which is such a waste of time & brain power. Focus back on the self. It's all you can control.

★
Mindfulness & Non-Attachment
★

10-13-23

Forward Progress

Really good meditation just now. It was focused on releasing toxic bonds. Obviously this focused on Ivy. The meditation was really effective in getting me into a detached mindset of acceptance. This was the mind state I'd achieved in weeks prior when things were best. Definitely a practice to come back to repeatedly.

A realization – Sort of had a flashbulb moment in the gym today fully seeing how much I've been holding myself back in favor of other people. I was dancing in the gym – dancing really well – when I reflected on how I hold myself back when other people are around. I become a bad dancer. This led me to realize that it's only me holding myself back. Why do I do this when my natural abilities are so good? I think interactions with Dad taught me that it's not ok to be better than other people. Fuck that. It's time to shine. Detach, settle into yourself, do what you want to do & shock the world.

How to best make progress today – Good job working out, meditating, & journaling. Write networking emails to be sent Monday. Present moment optimization. Parent & Guardian.

10-15-23

Conscious Direction

In order to find the right mindset consciousness needs to drive the subconscious to a specific target state. What does the target mindset feel like? Identify that & live in it. When struggling – even when taking into account that changing mindset is your responsibility – it's ineffective to simply hope that your mindset improves and have the brain aimlessly wander, randomly switching between different mindsets hoping one fits.

Even the mindset of an empty brain or giving no effort requires the drive of the consciousness towards that state of mind. You can't just say "stop thinking" because you're thinking to do that. It's more of "what does not thinking feel like," feeling that, and living in that & having that feeling drive all subsequent behavior.

This is the framework for foundationally changing your mindset which changes all down-stream thoughts, emotions, & behaviors. It's using mindfulness to reprogram the brain.

Being too needy. Remember everything without resentment to eliminate the pedestal. Become the power.

10-16-23

Searching For Authenticity

Today is the day the weed is being kicked for good. I'm all out of excuses to continue. My mental state has been slowly deteriorating every day I continue. Remember don't get attached to the thoughts.

Continuing to get more attached to Ivy. The attachment is leading to anxiety as I both strive to behave in a way that is trying to get her to love me and as I try to avoid making any mistakes that would "mess things up." Both of these things are you being inauthentic. Things are best for you when you're fucking with her. Remember, you're the man, the leader, the one with access to the Universe. Access that spirit.

Decide to be the best. Get in touch with yourself. Focus on recentering. Find the frequency of detachment. Of not caring. Focus wholeheartedly on releasing yourself without any effort or resistance. There is no place for anxiety in this. It doesn't make sense.

Try to reparent when the feelings take hold. If it's not the Inner Child being triggered then it's simply cravings that are making you irritable.

Change thoughts, change behavior.

You are no longer a smoker.

Everything in your relationship with Ivy is bonus time. It's impossible to mess this up now. Be yourself.

Re: Not Caring – It's not a faked not caring, it's realizing that you really don't care. That no one's opinion of you matters. That none of this is important. That your responsibility is to act as you want. To achieve a state of not caring, you must realize you really don't. But this requires you to ignore all the thoughts, behaviors, & habits driving you towards your old mindset. The mind would love nothing more than to maintain the status quo. It wants to remain comfortable. Uncomfortability either indicates you're not acting in alignment, or are growing. You know the difference between the two. Search out the growth. Like exercising, discomfort is growth.

You will never be or get who & what you want with the people-pleasing behaviors.

•

Just had a childhood realization. I never felt like it was ok for me to do what I want. Always feeling like I was doing something wrong & seeking validation and/or approval for my behavior. This has persisted into adulthood & I am constantly experiencing the same fear & need for external approval. No more. Integrate with the child and do you.

•

The all-important sensation is the one when you're able to see & acknowledge the thoughts & sensations but are able to detach from them

Or I?

– and then to direct your behavior despite it all according to your Higher Self.

These anxieties, triggers, hang ups & attachment wounds are the lowest of thoughts – the Parasite – dragging you down.

•

When you're feeling really stuck & jammed up, you're triggered or in a trauma state but don't realize it. These are the moments to use all the tools you have. The challenge is to not give up when things don't change right away & to keep battling.

★

The sensation I'm describing

is one of being above the thoughts

& emotions that exist & deciding what

to do from that POV

★

•

On emotional unavailability. I think I may have been the unavailable one the whole time.

•

Currently in a detached state. It's great. I feel like a full on human being. Feels light. Lots of struggle to get here today but hold on as long as possible. The key today was reading old journal entries. It is also in realizing my responsibility is to be my true self & that can't be dependent on worrying about anyone else.

•

The detachment comes when you internalize that it only makes sense to brush other people's actions off and that other people's behavior really should hold no sway over your state of mind.

Basically it doesn't make sense for you to be influenced by other people.

Become detached & become the one in control.

10-17-23

Instant Karma

Facing what I think is kind of an instant karma thing from the Universe right now. Things have been going great with Ivy. I'm fighting with all my might not to get attached but I can feel it happening. We've been really connected, chillin every day, watching TV & movies like never before. Etc. Well tonight we watch Nocturnal Animals. We're chillin, talking about the movie afterwards when Ivy out of the blue says that *The Exec* from *The Network* says that "the numbers aren't where we want them to be." She then goes on to say that he said that they should tell PR if they're dating anyone. Later says that *The Network* wants to see her dating. She talks about the fact that she went on a date with *The Guy* from *Another Reality Show*. I'm trying to stay as detached and cool as I want to be. But obviously hearing this hit that part of me that's still raw. Also obviously I immediately began to fantasize that she said this to see my reaction & if I would show any feelings. But Occam's Razor – the simplest solution is often the truth – she said it because she is treating you like the friend you're supposed to be. It's wrong to hold this against her or to be resentful. She's enjoying your company & your attention. That's it. Accept & don't resist how painful this is going to be. Identify this fantasy thought generator and become aware of the false hope it's creating. I'm sorry. Please forgive me. I love you. I thank you.

10-18-23

ADHD

Or I?

Today is my first day on Adderall. I just took it and immediately feel great. I think this is going to literally be revolutionary for me. Maybe weed tonight, maybe not, but I can already tell how much my desire for it is abated.

•

About to go to bed. What a great day. I am grateful. Definitely crashing a bit now but totally worth it.

It's interesting, the crash is a little acid like where you're kind of in & out of it. I could tell when it was wearing off when my brain just sort of slips into confusion & my body into anxiety.

The best part about it by far was the elimination of my anxiety. It was astonishing to experience living without it. I felt so free. Immediately reached out to and connected with a bunch of people. Literally immediately brightened my friendships.

Interesting effect on my confidence. *Her Show BFF* came over today before they went off to this *Clothing Company* event. I was as nonplussed by her presence as I could have possibly been.

Interesting effect on my perception of & interactions with Ivy. First off, through being more grounded, I'm able to see her more clearly. When she came back from the event and was telling me about it, I was much more clearly able to see how dumb the whole thing is. Again, was able to stay nonplussed/detached in a way authentic to myself. Also in seeing her interact with *Her Show BFF* I'm reminded of the change to her personality that I don't like as well as to get a glimpse into just how much boy talk/chasing goes on. The personality change is weird in that she becomes the subservient one kind of pandering to *Her Show BFF* or whoever else. It really makes me not want to ever be under her finger. Obviously the guy shit I hate. It's funny because I swear I feel like she could sense the difference in my demeanor & it drew her closer & closer. I honestly think she loves it when people don't treat her great because that triggers the "I'm not good enough" wound. She then needs to get that person back to reseal that wound. Rinse & repeat.

Anyways, I'm excited to continue on this journey. I'm so excited to feel like my confident self, to see clearly & calmly, & to know that everything is going to be ok. Thank you. Thank you. Thank you.

•

Text

The question is are you going to allow this feeling to control you? The answer is always no. But you've been saying yes for a while.

10-19-23

Adderall Test

Today's going to be a good test of Adderall's capabilities for me as I just woke up having slept very little & feel raw/dry/awful. Very unsettled mentally. Took the first dose @ 9am. Let's see how it affects my mindset & how I feel.

Very grateful for all the mindfulness/meditation & other work I did leading up to my prescription. All of these efforts still work on Adderall & are actually that much more effective with a quieter mind.

•

Today has definitely been an exhausted struggle but I know that it has been much better than it would have been otherwise. I also think that a lot of the shittiness can be attributed to weed/tobacco withdrawal on top of the extreme exhaustion. The other major thing is that I haven't eaten for like more than a day so my blood sugar level is extremely low.

Basically, what I read on reddit was wrong that this doesn't work when you're tired. It does but you're worked.

10-20-23

Mind The Gap

Or I?

AM: Woke up @ 7:30am and went to the gym. Slept @ like ~1am or so. Didn't sleep great despite being extremely tired because I took Adderall so late. Just took Adderall @ 9:30am. It's hitting now & is clearly benefitting my mindset despite my exhaustion. Although it's only day 3, I do see the downside to this stuff. There's a sense of being strung out. This should be improved with better sleep & less consumption. Currently settling into my relaxed self/proper frequency.

•

PM: Adderall completely done by 1:30pm (fully @ 2:30pm). Feel fine but out of it. Weed obviously contributing. Going to take another @ 2:45pm & check duration again.

•

Article

<u>Listen</u>

<u>by Scott Galloway</u>

"Communication is with the listener, and if you don't soften up their defenses with active listening, you'll never get to the beach."

10-21-23

Email To Psychologist

Hi *Psychologist*!

I've noticed a drastic improvement in my quality of life over the past couple days since starting Adderall, which I couldn't be more thrilled about. It's also become clear that the current dose is too low as it wears off after around 4-5 hours, making it hard to get through the rest of the day. Do you have any advice on how to manage this between now and the next appointment? Do I have any options or just need to wait it out?

Thanks

10-23-23

Catch Up

Catching up on some journaling having forgotten to do it over the last couple of days.

Ivy left for the UK so I'm watching Fido. Not missing her per usual.

Sleep has been horrible & I'm paying for it. A bit of a self-perpetuating cycle taking Adderall to cope then finding it harder to sleep as a result.

2 nights ago Fido kept me up all night with diarrhea. Sucked but felt bad for him rather than being frustrated with him.

The Adderall I've been taking (10mg XR *(extended release)*) is too weak. Need 20 XR w/ 10 IR *(immediate release)* boosters. Took 2 this morning @ 11am and was dragging by 3pm. Question for *Psychologist* – at what point do I take another?

Can feel a big difference in my motivation/productivity on/off Adderall. There is a cost though which is the comedown & feeling somewhat cracked out. Totally worth it though.

•

Adderall

The Adderall has made such a difference but the dose is way too low. Looking at my journal, my tolerance is clearly very high. By day 3...

•

The above was the beginning of what was going to be a massive rationalization as to why you should up the dose of the XR and get a 20mg IR. By the grace of God, I got distracted and ended up doing something else before finishing it. At some point upon reflection and, ironically,

Or I?

because of the research Adderall led me to, I came to realize that going down this path, one I would have easily convinced the psych was necessary, would have been utterly destructive. I honestly am so grateful to the Universe because this felt nothing less than a life saving nudge in the right direction. Thank you. Thank you. Thank you.

In reflecting upon this situation, I had a revelation about my compulsive behavior, especially as it pertains to addictive substances. This was born of the realization that it was the subconscious operating from a scarcity mindset resulting from the low supply of Adderall which drove me to think I needed – and should scheme to get – as much of it at the maximum "reasonable" dose possible (20mg XR, 20mg IR). This applies to how you've operated with all substances and most things. This deserves maximum attention.

Have thoroughly enjoyed singing again. It's crazy how much progress I've made. Also thanks to Adderall. The video I watched on YouTube was a major unlock, but, more importantly, the lesson spoke fundamentally to so much of the work you've been doing. That lesson was that you should sing from a place of ease & with as little strain as possible. This ease is literally the Resonant Frequency of your voice. The Resonant Frequency. Ease. Not straining. Being relaxed. Being unapologetically you because that's all there is. More and more these ideas come up & the more they do, the more they prove themselves to be core tenets underlying self-mastery & authentic self-connection.

10-24-23

Adderall Psychologist Mtg Prep

Avoid misuse & keep it simple. Godsend. Can't believe I made it this long without it.

<u>Intensity & Duration too short</u>
10/23: 11am-3pm (4 hrs.)
10/20: 9:30am-1:30pm (4 hrs.)

After doing my research it's clear the issue is one of duration rather than of intensity. Increasing mg doesn't necessarily increase duration, but may mess with the homeostasis you're enjoying while on it. As my mental state is the most important thing, it's actually illogical to increase dosage for the sake of duration.

I either want an IR booster or 2 10mg IR a day (4 x 5mg).

The problem with the XR is that there's a sort of lingering weird feeling that I never experienced with the IR. I do remember always preferring the IR in college but that's probably not the best reference point.

★

I like the feeling and everything but it's not lasting long enough.

★

Onset: Starts ~15 mins

Intensity: Slightly too low

Duration: 5 hrs. avg (usually under)

Negatives: Dry mouth, Sweating, Come Down, Hunger, Time Blindness, Slight Nausea

Positives: Myself, Quality of Life, Substances, Calm, Anxiety Gone, Confidence, Ease

•

All Set Up

Just picked up a new Adderall script. 15mg 2x/day. Think I'm probably going to take this in 7.5mg doses @ first. Think that's going to be the ticket. Would like to get real specific on the tracking.

Today: 10XR @ 11:15am → 7.5IR @ 2:15pm (XR not fully hitting): feel much better by 2:25pm.

Very tired today, slept like shit last night. Definitely hindering Adderall performance. Despite tiredness, was able to put down a 5 mile run this AM. Could feel the effects of weed on lungs today for sure. Bit of a

Or I?

wakeup call. Sleep impacted by taking XR too late. The IRs should resolve this issue.

It's incredible how much this drug has improved various aspects of my life. I'm so much more productive. Really getting shit done. I am also able to see how my brain is working on Adderall & to apply that to my sober mind.

Phillies game 7 tonight! Let's go boys.

10-25-23

Major Drag

Went crazy on the Adderall yesterday which caused me to stay up all night. Feeling lots of shame about it. Feel basically anxious/terrified. Was a bit of a wakeup call as far as my behavior is concerned. Right now is a real look in the mirror moment for me. This Adderall can be one of the best things ever for you so long as you don't abuse it. This abuse is clearly tied to this compulsion to binge anything that is limited in quantity or that I feel is being taken away somehow. The limited quantity of pills per prescription falls into this category.

Shame abounds due to my continuing to smoke weed. Again, this is something that I'm continuing to do compulsively because I feel like my desire to quit represents the feeling that weed is being taken away from me, which causes me to hold on as tight as possible.

Re: weed & all other habits/compulsions, stop shaming yourself for these things. There is no moral or immoral quality to any of these substances. The fact of the matter is that you can and do do whatever you want. So if you're continuing to smoke weed, it's because you don't really want to give it up. But that's ok. Just realize it's your responsibility to look after yourself.

10-26-23

Progress

Actually slept last night. Felt great to wake up with some Z's under my belt. Still tired but going down the right path. Also cut back on Adderall which I'm happy about. The smaller amounts are more effective for me. Right now dosing in 7.5mg increments. First today @ 12pm. Noticed the IR lasted ~3.5 hours yesterday. Longer than before. Also feels better physically than the XR which was giving me some adverse physical response in the body. Must be the pill coating.

Very happy with the progress I'm making with the singing. It's as if I was granted the wish to be able to sing yesterday. Very grateful for that. Thank you. Thank you. Thank you.

•

Articles

An Absurd Approach to Find More Meaning in Life

by Stephan Joppich

Life Meaning/Enjoyment

•

How Two Boring Sentences Helped Me Stop Feeling Lost

by Stephan Joppich

"It's alright. Take all the time you need."

The above article talks about using this statement as a mantra to alleviate anxieties around uncertainty. Living life itself & approaching everything with curiosity & as a challenge to solve is the point, not to meet societal and parental expectations.

10-29-23

Or I?

OCD & ADHD?

Currently trying to understand my OCD & ADHD diagnoses. In doing research online, there's debate as to whether these two things can be co-morbid. Or whether similarities in the ways they manifest (both are executive function disorders) leads to misdiagnosis. Adderall is seen to make compulsions worse in some with OCD. This is something to keep an eye on re: my stimulant consumption. I have been playing with my hair a ton.

Took 15mg Adderall today @ 12:15pm. Curious to see affect & duration.

Before taking – Frazzled. Out of it. Worrying about money. Blank but buzzing mind.

If there's one thing that's clear in all of this it's that you're not alone. You've been managing all of this raw-dog, now you should be able to manage more effectively knowing that this is the disorder talking. It's also clear that so much of the delusional thoughts & things I have been dealing with were symptoms of OCD that I didn't recognize as such. Negative self-talk. Sexual compulsions. Etc.

Trying to figure out if ADHD exists & how it plays into all of this.

•

Adderall – Took another 7.5mg @ 2pm to see what affect that has. The 15mg was working but still felt a bit "under." Seeing if this does the trick. I do feel much calmer/more able to ignore the thoughts that come up.

OCD – It's starting to seem possible that my compulsive substance abuse & inability to stop is fundamentally connected to my OCD. When drinking/smoking/doing any other substance there is this sense in my mind of getting the feeling "just right" in a way that reminds me of OCD. Furthermore, the feeling & anxiety that always leads me to cave is extremely similar to and feels connected to the "if you don't do this, something terrible is going to happen." Usually that terrible thing is that I'm going to sleep bad. But it can also have a kind of unknown & unknowable consequence.

ADHD – It does feel more like my inability to *write* that I've always struggled with is more related to ADHD, but there is a way to associate that with both things intellectually. If ADHD, lack of interest combines with lack of urgency & distractibility. It's only on time crunch that I'm good. If OCD, thoughts of "I can't write, what if I'm stupid?" turn into a self-fulfilling prophecy.

10-30-23

Article

The Struggles of Writing With OCD

by Ross Carver-Carter

10-31-23

THE POUCH
(Harry & Sally's Wedding Gift Alongside The Wedding Ring Pouch)

This is the pouch that held your rings. It kept them safe. It was their home.

The fact that they're on you now means that those were always going to be the rings you chose, and this was always going to be the pouch that carried them. The rings' existence was made certain the minute your relationship began, and, in a way, the rings were born in the pouch that day. But wedding rings need each other, as one has no purpose without the other, so they wouldn't commit to leaving the safety of this home until they were sure that your love would allow them to stay connected forever.

As your bond deepened, the pouch filled with the hopes, dreams, and promises of forever. The rings absorbed this and began to see the possibility of a life outside this pouch. Your engagement turned this possibility into a reality when, at that exact moment, the rings bound

Or I?

themselves to your relationship, knowing they would always be safe in your hands.

From then up until the wedding, the rings lived blissfully in the safety of the pouch, enjoying the home that made them, while basking in the reflection of all the memories you shared. Filled by the warmth of their reminiscence and thanks to the pouch's constant protection, the rings shined brighter than ever and were ready to step into their rightful role as both the embodiment of your relationship and the demonstration of its strength.

With "I do," "I do," the rings ascended out from the pouch and onto your fingers.

While the rings were for the first time apart, they remained united through the life you share. They began to experience the world without the pouch and found that by relying only on each other, they were able continue growing far beyond what they ever could have under the pouch's protection.

The pouch had done its job. Now, when the rings saw the empty pouch, it served as a constant reminder of their journey to you. They remember that it's empty for all the reasons you married each other. That it's empty because of the love you share. That it was always meant to be empty. That being empty means you are whole. With this they realize that the pouch was never really the rings' true home at all. Home was always sharing a life with the two of you, the pouch was simply meant to get them there.

Just as the pouch kept the rings safe until marriage, dating and everything that went into it fostered your future together. The pouch carried the rings to marriage like dating did for you. Marriage made the pouch empty and caused you to leave the dating world behind. The pouch and dating were the necessary stops for both the rings and your relationship on the way to marriage.

I hope this pouch reminds you of everything that led to "I do."

•

Coming To Terms

I'm slowly digesting the reality of my ADHD/OCD diagnosis and struggling to come to terms with it at times. It's often hard for me to differentiate between the two which makes it hard to know whether the medication is under or over dosed.

Experienced the same writing struggles I used to in college while writing The Pouch. Fortunately I was able to power through and ultimately it became one of the best things I've ever written. Two suggested techniques that seem to work are creating a framework for the paper out of bullet points that are used to structure it in advanced. Becomes easy to write words around this structure. The other is to force yourself to write without *stopping for* anything as you go along on the first pass.

11-1-23

OCD

Well had asshole surgery yesterday. Hahaha. Ended up having a thrombosed hemorrhoid, which means a hemorrhoid with a blood clot in it. Very proud of myself for dealing with this situation right away given how embarrassing the whole thing is. I attacked it head on & really wasn't even that embarrassed.

Have made great progress regarding confidence recently. All it takes is for you to remember how confident you are. Look at the above example. Your trouble comes when you attach to the OCD worries about your intelligence & worthiness.

OCD Practice – Remember the videos you watched which said that the most effective practice is simply to not believe any thought that comes up in your head.

OCD/Ivy – Pretty sure everything having to do with her was related to OCD. Going to look into the relationship between OCD & limerence.

Think I need stronger meds. Feel much better @ higher doses. It does seem like they may be having an adverse effect on the OCD although need to get a better read when sleep has been better.

Or I?

What's crazy is that all the advice related to OCD says to do the thing that I figured out how to do intuitively. Namely being mindful of the negative states that arise & training the brain both to accept/not engage *with them* and to softly identify/direct the mind towards the target state. This is the whole frequency thing that you've been working on.

11-2-23

Carry On

Realizing just how much OCD is driving the train for me. There is no doubt that you have that at the very least. Great to know so you can manage better.

What I'm working on right now is identifying the difference between anxiety, OCD, & ADHD. It is becoming clear that they bleed into each other. If I get anxious or am very distracted, OCD will follow & wreak havoc. Identifying trends will really help.

It is actually a relief for me to be in my right frame of mind. Here's what I've noticed with substances:

Coffee – Increases anxiety/ADHD which then leads to OCD/more anxiety. Not good for you at all.

Adderall – Hit or miss. Some days a godsend. Some days absolutely fucks my OCD. Feels good to be on it, feels good to be off it.

It's becoming clear to me that everything around Ivy is related to OCD & trying to get certainty. Remember: <u>I</u>dentify – <u>A</u>ccept – <u>M</u>ove Attention *(I AM)*.

When you're spacing out that's ADHD. The way you respond can lead to OCD following the path: Space Out (ADHD) → Loss of control/fear of judgement (Anxiety) → OCD (latch onto anxious rumination). This is one specific way ADHD could catalyze OCD when ADHD is making focus/conversation/active performance difficult (ex. GOLF: Poor Focus → anxious about performance → OCD obsess about bad shot → worse performance all around/OCD stronger).

Again, it's all about finding the true you under there & operating as the main character with everyone as extras. You know when you're in this because you're actively taking the situation in and deciding how you want to respond rather than reflexively responding on ADHD/OCD/Anxiety auto-pilot. The best mental state for inner work is when you are feeling triggered & are able to accept those feelings while holding space for the true you to operate autonomously.

The fact that you've made it this far with everything you've been struggling with makes you a fucking animal. Actually can't believe how confident you are underneath it all.

Before smoking – Brain fog, confused, anxious. But also slip into & out of being grounded. Feeling both hopeful & anxious.

After smoking – PANIC. Black feeling. Confused. ADHD spike (don't know what's going on). Yea this stuff is probably the worst thing for the ADHD/OCD. Now settling into some of the calm but head is still buzzing. Remembering the OCD paranoia I used to get in college, which was the foundation of my smoking. Yea this activates the OCD big time. Ok now you know. Make a choice. It's very clear that this is a major net negative. What this give you is stimulation. That's why you always want to keep doing it. That's why you want coffee. Both things really fuck it all up.

Dose ~30 minutes ago. 7.5mg. Instant relief in a bunch of the above. Instant anxiety relief. Executive function online. The lower dose is better. Compared to last night this is so much more the ideal zone. Too much exacerbates both OCD & ADHD. I think 10mg is going to be the sweet spot.

11-5-23

Work To Do

I'm currently being shown that there is a lot of attachment/OCD work to do regarding Ivy. From my POV we'd gotten to one of the best spots we've been in since she got back from the UK. While she was gone I didn't really miss her I don't think. Although with Fido here she was

Or I?

ever-present, so I don't know. *Telling her about* the hemorrhoid, her trip home, Fido *getting cancer*, watching *her show together*, talking until 2am two nights ago, and really all of it accumulating to a newfound level of comfort made me realize that there is no one I feel more comfortable around. Melting around this realization made me the most myself I've ever been around her. This brough us closer too. When talking after watching *her show* she asked me what I'm doing this weekend with the most interest she's ever had. I told her about meeting up with *some friends*. Her reaction revealed nothing. Up to this point all's well. However attachment & expectations/hope were significantly ramped up by all of this. This is where issues begin. She has been super distant since I got back from *my friends' place* last night. Uncharacteristically went to her room all night last night. Spent a ton of time talking on the phone right at the threshold to her room. I've been OCD ruminating about this call. Weirdly let Fido stay out with me when she went to bed. Then straight to her room since getting back from her showing a couple hours ago. The distance has revealed my attachment to her. I've been constantly ruminating & obsessing over what everything means & her dating since. I've been obsessed over that call thinking that it was for a dating show or something & that this is the reason she's being distant & doesn't want to tell me about it. Been obsessing with worry that when she asked me what I was doing this weekend, that really she was hoping for space. Realize that I got my hopes up that she was developing feelings & sad to have that hope challenged. Regardless she's done nothing wrong. I'm feeling resentment and upset build but that's on you. Remember not to feed the OCD. She was talking about moving on yesterday. She is dating other guys. She doesn't have feelings for you. She is discarding you right now. Your relationship is going to die at the end of this. And worrying anymore about her is a waste of time. Detach & be grateful. Enjoy the remaining time. But only focus on yourself. Settle into & use the comfort you have around her. Accept feelings but don't buy in to anything. Impress yourself. Love yourself. Parent yourself. Remember yourself, that you are content, and live in that confidence.

The big thing you realized which led to all the good is that everything in your life is completely in your control. It is actually insane how much this is true. Every time you really really embrace & embody this realization, the vibe around you & the quality of your life truly changes.

All you have to do is to decide how you want things to be & they will be so.

Right now all I want is to be me. So that's who I'll be from now on.

●

I am and have been absolutely bugging since I got back here last night. I can just tell that the energy is so different with Ivy and not knowing why or what's going on is driving me insane. She's literally been in her room since I got back here yesterday. What in the fucking world. I'm getting really wound up. Feeling very depressed. Anxious. Almost panicy. The reaction that I'm having is definitely over the top & is making me think that some sort of childhood abandonment wound or some other trauma is being triggered.

How can I find my way back to focusing on the internal? But also for real what the fuck is this that she's doing? This is weird. What other explanation is there other than that she doesn't want to be around you? There are obviously. She could have met someone. But when? What was that phone call? The way she talked just in ear shot and hasn't mentioned it and that it's in the middle of all this makes me think that whatever's going on is centered around that. But let's play worst case scenario. She realizes she hates spending time with you, doesn't value your friendship, met someone, has never really cared for you in any way, and is never going to spend time with you again. O.K. I can deal with that. So I can deal with any of this.

At the end of the day she's entitled to whatever space she wants and doesn't owe you anything. You're having the reaction you've wished upon her a thousand times. You also believed your absence/distance would have this effect knowing how this would affect you. Obviously this is highly flawed, Ego-centric logic. Your feelings are real and valid, but they're over the top & ones that need managing. If she's avoiding you let her. And if not then this is all the more misguided. You're making this all about you & the external. Nothing she does has anything to do with you. Let's try to focus on not taking things too personally. However, this does hurt and that's real.

11-8-23

Or I?

Well it happened. After literally days of agonizing over Ivy pulling away, I finally got over it and of course that's the minute she tries to reconnect. *Cleaning her* closet Sat night after *my friends' place*. Closet Sunday. Filming/silence Monday (somewhat tried to talk *about my job* interview "how do you feel about it?). But lying on the couch dejected silent rest of night/room early. Yesterday *I* left when she got back *to go to* gym/Miramar. She's in room by the time I get back at like 10pm. Maybe earlier. Today I immediately left in the morning. She was trying to be warm but with her false tone "good morning!" "How are YOU." "Good, got some shit to do." Go to leave. "I'm going to the dentist." "Ugh. Brutal. Good luck!" Walk out the door and leave. Get back from Miramar @ 8 and go to the gym. She's not back from her meet & greet @ the consignment shop. She's here when I get back from the gym @ 9:30pm. Super warm trying to draw me in, and clearly now dropping the distance, "Hellllo" Petting Fido "Soooo windy" "Hey what's up" "How was your day!?" "Good" Go to my room, come back out, get my keys "I'll be right back." Come back, no "Hi" from either of us. I shower. She stays in living room with a TV show on. Curious. I go in the kitchen. "OMG those TJs spicy chips are so good!" "What" (headphones in clearly listening to something – pause) "Repeats" "Oh, nice!..." "Did you watch Beckham" "No I didn't start it." Then sat there eating my food, listening to & laughing at this YouTube video. Finished. Got up, put away the dishes, & without delay said "Goodnight, sleep well." With a notable beat in-between, she said "Goodnight." She stayed out there and I went to my room where I continued to laugh at the videos.

Right now I feel free and done with her. I don't want to continue to be fucked with & I don't want to suffer so badly as I just did because of her ever again. That means no more closeness. Having just come out the other side, I feel a detached apathy that I'm loving. I don't care if it gets super uncomfortable in here. I'm done with her. But I think the best course of action is to be polite, but totally disengaged from her. And most important of all, to give literally no effort towards her. There's no more investing, she's proven her worth to me. Also most important of all is that you must act in a way that is completely true to you. The indifference/apathy/etc. needs to be authentic. You're dealing with a pro so it must be on point. Also don't be mean. Put the best vibe out there, just none for her. She obviously now knows that shit's fucked up when I'm not asking her how her day was or engaging really with anything she's saying. I just don't care to waste my time anymore. I'm going to rein in the rudeness, but my attention is too valuable & she has used too much of it up for me to be wasting any more on her. You are now in the power position because you really don't care. She is hanging on by a thread right now.

11-9-23

In The Thick

In the thick of it with Ivy. Enjoy this. No butt hurt. Every girl wants to fuck me. Every girl wants to fuck me. Every girl wants to fuck me. This is completely her loss. I am the best guy. Sucks for you you don't get to be a part of my life. I'm light. I'm free. This is great. Have as great a time as possible. All energy into you. Your attention is pure gold. But HAVE THE BEST TIME. This is payback for everything she's ever done. This is don't take my kindness for weakness. This is you being the best you. Always keep in mind not to be coming from a low frequency place. That's just dragging you down. When triggered (1) Completely stop trying & (2) Tap into high frequency (I'm sorry. Please forgive me. I love you. I thank you).

Remember why you're doing this. Remember that the pain/discomfort is something you enjoy. It represents growth. Remember that this pain now is nothing compared to how painful things will be when you get discarded again after getting re-attached. It's over. You're happy. You've already given everything. Model your man. Remember anti-fragile.

YOU'RE KIND APATHY

•

What's Happened So Far

She tries to be really buddy-buddy again this morning when I saw her. Asks about sleep and tries to use that to excuse her distance "Slept so well, I've been soooo tired recently." I go "That's good!" Immediately start doing my own thing. She maybe asks me something else that I dismiss. I'm in my room when she asks if I will watch Fido while she's out of town Tues→Fri next week if "I want some extra cash." Another test of strength. The money part pissed me off too. I said I'd think about it

Or I?

then told her no. That I'm in LA too much next week. We sit in silence after that for a while. I leave for an errand but tell her so to be cool. She gives me a warm response. We don't talk when I get back, sit in silence until she eventually goes to her room. Remember to be your amazing self, she just doesn't get the attention.

11-10-23

Misc.

Greatest efficiency *running* when knees & feet can be used as shock/spring system. There is a moment of bounce back of energy from the ground into feet that is indicative of maximum efficiency.

Melting into yourself. When you feel tension internally & are battling yourself, that's trauma manifesting. Recognize this, accept/make space for it, melt into your authenticity & be truly you regardless. Mental jam up & angst expecting to be able to read people's minds to predict what they want & to act accordingly all at once.

Remember your complicity with Ivy. This isn't all on her, you allowed this to happen too. Avoidant attachment is clearly her primary style. Our traumas complement each other. I've been complicit in allowing her to walk all over me. Research shows she will always have commitment issues. While the behavior is understandable in how it develops & manifests in relationships, it makes it easier to understand & depersonalizes the situation, but it doesn't make it acceptable. I have a lot of avoidant in me. I'm likely disorganized in my attachment. She will not understand my reaction. I'm planning on softening up a bit but she's still got to earn it.

"The secret of happiness, you see, is not found in seeking more, but in developing the capacity to enjoy less" – Socrates

"The greatest wealth is to live content with little" – Plato

Happiness is 100% internal & in your control

•

RE-TRAIN
THE VR
SUIT
MIND

•

Written To Prepare For A Talk

You very clearly wanted space. So I gave it to you. But you've done versions of this a million times. So I knew what was going on. And it's been a long time since this has hurt me, but it's just so fucking disorienting because it always comes at a time when things are going great. And the turn to ice cold is whiplash that's like – at least from my perspective – let me show you how little I care. But then I realize, because of just how many ways you've shown me, that really you're just trying to get out of there to avoid having any sort of real connection to me – PLATONIC connection – that you're just like "ugh too much I'm out" without a care in the world about what that might feel like on the other end. But, again, you've done versions of this so many times that it's something that I just shrugged off because it was just bullshit. The only thing that ever really continued to bother me about it, and unlike everything else, made me more just like, I don't know, a different kind of upset/hurt was almost more disappointment that this was going on. Basically I started to feel like a little more of a fucking idiot for fighting so hard for a relationship that was unbalanced in every way against me. I really don't know if I should say this because I don't want you to feel like I'm taking shots – I'm not – I'm just trying to articulate the scale of just how one-sided things were between us – a situation I completely *co-created*. But when I think about the fact I developed feelings for you *it brings* me immense shame because I was aware – even before & at the time – just how little you gave me. I always knew that. I never really gave a shit in the beginning. I never really gave a shit for years because I always knew that I existed in this sort of weird lesser than role than people in your life outside of our place. I'm not saying I didn't like you as a person, I did, we were boys or whatever, but I just knew that it was all meant to be surface level. But the thing is that you're fucking cool and we just had an easy vibe, so I let you in. And this is where it all gets fucked. And, before I go any further, I know that I am completely complicit in this. It takes two to tango & I danced well. I played my role, and if I hadn't none of this would have happened. You've seen that I hardly let anyone into my life. That all of my closest friends are people I've known my whole life. And I hate that about myself, because I don't want to be alone. But what I am protecting is the fact that once I let someone in for real, that's it, that's for life, and I will do whatever I can to help you even at the detriment of myself & even when that person is doing nothing for me – or even hurting me – because somehow in my mind it's like I can't go back on the commitment I made to them as a friend. So I really didn't want to let you in, because I already knew just how much I was going to give, and just how little I was going to get in return. But even early on there was so much shittiness going on in your life & whether someone's really my friend at the time or not, I'm going to help anyone even remotely in my life if they're struggling, so of course I'm going to go out of my way for my roommate. And at some point in all of that and with everything you were going through, I couldn't help but let you in for real. If there was ever a doubt about this for me, I knew I considered you family-level close when it all really hit the fan with *Our Last Roommate*. My knee jerk, "I'm never talking to you again" reaction is exactly the type of reaction I only have for a few people. It's almost straight up subconscious where my body & mouth are reacting quicker than I can think. And, yea, as you know I didn't talk to him again. It's not like we were that close for real or that I felt like you knew me or something, but you were in my mind and the loyalty showed up.

Now obviously spending 24/7 together with COVID and us being solo down here together we got much closer. While there was always this weird distance I couldn't quite put my finger on, and maybe I was even responsible for, and while things were as one-sided as fuck, I knew to expect all of this from the jump, and so in my own delusional rationalization, feel like it's unfair to ask for anything different. But this is where my complicity is at the root of this because I was an active participant in it. So I saw how we only ever talked about you. I learned to keep my problems & details of my existence to the bare minimum seeing how quickly you would go to your phone, somehow eject, or otherwise disengage from the convo. I saw that I would spend days, weeks, months, years at a time giving you my undivided attention, discussing anything and everything you want about your life, while I'm concerned that any discussion about any issues I'm having with myself – big or small – beyond 1 time & more than like 10 minutes, is like annoying you. I noticed that despite spending so much time together, we never did anything outside of here together. I noticed that you would throw me token bones to do something with the group outside of here like 2 or 3 times. I felt so uncomfortable to ever ask you if you wanted to do anything, because, especially now with *your show*, I understood the sensitivity to you living with a guy and didn't want to give off any mixed signals. Whether unfounded or not, the idea was locked in stone when the world opened up again after COVID that I wouldn't be included as a part of your life outside these walls. This stung but *I* convinced myself that despite everything in here, I had no right to ask for any time or attention outside these walls because that would be too much somehow. Again, I'm being complicit in the dynamic here & this is where fractures begin because this is where I, not all the time, but at times begin to feel like I was beginning to have trouble justifying just how lopsided things were. Like think about what that was like after all that time & support to then realize you're really a part time therapist, part time attention provider, & full time support to the life you're living that I'm not a part of. But I didn't take it personally, I just took note. So I don't know how it was that the combination of me going through everything at work + me realizing that I didn't have a place in your real life led me to develop feelings all of a sudden, but it did.

Kind not weak. My choice, not manipulation. But now new choice.

11-11-23

Trudge Today

Oof, have that "I'm a raisin" feeling right now. Slept not one wink 2 nights ago because of taking Adderall too late, then stayed up until ~4am last night. Woke up @ 9:30am feeling unable to sleep more, but obviously I'm totally out of wack. Drinking water would be a good priority today. Same with eating because you're beginning to be malnourished. However, the flip side to it is that really this isn't so bad. People do this all the time for years. Think Elon Musk.

Careful around Adderall today. Going to need more due to exhaustion but mind the OCD/overdose. Took 10mg ~10am. Considered taking more due to exhaustion, but wanted to wait & see. Glad I did. It is

Or I?

starting to kick in & provide relief ~10:45am. Just need to see if 10mg is enough considering my exhaustion.

Continue the focus on brain training with a new focus on driving change through navigating & regulating body. The "what would ideal state FEEL like, identifying the feeling, and live in that which drives bottom up regulation to the brain." *A Lifelong Friend* mentioned just how important body is in all this yesterday. Added benefit is that, by taking focus off of mind driving all changes, the brain is able to conserve energy and focus where it's actually needed. It's less stressed & is free to operate with more space & Source input.

11-12-23

Made To Help A Girl From High School

★The Resonant Frequency★

In objects the Resonant Frequency is that special, specific frequency that thing operates best at.

An example would be when a glass makes noise when someone rubs the rim with the right force.

In this state the "atoms" within an object are in alignment & operating in sync.

I believe this applies to the human brain too. The Resonant Frequency is your brain's personal ideal wavelength. The wavelength where you operate with ease as yourself. This state is defined by 2 main qualities. (1) An "Empty Mind." & (2) Complete Autonomy. Stop Trying. Detach.

Empty Mind: Can mean literally empty & living in the blank space which is actually the Source connection to Universal intelligence. This is the ideal, ideal state which any ancient eastern philosophy defines as enlightenment & is extremely hard to hold onto. More practical, the empty mind can also paradoxically be identified & pursued with mindfulness when things are crazy in there by recognizing, accepting, and separating from (BUT NOT RESISTING) those thoughts. Now identify with & melt into consciousness which is the calm observer of the thoughts. Operate from this new perspective.

Complete Autonomy: You should feel completely distinct from everyone else while also feeling weirdly connected & one with everyone & everything around you. When in this state everything is easy and external influence slides right off because the only one whose acceptance matters is your own.

↓

This is the wavelength/mental space that is the seat of your consciousness. When in it your consciousness is driving & controlling the VR Suit. At your best they operate in sync & as one. In tough times, the consciousness is aware that the Suit is going haywire, but does what it wants in spite of that.

Mindset Hacks

When "stuck" → best way to get back into the RF is to literally STOP TRYING. This doesn't mean try not to try, this means literally stop trying & let go completely in that moment.

Experience not trying (as redundant as that is but it has to be experienced to be believed) and therefore begin to experience detachment from external influence/people/judgements. This could also mean detachment or non-identification with intrusive or discordant thoughts.

Important Distinction: Not trying does not mean being lazy or apathetic or anything like that. It means realizing that you already have all the answers & so don't need to try so hard to access them. Or you don't in which case it doesn't make sense to strain for a response. In that case just say so, it's OK not to know.

•

Higher Self

The Higher Self is the ideal future version of you who has reached whatever your full potential is right now & who carries within him all the knowledge & insight that experience brings with it.

Inner Child work is the best for resolving past traumas that cause contemporary problems. But when past trauma can't be determined to be the underlying reason of whatever it is that has you stuck, looking for guidance from the Higher Self is a similar practice that can provide great clarity & perspective. Can be particularly helpful in figuring out what to do or how to act in certain situations & conflicts.

How It Works

To use this: visualize the ideal future *version* of you in your mind's eye. Where is he? What is he wearing? What is he doing? Who's he with? House? Family? Kids? Job? Anything that comes up & as much detail as possible. Once the image is clear, notice what does it feel like being him. Embody this feeling, and, from this perspective, advise yourself on how to deal with whatever's going on.

Through this process you are necessarily self-reliant. Especially as impactful is the fact that, by using this change in perspective as your guide sight, all thoughts, decisions, actions, & emotions are in line with & put you on the path towards actually becoming the Higher, ideal Self. The more you do this, the more you essentially become that person. The image of the ideal self that is used to guide you can & should be updated when intuition dictates that the current one is no longer accurate.

This is self-actualization

•

ADHD/OCD Interaction

ADHD can lead to OCD – Example Below. If the rumination is engaged with/fed, the OCD is reinforced. It is always only getting stronger or weaker accordingly.

Potential ADHD/OCD Route

When you're spacing out that's ADHD. The way you respond can lead to OCD following the path: Space Out (ADHD) → Loss of Control/Fear of Judgement → (Anxiety) → OCD (latch onto anxious rumination). This is one specific way ADHD could catalyze OCD when ADHD is making focus/conversation/active performance difficult.

- **At work:** Distracted/All over the place (ADHD) → Performance, email, meeting, or any other kind of work-related anxiety → "I'm

an idiot/fundamentally flawed/going to fail/going to get fired/or whatever OCD related thought → Latch onto thought/ruminate (OCD) → Neural pathway specific to that rumination either established or reinforced & rumination primed/more likely to recur → Dopamine spike resulting from rumination or completing compulsion satisfies ADHD → OCD remains.
- **Addiction**: As OCD is essentially an addiction, this process shows why substance abuse is so common *when combined* with ADHD. Distractibility (ADHD) leads the brain to seek out substances as stimulation instead of satisfying through rumination.

Adderall & OCD
I think why Adderall is usually helpful in minimizing OCD despite how increases in dopamine can wreak havoc on it is because of 2 things. (1) Raising dopamine to baseline and the subsequent improvement to executive function keeps distractibility from causing the brain to both produce & latch onto intrusive thoughts. (2) Improvement to executive function allows the brain to more easily avoid latching onto intrusive thoughts & to refocus on task at hand when a thought is *activated*.

Where problems arise between OCD/Adderall is, first, and probably most impactful, when OCD is either undiagnosed OR too severe to make the potential of Adderall ever exacerbating it prohibitive. But specific to me, bad sleep makes Adderall less effective but still pumps the dopamine levels up in a way that elevates OCD. At the same time, exhaustion is already exacerbating both ADHD & OCD, alongside all the other ways the brain & body are already dysregulated by being tired. The confluence of factors can cause OCD to spiral. Still, awareness of what's going on is beneficial & still leaves room for mindfulness to be effective, as always…

11-13-23

Really crazy fucking situation with *A Girl From High School* unfolded between yesterday and today. It was wild. Check the text messages at some point in the future to determine just how harsh you were. I feel very proud of myself for how I stood up for my needs and didn't back down when challenged. I feel great about the way that I responded to her. She was really going after it. The Adderall allowed me to address the situation for sure and it also definitely makes me harsher. Also nicer at times in that I'm able to delicately articulate things when needed. This was a big step though. Really all the information about what went down and what I felt about it are included in the text messages. I was totally honest with her despite her declarations otherwise. She is so willing to reach out to anyone and she gave me good advice earlier on making it clear that it really isn't a big deal to reach out to people and that I've been negligent. Really actually look where reaching out to people has gotten her. And the more people get to know you, the more their decision will always have been validated by your performance and who you are as a person.

The interesting thing about yesterday is that I was able to apply what I now understand about the INFJ *(My Personality Type)* Door Slam. Basically this was an updated Door Slam according to my growth where I was able to re-examine and be more nimble with the how much loyalty I ascribed. It wasn't so deep. And I understood how little I owed to her because our connection was weak. So the weight of this new stuff combined with how I was about to replace the situation with Ivy with a new, frankly even worse one with *A Girl From High School,* which was too much to handle.

The analogy that I've been using *for the Door Slam* is that it's kind of like a see-saw that's completely weighed down on one side by your loyalty and care for people. You don't know how heavy that weight that's holding it down is. The more bad things that accumulate over the course of time, the more weight is added to the other side. At some point whenever the weight that is being accumulated through the experiencing of bad events outweighs the weight of my loyalty, the see-saw flips to the other side and is now stuck there. All of my loyalty and care is done. And its weight is now significantly reduced and the weight of the accumulated bad experience remains the same. It's now very very hard to reverse the direction.

I now understand how my brain works regarding relationships and I'm very happy for both the understanding and its natural disposition. The underlying feature of my INFJ tendencies is that I really don't hold grudges. It's not that I will allow people to continue to mistreat me, which is what it looks like from the outside, but that I am assessing whether I can get over each situation a la cart. Once that situation is resolved I let it go and don't continue to let my hurt from this issue affect my determination on the next one. This is what allows me to carry forward with these relationships with pure engagement and care.

The **DOOR SLAM** is a straw that breaks the camel's back moment. At some point if mistreated long enough – and the length of time I will allow this to happen varies according to the length of the relationship – I can now no longer avoid considering all of these events I had previously considered a la cart as individual instances and view the whole thing as a collective. At this point my image of the person is shattered and their attachment breaks clean under the weight of this new perspective.

The key unlock here is to use resentment as your guide. Resentment is the key. As resentment builds, there are things that need to be resolved because your subconscious is showing that it's keeping score & the seesaw is gaining potential energy as further infractions accumulate. So even though you've processed & forgiven whatever sins *exist* in your conscious awareness, resentment is showing you there is still an issue.

But what to do about the fact that resentment often completely dissipates in the good times?

This is a judgement call. You know the difference in the feeling now. The best thing is always to nip it in the bud.

Simply put – Don't get into another one of these relationships again knowing what you know now.

And if you do, by or by no fault of your own, get out of it as soon as you recognize it, like you did with *A Girl From High School*.

•

Ok holy shit. Massive massive unlock. I'm INFJ/FA *(Fearful Avoidant attachment style)*. INFJ is foundational. FA makes me delusional. *HS Girlfriend* was the inciting incident. Think that's why so much healing after *seeing her at Harry & Sally's* wedding. Although I really wasn't thinking about her.

EVERYTHING IS HAPPENING FOR A REASON. SHOWER THOUGHT!!! SHOOTING STAR WISH. SELF REALIZATION. SHOOTING STAR THE OTHER DIRECTION!!! THANK YOU THANK YOU THANK YOU.

Or I?

Then...self-check on the FA/DA *(Dismissive Avoidant attachment style)* dynamic to re-correct my self-righteousness.

Fearful Avoidant *Attachment Styles*

VOLATILE FA – Most common. Been through a lot. Under the radar trauma. Lots of fighting. Controlling/Manipulative parent. Think it's the norm. Can be the more extreme things too – alcoholism, cheating, etc. Not hot/cold but accompanied by emotional outbursts. Can be angry. Critical.

CONTROL ORIENTED – Relationships triggering. Feels like everything goes out the window in a relationship when you were totally good before. High achieving trying to be safe. Perfection in childhood was good. Very controlling of yourself. Controlling of who you have in your life.

INTERNAL EXPERIENCING – Experiencing all this hot/cold and anger and all other emotions but other people can't see it. Emotions outwardly in check. Relationship example – it's early in the relationship or don't have leverage so keep emotions under wrap but can explode.

FA LEANING ANXIOUS* – Over giving. Open/present. Enmeshed. Co-dependency. Intentions so good. Want to connect. Clings too much. Or pushes away when people are trying to get close. (THIS IS ME)
- Won't always be triggered by abandonment

FA LEANING DISMISSIVE* – Can seem really warm and close but will pull away and not say why. "Most damaging"

Both *have a* difficult time seeing the other's needs. FA can see any disconnect (i.e. *me with* IVY)

DUDE YOU'VE DONE AN AMAZING JOB ALL THINGS CONSIDERED. THE FACT THAT YOU ARE SO CONSIDERATE WITH THESE ATTACHMENT ISSUES IS INCREDIBLE. THANK THE LORD FOR INFJ PERSONALITY TYPE.

HELPFUL WEBSITE (freetoattach.com)

★11-14-23★

The Golden Boy

I am the golden boy. The perfect one. The smartest one. So smart his parents wouldn't even tell him his IQ. But they definitely let him know he had one to hide that couldn't possibly be shown. He just wanted to know what he was dealing with so he could plan accordingly. But now he knew for sure that he was the smartest boy around. Maybe even in the world. He was so good at every appointment, every adult party, at the dentist. His Mom was so proud. She told him so when they'd leave. "You were so good, you didn't complain at all." It felt so good. Ahhh what amazing approval.

He was absolutely the cutest boy. Omg the cutest. I don't think there was ever a cuter boy. Oh look at those eyes. Those cheeks. That nose. It felt so good that everyone loved his looks so. Because what would he be without them? But luckily he knew he'd be a cute little boy forever & everyone would love him so. Luckily Mom always told him it was true.

He was a skinny boy too. THANK GOD. Too bad he got his Dad's legs & feet though. At least that's what everyone says. Sounds bad. But who knows. He'd never had any problem with his legs. But he had his Dad's legs, so he knew he'd find out sooner or later. Weird though because *Dad's* so awesome at biking. So yea his Dad's legs ARE nice but there's no way he could come even close. And even though Dad's look a lot stronger than other people's, and even though Dad can bike 100 miles, his Dad's legs are pretty skinny. Wait, then his legs must be tiny! He looked down & saw for the first time what Mom & Dad had been trying to get him to see all along – he really was so unlucky to get Dad's legs. But now he realized a more insidious truth, everyone had just been trying to make him feel good all along, because he didn't get his Dad's legs, his were so much worse. So skinny. Too skinny. Abnormally skinny. Flawed. Ugly. But honestly, what a relief, he now knew the truth so he could make sure to hide his legs at all costs. You never know what might cause someone to notice. He was exceptional in his subterfuge. No one even said anything when he wore shorts… That's when you know you're good. Hopefully he can keep this up! And it's so fortunate he was preparing because little did he know that one day, many, many years from now, one girl would make fun of him one time. And then he would make out with her.

Or I?

And thank God he doesn't have hair. He hates it so much. It's so disgusting. Even Dad shaves his legs for biking. Ugh when he sees those disgusting hairy men in their swimsuits he could just vomit. Ughhh that one boy at the swim meet that time. You could see his disgusting hairy pubes & butt!!! It was so gross. He would hate nothing more than to have hair like that. He wouldn't be able to live with how disgusting he'd look. No one would like him then. He could never find someone to marry. Oh please God, don't let me be hairy. Oh. My. God. Has asking God for something so careless & selfish made him hate me? Am I going to go to hell. OH. MY. GOD. He's going to make me hairy as punishment, isn't he? "FORGIVE ME LORD, AMEN." "I wonder if that worked?" "I hope so because that guy is so disgusting." "OH NOOOO" "God is going to punish me for saying that too, that was so mean." "FORGIVE ME LORD, AMEN." "Whew, ok, I think that might have actually worked." "I feel much better." "Definitely got to keep doing that if I do anything bad, I don't want to go to HELL!" I mean I really do hate hair but I'm so lucky Mom surprised me by saying she'd be happy to – have to – pay to get it lasered off. I mean what other option is there?" "THANK GOD." "OH NOOOOOOO! I've taken the lord's name in vain. Now THAT has got to be bad." "FORGIVE ME LORD, AMEN." "No, that didn't feel right for some reason. Better do it one more time to be sure."

•

Relationship Adjuster

It's time to make some adjustments in my relationships. The recent realizations I've had around INFJ & my Fearful Avoidant attachment style have been revelatory in light of Ivy break-up. Using my relationship with her as my guide sight, I'm seeing similar patterns in many of my other relationships. The change in dynamic with Ivy has been so empowering. The cut-off of *A Girl From High School* was so empowering & clearly self-care – although I'm sure I was pretty harsh. Both of these things have showed me that this is necessary elsewhere. As you've uncovered, deep resentment is the indicator that I'm far down the line towards a Door Slam.

People who are on the hook in order of risk…
Aston
Gilly

Harry

People I've slammed door on:
Loki (a lifelong friend on the other side of the country)
College Friend
HS Girlfriend
My & Ivy's Old Roommate
First LA Roommate
Biergarten Girl

I would say that Harry/Gilly are not necessarily close to being at risk, but it's clear I need distance. The weird thing I'm realizing now though is that the only reason I feel loyal to them right now is because I did Harry's wedding, and Gilly complimented me there. Actually Gilly isn't at risk at all, but boundaries need to be set with him. You started that yesterday when you chirped back at him.

Harry on the other hand – I don't know what to do with him. I think he may be FA too?

I'm very close to being done with Aston. I need to have a conversation with him. He's a net negative for me. Takes & takes. Comfortable because of distance. Disaster when close. Think he is also FA with an anxious lean. He's been hot/cold with you a lot. Also definitely has narcissistic tendencies. But I think his level of self-awareness trumps this. With him, I'm going to set some boundaries & then we'll see if I need to take subsequent steps towards further detachment.

This is all possible because I'm able to more clearly see the "see-saw" in my mind's eye & how it should really work.

(Instead of weight on see-saw, think of Jack in the Box?) – Trying to come up with analogy that speaks more clearly to the "all of a sudden" nature of *the Door Slam*.

•

Mistreatment To Conscious Or Subconscious?
Bad events for conscious awareness OR subconscious repression. Key – Either way these are events that I viewed as extreme enough that I should really think about whether I'm going to end the relationship or

Or I?

not. Remember, no conflict so looking to forgive everything that's not big enough.

•

Can't trust OCD because can't trust myself? Checking *if door's locked* while looking at door knob.

11-15-23

Little Sleep, Adderall, & Relationship Mania

Basically *the Door Slam* happens when something happens that's so bad that it irrevocably ruins the relationship no matter how much I like the person.

OR

It's the straw that broke the camel's back.

I thought this was a straw situation. Really it was the first one in disguise.

•

Your actions told me that you didn't value any of the effort and it was the most painful thing in the world for me – like that I've ever been through – and I felt like you were showing how easily you could just discard me. And maybe sub-consciously you were doing that – which I get too – because as I'm about to show, my subconscious motivations were fucked too.

But weird because this is something I'd gotten used to. But I was so unbelievably triggered this time. Maybe more so than ever. Which made no fucking sense to me. Because I was in the purest place I had ever been with you.

This trajectory had all began a little before Fido got sick. Came home on a random day and had the epiphany *about feeling comfortable around you again*. Then Fido got sick, got even closer. This all led to me feeling closer than I had ever felt to you in the purest and most honest way right up until your withdrawal.

I was so proud. It was the most earned relationship I had ever had (proof that it wasn't romantic is the avoidance – also proof of my care was the admission of feelings – sacrificed myself for the relationship. But hot cold killing me and rejection of true self trigger).

For me it really is all about helping people and doing right by them and trying to get people around me to have better lives. My motivations also have to be completely pure or it doesn't mean anything to me. Like if I do something nice for someone but I have ulterior motives and I know it then it's actually a negative for me. I was losing the ability to tell when I confessed my feelings for you which is a big part of the reason *I did* and I needed the connection to be pure or else it was like tainted to me or something. Idk. But what's very strange about it is that there is only a small, select group of people who I actually care about. While I'm kind to everyone else – and kind is the key word, I am not nice. I have been nice and that's now a real fucking thing I need to look out for which indicates that I'm in a subconscious anxious state. Because I'm not nice – I can be brutal – but I've been hiding that part of myself big time. To avoid blowing up from all the repressed needs. Everyone else doesn't really matter to me – I don't have strong feelings for them at all. Feels kind of weird actually.

For the "special people" – this is the best way I can describe what happens for me as people get closer to me and I decide to let them "in."

I have this thing at *that* level about what friendship means. And it's totally totally set in stone/unchangeable from a value standpoint. And that is that my best friends all get treated like this. If they do something wrong, as long as we can get through it I won't let it affect the relationship at all.

There's an irreversible path resulting in completed Door Slam once I start having trouble accepting new things that are happening which aren't even as bad as a bunch of things that have already happened and been accepted into the trash without consequence. What's happened here is that I haven't properly established boundaries up to this point and this is a point of no return. I know it doesn't make sense for me to have accepted these past things, and then not to accept this new thing. It's inconsistent with the rules. If I rejected this I would have to address everything else.

Or I?

Closeness affects how much I'll take from someone. Obviously this is the case for everyone but for me it's extreme. Example of threshold passed.

I will do everything for you. Completely locked in place. Almost.

Trash bags – hold space in my head for each person. Imagine this is represented by a trash bag. Anything that's done against me is judged for am I mad about this? Should I confront this? Etc. If I accept the thing it's accepted forever. Even if I get frustrated about it later on, I will remind myself that I already accepted it and it's not fair to go back on that to the other *side*. If I accept something one time, I have a hard time saying that it's not cool when it happens all the time. Even if it's not cool. Because I'm like I don't know how I can rationalize that there's an amount of times that's appropriate. It's either ok or it's not.

Every issue that comes up where I feel violated, used, disrespected or whatever is something I consider as its own thing. The other events that I've already accepted have no bearing on it. This is how I'm not holding grudges. Every new infraction gets put in the bag. The seriousness of the issue is represented by how much it stretches the trash bag. This thing is like 20X more stretchy than a normal person's capacity and I also understand people's motivations so clearly that I will always put myself in their shoes and often rationalize behavior away.

But I'm not really actually letting these things go. It may seem like it because my capacity to hold on to hurt is so great, but really it's just that the hurt isn't taking up too much room. But one day, something happens that's the straw/camel. At this point, the trash bag breaks and all that trash I had been ok with alone is scattered all over everywhere – and when I'm looking at it all together for the first time, I see just how clearly this is bad for me and it's basically a rational decision made by my brain without my control really that I'm done with that person. Despite the accumulated mistreatment, my care for and commitment has been unwavering and is at the same level as even my best best friend. But the minute the trash bag breaks is the minute that person falls completely out of their spot. I am about as unaffected *by* this as you can be. It's unsettling. And the feeling inside me is unmoving. I had never felt closer to you a couple days before and now I'm here not even caring about your presence or the impact I was having whatsoever. In this empowered state – which is extremely unmovable by anyone – I am willing to take *on* pretty much anything within reason at this point. Sometimes I can go out and confront other people who've been really messing with me and

I've known the relationship is dead for a while on my end but haven't been willing to get the balls to end it.

I was as depressed and spiraling as I've ever been right after you pulled away. I didn't understand because I had dealt with my feelings and was coming from the purest place possible. It was very very confusing. This was actually the most triggered I'd ever been and I really felt like I was losing my mind. I think actually in a way I was as the false self I'd been presenting for the past however many years was dissolved and the part of me that has been hidden all these years began to emerge.

Did the opposite of what I knew to – stuck around, lingered, hoped you'd re-engage, didn't want to believe what was going on. Day 2 *(11-5-23)* still waiting but getting dark now. Day 3 *(11-6-23)* still here but by the end of the night my patience was through. Went to parents' *house*. Still bugging for a day. Really really crazy emotions that were so painful.

The next day, what felt like all at once, I had an immediate relief and was no longer negatively affected in any way. I was at peace even though I knew I was going to be extremely brutal. While spiraling my mind was quickly showing me all the things that had been held in the trash bag. Some of them I was actively aware of and constantly managed through (never hang out, one-sided convo, feelings convo, feelings aftermath). I don't re-appraise anything in retrospect. Like I don't look at something I'd already said was ok and then change my mind. It's more that I've never looked at the whole mess before. And now that I'm seeing it all out there for the first time I now consider it all at once, and the evidence is so overwhelming that the decision isn't even a question. It's final and it's clear.

The reason the Door Slam doesn't stop once it starts almost ever is because I'm all or nothing. There is no in-between. So to stay in contact with this person who you had such a strong bond *with*/protection over in any way just makes it impossible not to give.

I was completely comfortable continuing with *the Door Slam* once you'd left *for your trip*. I could see that you were getting upset and I just would consider how bad you treated me this whole time – again with the false image of myself/perspective on things. It was very very unsettling because a week before I was thinking about how you were literally one of the most important people I will ever meet. So I was super fucking confused.

Or I?

I remember doing this to a bunch of other people. Then start researching to try to figure out what was going on. I'm really not thinking about you at all and am not dissociating whatsoever. I couldn't be further gone. I find the answer that I'm looking for when I come upon INFJ Door Slam. Major Unlock.

I'm reading into this to understand. Major relief on something that's a massive core wound. This power and this darkness. Completely juxtaposed to GOOD BOY. Also reading this now sort of soothing myself for what I'm doing to you. Because now I'm starting to de-activate and come back to myself. I was still fine with the Door Slam, but the more I come back to my own mind, the more I realize that this is very cruel to you given your abandonment wound. For some reason this – the most sensitive realization I could have – had *only* a minor effect on me *and* I was able to easily brush it off. The decision I made at this point was – because I was always the one who had to bridge the gap, and because I assumed you knew this was your fault, which I now know you probably had no idea – that despite the fact that I was totally done, I owed it to you to give you closure. So if at any point you had reached out to me to see what was going on I would have engaged then and there. If you didn't engage and things went sour, I was going to wait like a week and then give you the closure and offer to move out that minute. The closure was going to be completely amicable – I was all about not being mean to you – and was meant to provide *you* with the blueprint for attachment changes that need to be made.

I'm still very unclear what's going on though. Now I understand what I'm doing and what I've done to many more people than I realize. I realize how cold I can be to some people. This all flies in the face of the INFJ thing and also the image I have been using for myself as this great, only nice guy.

At some point I start really trying to understand your perspective against me because I just can't shake the feeling of being so left behind and detached and like you never cared about me at all if you're willing to *discard me like that*. What I realize now I was always looking for was simply clarity. So I'm ruminating on this situation like it's going to give me an answer. I'm doing what I do best which is try to put myself in your shoes to see how you could be so careless with me when I've been so careful with you. Like what would that feel like. Holy shit starting to see how detached I'd have to feel in order to be comfortable playing someone like I thought you played me. I'm really visualizing it. I get the feeling and hate how careless the attachment feels. I know I like this person and they add value to my life, but I'm kind of apathetic to them. I will immediately forget them if they're not in front of me until I randomly remember that I haven't talked to them in 5 months and reach out. I will think this is normal. If the conversation goes on for more than a couple exchanges, I'm completely done. No joke as I'm having this visualization I have a crazy "wait, what the fuck…" moment when I realize that I'm able to visualize this so easily because I know this feeling. And what I'm visualizing and what you did to me is something I've done to a bunch of other people. "Holy fucking shit" I think. And I run to my room and immediately do all the research that I have now.

Through this, and with extremely little effort now that I knew what to look for, I had my world shattered again when I came across a video for "Fearful Avoidant/Dismissive Avoidant Relationship Pattern." When I say this was one of the most eerily accurate representations of our dynamic, I literally cannot emphasize it enough. My jaw was on the floor. And herein lies the big paradigm shift for me.

I learned that I have a Fearful Avoidant attachment style – which is the rarest and most complex – also coming from the most trauma. Your attachment style is 99.99% Dismissive Avoidant. Our attachment styles line up perfectly for each other to have a slight push pull dynamic going on all the time. But it's very slight because we're both primarily avoidant at our core. So while we both want intimacy, we both avoid it and the person who could provide it to us in different ways. So subconsciously we were both keeping the same distance apart. We just were doing it differently.

I really want to be close to someone more than anything but will either keep that person at arm's length and/or self-sabotage the whole thing. Very good at reading behavior/emotions – *from* reading *my* parents for mood. INFJ on top of this.

You want intimacy too but avoid it in a different way. When you start to get close to someone – platonically or romantically – who really is a possible healthy attachment for you, at some point your body will reject getting any closer. This should feel something like that knee jerk "I gotta get away now" feeling that is confusing and you put on the other person which is when the hot/cold behavior cycle starts.

Or I?

For *a* Fearful Avoidant, on the other hand, I experience the knee jerk trauma response when someone pulls away once we're connecting if they're more avoidant than me *(if I'm* anxious more *than them)*, or I will pre-emptively pull away if I feel things are getting closer or are showing too much potential *(if I'm more avoidant than them)*. I'm hyper critical of problems. The amount of anxiety depends on how bad *the attachment issue is*. Anxiety *around everything with you was* awful at first. *This* whole thing healed me.

Where this would go extremely out of wack was when we were trying to reconnect after the feelings portion of the program. Basically the way the cycle works is that, just like what happened with us, the Fearful Avoidant & the *Dismissive* Avoidant get into a cycle when they get disconnected like we did where the one person is ready to close the gap at the same time as the other person is as angry as they get. And both people are confused now because they have been mad about so many different things that both people are stubbornly like "I'm not going to be the one to say something."

The fact of this attachment style is revelatory for me is so many ways. And what many would view as a negative – *because* everyone wants to be *securely* attached – is one of the most positive and revealing things of my life. If not for this I would have believed I was totally fine and everyone else was fucked up forever. I came to fully understand my family dynamics. I came to fully appreciate that I had been unfairly holding you primarily responsible for *our relationship issues*.

I have never stopped *the Door Slam* before. I've never even heard of that happening. I woke up and was completely fine and completely done. I was calm. There was no angst. And the dark power feeling I have inside me was fully re-activated again for the first time.

You were dead to me. I was always going to be nice but took 3 hours prepping my mindset and I still fucked up when I got back here. I didn't want to be mean at all. But this thing lives off resentment and was just pumping me with it. Was scarily unaffected. Now I'm so fucking confused. Because I'm also liking this and I have no idea what's going on. No part of me wanted to shut you out.

Bad things – judge a la cart – put in trash. Never let it affect the next decision.

I view *the Door Slam* as totally fair, justified, and completely earned, so therefore I don't have to have any anxiety over it.

Core wound – **Fear of Rejection**. *Feelings admission* proves relationship more important to me *than avoiding this fear* and *that I* would sacrifice myself on the most dangerous/scary of places for it. I did that. Staying around was living in my personal hell. Relationship still more important than that. Healing beginning at this stage as I learn how to manage my anxiety in the most anxiety inducing dynamic for me. **Good/Perfect Boy** – Hiding any imperfections. Hiding dark power. Shame. Deformed. Issues with relationships started being hidden. Emotionally knew problems *existed* – hidden. Hide. Hide. Hide.

Ok so now what really happened in all of this. FEELINGS *CONFESSION* – Feeling so close, especially being at home. *Those 2 comments during the Super Bowl* that I took as direct shots to the core wound of *the* true me not being accepted because in general and with you that was the most it had been out in years. Directly triggering core wound is what drove me so hard to do *confess feelings* right away with such bad timing. Never understood that *before*.

REVEALING FEELINGS ABOUT AVOIDING DOOR SLAM – Was about to go. Needed clarity. Another sacrifice. Literally could not do it anymore.

FIDO CONFRONTATION – Instead of DOOR SLAM. Trying to take some trash out.

Something happened before *going to* Park City *for Harry & Sally's wedding* where I was on the verge of the Door Slam for real. And then it dissipated. In Park City I stayed for so long because I was deciding what to do. I didn't know about the Door Slam at this point but thinking about the feeling, I was right on the edge. It was almost like acid reflux that I was just holding back. But basically I sat myself down and told myself I would figure out if I thought I could move forward with the relationship with absolutely 0 expectations and just pure gratitude over everything that happened. I didn't know if I could. I was so bitter and hurt by you now. Also when I'm away for a long time my avoidance really kicks in and it is physically hard for me to come back. But what I didn't realize is that the Door Slam was just festering in there. If I knew about this then I would have known it was at critical mass.

Or I?

During my drive back I was able to resolve everything and move forward without any negative. I knew you'd likely be upset I was gone so long, but I needed the time to figure out if I was going to invest in you for the rest of my life, or if I couldn't do that with all of what I saw as mistreatment.

After that was the progression discussed earlier. So close. So comfortable *once again*.

Euphoric realization. A feeling I've never felt before. I'm wondering if I've ever felt I could be more myself around someone. No. That feeling was the most I'd ever felt myself. I could feel there was a lot of work left to do but I distinctly felt myself back in there. I wanted to cry.

The last two days *before you withdrew* were so amazing for me. I think for these two days I had achieved secure attachment to you. I had really really worked through everything. Even the vestiges. I had resolved my relationship anxiety in these dynamics. There was no more acting/re-acting for me. I also didn't care what you did who you went out with whether you included me or not, whether you talked to me or not, or anything. I simply was purely grateful for the relationship. And especially to reconnect with you and to be able to sit here comfortably together without even talking. I realized that it probably wouldn't be possible for us to really continue having a relationship after this because it would keep us both from being able to grow into that next relationship. I knew that being as close as I felt right now was going to cause leaving to be one of the most painful experiences – because in that moment I was allowing the last walls to come down – walls that had been up with you the whole time – and that I had not let down for as long as I can remember. Maybe never. It felt so good and I felt the best I'd felt in years. I was so excited that it looked like we were going to complete our story arc and that this would end up being a growing experience for both of us.

I was really excited to just literally sit in the next room as you the next day. My energy was totally calm and I remember for the first time in as long as I can remember having this feeling of coming home. Again, between *Last Company Name*, the feelings that I was hiding for a minute, my personal post feelings hell, your bday, no bdays really together, and our relationship being very delicate, I was exhausted and was really really feeling it more than I can ever remember. I think my brain was releasing all the stress that had accumulated.

I came in and felt a chill immediately. I knew something was off right away. Everything about your demeanor, tone of voice, etc. was pushing me away. I thought I might be imagining things. You said you were cleaning your closet. Every once in a while you would come out acting "normal" but with different everything – not *just* being cold like usual during these. I still refused to believe. In these situations when it's clear you're looking for space I had gotten really good at leaving right away when I saw this. Instead I knew I was making a mistake but I was desperate to reconnect. I stuck around on the couch. I knew this might drive you away further, but I refused to believe you would remind me once again how easily you would throw me away. You never came out again for the rest of the day. I did not understand why I was being so emotional when this hot/cold hadn't bothered me in a long time. I knew I was feeling the weight of some work stuff and so wondered if I was just having existential issues.

By the end of the next day when, now you'd come out of your room, but could not have been more detached on the couch. No engagement, obviously didn't want me to, on phone the whole time despite being here. *Those* two days, and this one, despite being emotional I kept hope alive, despite the sinking feeling in my stomach knowing the truth. Like I said, the vibe felt very off and to me it felt like a massive paradigm shift had taken place. I started thinking *about* just how hard it was for me to eat the shit I needed to in order to get to the other side of the feelings and prove myself to you – I thought about your reaction to my feelings declaration, I thought about how besides staying here I didn't feel like the crime for the feelings fit the punishment at all. Everything started flooding me all at once showing me just how much I'd let myself get taken advantage of. My body started feeling extremely strange. Mentally I was ok with you, physically the thought of being near you or even having to talk to you seemed actually impossible. I went to my room that night starting to feel very very strange in a way that I couldn't place. The next day I found things had progressed to the place where I couldn't even be around you. Luckily I had a meeting in LA so I would be out. This is literally all I thought about the whole way up and back. I was defeated. I thought I was done with wondering what the fuck was going on. An extreme resentment bubbled up.

I'd cooled off at this point and was planning on showing that I wouldn't run away from the apartment to make you feel comfortable and *to let you* know I was good. I got back home and was waiting here thinking, "ok, yea idk what's going on but I'm feeling a bit better, it will be good to get this over with." I was in the kitchen when I saw your car *pull up*. Everything in my body screamed at me to leave. My brain did not know what the fuck was going on because it was totally good. It knew this need for space was whatever. It was just like every other time. But I don't think it actually was. I think there was something bigger going on with you. But even if I'm wrong, I realize that this distancing wasn't a little deal for me at all.

I went to get something from the kitchen when I saw your car. I saw you coming back from somewhere – the first time I'd see you since *I realized* how much I sacrificed of myself to you to get here. How I took the abuse after my rejection. How we never hung out outside of here. Watching you walk into your room that night, I felt the relationship end the minute you closed the door. In my mind you had just abandoned me as aggressively as possible.

But I was willing to go back to the well of existential pain one more time with you in order to be able to enjoy the last couple months together. At this point I wanted to spend as much time as possible with you before the end of this. This is a dangerous realization around a dismissive avoidant. I'm sure you felt this and this was the revolting feeling that led you to need some space all of a sudden.

Now what really happened the other day. Comfortable. Grateful. Prideful. Story arc. Ride into the sunset was all I wanted. Who knows what happens *after that*. Never felt more comfortable around anyone.

What had happened to me is that for the first time in my adult life, the parts of me that I had been hiding. The parts that are the most vulnerable. The parts Mom and Dad denied the most. The parts I'd been slowly finding over the course of my progress over the past however many months. Those parts – my core wounds – found their way beyond my protective layers when I had the euphoric sensation of realizing I could be myself around you. I was myself for a day or two. And then you withdrew.

To me you rejected my core wound. My authentic self – which had just come out for the first time. This is why the reaction. The Door Slam wasn't even close *before this*. In fact I'd felt like there was nothing that could break our bond now.

Your rejection of the part of me that is the core wound was the final step in my rebirth. In going through the next couple days and feeling like I was losing my mind, I think the false self died, and the pain was the core wound experiencing the rejection I'd experienced from Mom and Dad which led to the wound.

My mind, now seeing everything that happened all together – i.e. the trash bag broke – decides, enough. She rejected the core you. You have nothing left to lose anyway. "I'm done." Immediately the space for you in my brain is eliminated. I can't feel you anymore. You're gone. I think, if you're constantly running, you were never really here.

I come back and am completely disconnected. I feel apathy for your hurt. I feel numb. I now know this was the part of my body protecting *my* Inner Child by numbing me. I feel great even though the most important person to me over the last however many years is suffering at my own hand. This is typically unbearable. Ok – what the fuck is going on. And this leads us to here.

∞ 11-16-23 ♡

Less Sleep, More Adderall, & More Mania

I re-integrated back into myself for real and that was the final thing.

Would have never gotten here or would have taken a failed marriage or serious relationship or something without you.

My life is going to be so much better because of you and I just really realized it. I want to tell you how.

The closer I get – the worse I perform because I'm protecting my true strength which I'm scared of. Because I gotta go be an asshole but in a different way. I got to be myself who I think *is* an asshole. Scared I'm like my Dad. I am but the best version of him and my asshole is really just about doing what's right at all costs. For me and for the world. This is in work too.

Or I?

For you – the closer you get, the more you protect that part of you, which needs to get out. I saw your vision board or whatever and I started laughing because *your ideal man* was a version of me. But you'll never get that version of me if you don't show both *sides of yourself*. If you gotta run away.

I caused you problems because I reinforced that outside part of you *(the mask)*. You were able to have it both ways because you got the validation from me *who saw* this version that *was* the inside part, the sweetest part of you at our closest.

Both of us are affected more by the opposite things. That's why things could deteriorate so weirdly in the bad moments. When things were good obviously neither of us cared what the other person was doing at all. We were happy with the homeostasis. When things got bad I controlled the distance between us on the inside. You controlled the distance between us using the outside. Like actual separation affected me more and emotional separation affected you more. I would manipulate more internally and you would externally. I'm here or I'm not physically when things are healthy and you don't care. But when things are unhealthy I'm manipulating with my distance and that upsets you. For me when you're here you can manipulate with your attention and I don't care when it's healthy. When it's not healthy you manipulate with your space within the apartment. When I had feelings I worried about your feelings and behavior on the outside for the first time.

For me – the closer we got the more you saw the inside part of me. But that was also when things were at their best and realest on both sides. That scared the fuck out of me because I knew that meant it was much more in my control than you. I'm sure that scared the fuck out of you because you realized that we vibed better than you thought and we were bonding more. AND THIS is when our fear of intimacy both gets triggered. We both got triggered. But you and I need the exact opposite thing at that time to soothe ourselves to get out of our discomfort.

•

Looking for any possible way to stop *the Door Slam*. I knew this was impossible because I had done so much research grieving depressing answering, working, calculating – all the things. So I was totally good with what was going on – had absolutely no intention of stopping it. And actually it was originally going to be way more brutal. The amount that I was holding myself back once I flipped *to the other side* was A LOT. When

I knew it was for real was when you left for your trip. And I was totally content and good with it. But I was still extremely confused about everything that had happened. My response to something as big as this without knowing what the fuck I know now is to try to get to the bottom of it internally. So after you left I pretty much spent all my time trying to do just that.

But with the feelings and the aftermath and all of it I just could never figure out what the fuck was going on in our friendship and I have spent so much fucking time thinking about it.

•

I run away through distance. You run away through disconnecting emotionally.

So you controlled and were able to manipulate with the physical distance more effectively. And I was able to manipulate with the emotional more effectively. Where things got wonky was when we either manipulated too much in our "realm of expertise" OR when we started fucking around in the other person's realm. I think. What I mean by that is this. So I can only speak for me but the latter was when the really big problems were going on. Because that's where we're most sensitive. So like I don't really care about physical distance or manipulations with it as much *as a securely attached person* because my Mom was *always* gone. I ALSO am *comfortable with it* because my mom was always gone. So I'm used to it. But when the manipulations in that realm are really big then I'm like wait what the fuck.

When I get close to achieving something really great I fuck up because that would validate my worth. My problems present themselves when I EITHER don't want to show how worthy I am OR don't want to see how unworthy I might be at things that are important to me. I didn't apply to Harvard, etc., because I didn't want to prove *my worth*. This applies to everything I've ever done. Golf. Singing. Plays. Etc. Always not reaching potential to *hide* it. Applies to job/career – *sabotaging* myself & making up excuses to throw people off the scent. Or doing things that are impossible to succeed at because then that will prove my lack of self-worth. The problem is that my natural abilities are able to outshine my absolute fucking hatred for myself. And I think it's the things that I'm feeding to hide the best parts of me that are *leading to success* – when really it's when the best purest parts of me show up that do it. And it's the same for you but in a completely different way. It just depends on the things/realms that are important to you where the problems show up because you're able to "prove/not prove" your value in those realms. That's where you split the most. This is where the "pressing" comes from. When things are going bad you're "pressing" on everything to get out. Especially with depression. Adderall has given me a reprieve from the pressing which has cleared the way for these revelations. The realms of importance are where things get weird because – since they're important to you – this is where you can prove the things true to yourself that you're afraid of the most. So for me CAREER, RELATIONSHIPS, GOLF, and then whatever else gets added to the list over time. This is where things get weird. When you decide more things get important to you then they'll get weird there too. This is both in career and relationships. CAREER & RELATIONSHIPS are the ultimate two because they're the ones that are most important to me. Then lots of problems show up in golf because that was something I was uniquely good at. And singing because same there – voice problems resolved. And then THE MOST problems came up with my brain because it's the most unique thing about me. WHOOPS see that right there is the old stuff. I'm saying it's the most unique thing about me as if it's a fact but really that's the Ego/conditioning I'm trying to undo right now. Saying it this way would have actually been reconditioning the old programming because the brain defined itself as *important*. Wow. Good catch. In detaching from the importance of these things you're then able to define yourself less by them and then act more naturally within them. This is why detachment is so important. Expectations. With attachment comes expectations. For me those expectations are more around external control and for you they're more about emotional control. Meaning the difference between a literal "where the fuck are you" and a *figurative* "where the fuck are you." We're both comfortable with physical and emotional distance. But I'm just a little more sensitive to the physical distance than a Dismissive Avoidant.

Your problem with writing has been that you've been trying to forcibly write according to the normative rules as ascribed by normative society. As INFJ you're statistically very unique and with OCD/ADHD/whatever this is you're mentally very unique. As a result of the latter it is not effective for you to write chronologically and it doesn't make sense for you to write the way "normal" people are taught. It doesn't make sense to your brain.

Don't write chronologically.

When stuck don't force brain down that path, move to another.

Be nimble with your attention – nurture what it goes to so long as it's still associated with the realm that's productive for you at the time to achieve your goals.

You don't like things that are monotonous continuously. Also you won't realize it but focusing on the same thing for too long – or for longer than you should will start to seriously affect your performance through focus loss and then the effects of OCD rumination will start to deteriorate mental state leading to self-conscious episode/ruminations/loss of self-confidence.

WHEN YOU FEEL YOURSELF SPACE OUR OR START TO FIGHT – TAKE NOTE – THIS IS WHEN IT'S TIME TO DECIDE IF YOU SHOULD MOVE ON OR PRESS THROUGH. IF PRESSING THROUGH STAY VIGILANT ON HOW YOU'RE FEELING.

WHEN YOU SPACE OUT IT'S BECAUSE THAT'S THE END OF YOUR ATTENTION SPAN ON THAT THING FOR THE MOMENT AND YOU NEED A BREAK – HOWEVER LONG. BUT ALL OF THIS IS MADE WORSE WHEN YOU'RE PRESSING AT THE SAME TIME. IT'S ACTUALLY MAKING IT LESS LIKELY THAT YOU'LL COME BACK ONLINE. THIS ONLY HAPPENS WHEN YOU'RE RELAXED. AND THIS IS WHY YOU FEEL FREE. ANY STATE YOU'RE RESISTING TO FIGHT, YOU'RE PRESSING AND LIKELY TO MAKE IT WORSE.

This applies to relationships too. The harder you fight against something that's natural to someone, the more you're going to push them away. Personality disorders and attachment styles become another person to consider in a relationship and come with *their* own set of rules additional to what normal people have around things that will be extra resistant, *determining* what can and will *push people away* and what wont.

I split because it was the ONLY way for me to stay with my parents. I killed the killer off when I stayed with Dad. Did it forever with Mom. Kill things off emotionally to blind yourself to their mistreatment. OR kill things off that would allow you to deal with it effectively.

●

Or I?

You can't do the same thing over and over again forever or you'll die. This is why *entrepreneurship* & psychology are both appealing. This is why office job is not. Can not do that. That's when I'm dying. Need something that's different all the time. I will lose focus and then hate whatever. Both within specific jobs and within an industry itself. I think I just lost fascination with Hollywood more than anything. It's just not interesting to me anymore. You don't care about TV shows anymore. You still want to be around famous people and all that but the industry is done. What you've really been wanting is success and you still think you can achieve it because you saw it there once and there's an inconceivably little chance you could do it again. But you can't.

DON'T FIGHT THE LOST THOUGHTS OR LOST ATTENTION. RECENTER AND DO YOUR BEST WITH THAT. THAT'S WHERE YOU'RE AT NOW.

•

Just copied and pasted *the above*. Wrote for like IDK an hour, hour and a half and then see that it was 5 pages. I THOUGHT I'D WRITTEN NOTHING. You just proved to yourself once and for all that the fear around writing and writing speed were all bullshit. I also above just proved that your ADHD has been true the whole time and that *writing* is *one* way that OCD manifested itself around it. It's when you just forced yourself to try to pay attention to *what* you didn't want to pay attention to over and over again until your brain found a way to describe the way it didn't want to focus. And you caused this problem yourself because you didn't go to class or do fucking anything and this was it.

It's the same thing with women. You just don't actually want to do it the way it's supposed to be done or to be as nice as you were taught you were supposed to be. So it's not natural to you and you don't want to do it. You also don't want to just fuck so you get weird around that because it's not natural to you. So you've created all these problems in your head for yourself around these things to prove to yourself that *you're flawed*.

And with Ivy the same things applies. I "accepted" things that were against my shit because I didn't want to get in an argument. When I had resentment these were those things. More confusing because I'm more accepting of these things than a normal person. But I wouldn't want to say uncle when it was too much so I let those go. Those things bothered me. Didn't have the balls to say it. I also didn't want to seem weird. Like you I'm cool with a lot of distance but just need an *invite* every once in a while on the external. But on the emotional I got problems and need to feel like I am constantly connected to you. As long as I have that I'm good forever. I constantly "accepted" unacceptable conditions because if I saw how bad they were I'd have to freak out. And the thing I was most scared to say was – "hey I'm sensitive to you in particular emotionally. Because I'm in a bad place and fragile right now in general, like any person would be, and you're the most important person to me, you're where I'm most sensitive because you mean a lot to me, can you please be gentle with me?"

BUT HERE'S THE THING. YOU HAVE BEEN THE THING I HAVE BEEN MOST SENSITIVE TO. I HAVE BEEN LIVING WITH YOU. I HAVE BEEN GETTING TORMENTED BY YOU. THIS HAS BEEN THE MOST DIFFICULT THING EVER. AND YOU SAW *THAT* THE WHOLE TIME. AS MUCH AS I'M SAYING I WAS FREAKING OUT AND I WAS. YOU SAW ME. THAT'S WHERE MY SHIELD IS. IT'S IN THE MIND. I CAN LOCK MYSELF UP SO TIGHT. I THINK NO ONE CAN SEE BUT OF COURSE THEY CAN. THAT'S BEEN PART OF MY DELUSION. "I know I'm being very distant but she probably hasn't even noticed." I thought you didn't care and that my distance didn't even mean anything to you which is why I was comfortable doing it.

I was forcing things I didn't want to do. Forcing acceptance that I didn't want to accept. Resisting some of the biggest parts of myself at the same time to make it all happen. And lying to myself about it the whole time. I didn't even know who I was anymore at all. I had lost it all and in the process completely lost myself.

But because of you I completely found my way back.

I want to see you at your wedding smiling so proud because of who you are. Because of who you've become. And because you're with a man who is going to care for you the right way and who you're going to have a great life with no matter what happens. If you continue doing the same things – and I'm not talking about doing something different or changing paths, *but behaviorally* – you're doing this because you like it and *are* including the parts of yourself you're comfortable showing – and because *you're on* TV and everyone is seeing it, you're only putting the parts of yourself on it that you're comfortable showing. You're fine being judged on those qualities because they're the ones that you were either told are ok, are ok with yourself, or whatever. But it's always been so interesting for me to watch and I could never put my finger on it until now. The parts of you that are most scary to you and the most vulnerable are the ones you hide the most.

BUT FOR YOU AND ME BOTH – I think we're both different. I know it. And I don't mean this in a we're so special way. That's something that I absolutely need to stop thinking about myself because its feeds into my core issues. The idea of being better than – of being perfect. And I'm able to use privilege and wealth and things like that to prove that to be inherently true.

Unemployment particularly difficult for me because it *feeds into a* core wound. But this core wound. You core wound. Job. Relationship. Mental Health (brain) perfect. Asshole Thing (body perfect – omg if anyone finds out). And then complete loss of you just happened.

It's like only when I really and truly lost everything that I held dear *that I found myself*. And I know that I still have work to do because my biggest crutch still exists – it's my parents – and they were the source of the problem. But I don't need to detach or lose them anymore because I now know exactly who I am and what my problems are. I can address them and healthily move on if they don't agree. It will be sad but it will be best for me. I can't hide things that bother me or do what's best *for them* anymore.

HAD MADE DECISION TO ACCEPT ROLE WITH YOU AND MOVE FORWARD WITH IT. DIDN'T REALIZE THAT THERE WAS ONE THING I WOULDN'T ACCEPT AND THAT WAS BEING EMOTIONALLY CUT OFF ON TOP OF THAT.

MISC

Really knew I had healed before *your trip to* London. That was me really wanting to watch Fido. Had nothing to do with you. Actually the money made me not want to do it and that was what I was sensitive to. For me my issues are really more about when I decide *about* these weird moral rules but it's like I expect *other people to have* the same rules. Don't tell them. And then get pissed when they violate *them*. Then get emotionally manipulative – although I can't help it because I don't realize I'm triggered – it's just that I literally just can't help but do it.

I see that you didn't really think you were doing anything at all *when you withdrew*. Because you needed space but didn't actually leave. It was actually a HUGE step forward for you. You kept coming out and acting normal. I took this as what the fuck (realization about healing/old part of me Door Slam). OMG NOOOOOOOOOO IVY I AM SOO SORRY. OMG FUCK. Oh no. The amount of time you were gone I took as like further fucking distance. I was crumbling. You had decided to stay. You slightly came out the next day but still needed some space. You weren't fully ready. At this point I was completely done. The next day you were ready and I was now gone.

WORK
GET GOOD AT DECIDING WHICH THOUGHTS ARE DISTRACTIONS AND SHOULD BE IGNORED TO CONTINUE THE CURRENT THOUGHT WHICH WOULD GET DERAILED OTHERWISE. OR WHEN THE NEXT THOUGHT SUPERSEDES THE QUALITY OR IMPORTANCE OF WHATEVER IS CURRENTLY BEING DISCUSSED. ORRRR WOULD BENEFIT WHATEVER YOU'RE TALKING ABOUT TOO MUCH TO BE IGNORED.

LIFE EFFICIENCY
You will be at your best when you switch from thing to thing and activity to activity quickly when your attention wanes on what you're doing too much.

SUPER SECRET – I don't care. I didn't care. I do have that. I was done. There are times I don't care about shit at all that I pretend I do. But it's not like normal people. It's like an apathy or whatever. But *the emotion is* just not there!!!!!!!!!!!!!!!!!!!! This is the missing piece. Got to find that part next.

THE PART THAT WAS SQUASHED DOWN BY DAD IN ORDER TO STAY IN A RELATIONSHIP WITH HIM.

Or I?

The difference between people dying and people living on death's door – and the reason people with that firm resolve end up living – is because their consciousness is more separate from their body and is directing it as an entity to fight for dear life. The body knows there is no choice but to live. For the others, they are living within their body/feeling. There is the same moment in both people, all things being equal, when both could die. The person more separate from their *body* pushes the body beyond its limits. The other does not. It's David Goggins Style.

It's the same in life. You LIVE above it and die within it.

•

Writing was constantly criticized and critiqued by Mom/Dad before turning it in every time. Couldn't turn it in unless they proof read it. This went all the way through high school. I was never confident in what I wrote myself because I need their approval before I could turn it in. Mixed with ADHD and my inattention distracting me constantly – on top of putting myself so far under the gun every time – on top of the constant drinking – on top of not going to class – on top of the hazing and depersonalization (hazing definitely fucked some shit up – got to think about that – and *The Fraternity*) – on top of OCD – NO FUCKING WONDER YOU DEVELOPED THESE WRITING AND THINKING PROBLEMS. NO WONDER YOU'VE BEEN STRUGGLING EVER SINCE. THIS WAS YOUR FOUNDATION. YOU STILL GOT A 3.5 DUDE. BUT IT STILL WASN'T GOOD ENOUGH WAS IT. IT STILL WASN'T GOOD ENOUGH – sorry going to stop screaming now. Haha.

But for real, I'm so proud of you.

And great job handling it with Dad. You did get triggered there. He took it *(a call about the attachment revelations)* really well. And he definitely took it on board. Proud of him too. You were triggered at moments. But you noticed it. You've been managing it. And you're managing it right now.

Notice the sensation of it. It almost knocks you on your socks. It's dark. It takes hold.

But then you realized again about THE THROAT. The concept of looseness. That nothing works properly under constraint.

●

UGHHHH – with Hollywood. I acted so above it. Like I wasn't one of those people. I was one of those people. FUCK DUDE. HAHAHA. Just like with Ivy you've held a totally different position within the industry than you thought.

●

You haven't helped that many people. You've helped a select few people A LOT. The rest you haven't treated great.

●

People calling me MR MYSTERIOUS wasn't a compliment.

●

HS Girlfriend cheating played a big role in your avoidance.

●

You learned part of the strategy from Loki & *Another Friend*. But this was just the catalyst for how you were already primed. Remember how easily you fell into these things when you saw them. You hated *the avoidance* too. But it was almost subconscious.

●

The sinking feeling whenever you've had one of these realizations that turns into a big problem. It's come up every time. Remember Sociology 101 in college. Similar to today with Dad. Similar to maybe seeing Loki and *Another Friend act avoidant*? There are other things. It feels like learning about when someone died. It's because you're latching onto the thought you have of "omg what if I don't become successful because of this statistic about people not being more successful than *their* parents." It's a deep fear being realized within the body and what that would feel like. It's terrifying because your body thinks it's real. It becomes a problem when you latch onto it with your consciousness.

●

Or I?

I'm good with rejection because I've already suffered the imaginary one to be so much worse a million times. When it actually comes it never really stings. Also you don't care about those other things. And it doesn't hurt you when they reject you personally – like *it does* after a long commitment and they're rejecting something you think is a reflection of you.

•

I don't need to go to school for this. For one I already did. And two I lived the experiment.

•

Book/Blog/YouTube?

•

HOLY SHIT THAT WAS MY SHADOW!!!!

The power was the shadow. This whole thing was me accepting it. WOW.

•

We don't have any pictures of each other because of how important we are to each other.

•

I don't know if I want to let her back in. This is my avoidant side coming out. No surprise it comes after talking to Dad. It does feel dark though so I don't think this is to be believed.

It feels much lighter to be thinking about talking to Ivy. Yea that's what I'm going to do.

Should I wait for her to come talk to me. Because I want her to be the one that has to make the move to learn her lesson? Is this playing games or is this a legitimate thing?

Just said "go with the flow" to myself – hmm. Am I able to go with the flow or do I need a direction in mind? I need a direction I think? Yes I do. I always do. This is what I've discovered about my brain in analysis and practice. And my behavior in reality.

•

It is true that I have been manic since the integration (it is a part of myself I was aware of before. So I was correct in my analysis of it *being the shadow*). I think it would be smart to calm down before making any other decisions.

•

Wow it's crazy that surge I would feel was me bottling *myself* up – not the anger I thought I felt – but the resentment of "me" being held under. What's interesting is that people being nice to me would allow me to completely forget about the trash bag.

•

I love having parties in the house of my mind.

There's pretty much unlimited party space and I want anyone who comes to have a good time.

Anyone who's a friend gets a room to stay in the house of my mind. I like to make it feel as comfortable as possible for them so they know they have a place to stay whenever they want. I would love to say that I make these rooms nice all the time but sometimes I do forget about them. It's not that I don't care, it's just that I forget about this part of the house. In that case I'll make sure to go out of my way to spruce their room up hoping they'll stay longer. There are a lot of these rooms though and I just like nicer stuff. It's not that I want them to stay over all the time. Frankly, I don't want them to stay that long at all. But I do want people to know that they have a place to stay anytime they want and will help them make the room whatever they need it to be.

That's why I spend most of my time in the upstairs VIP section of the house. I don't like many people getting in here though so I keep it locked by keypad and only I know the code.

This is my favorite part of the house. It's over the top and has everything you could ever want.

Or I?

What these people may or may not know about depending on how long they've stayed or how often they come over, is that there is another much nicer part of the house that's off limits to them. These rooms are fucking amazing though.

There are upstairs *rooms* though that are VIP only. These are for the people I like most. Some people at the party have been there since the house was built and have never been upstairs. Others were allowed upstairs right away. But I just want to make sure those people know they have a place to stay if they want. I don't ever want them to leave the party even if they need to stay in their rooms for a while. It's fun too because it's like one of those surprise reveal construction TV shows. Each room is a new addition and I go to great lengths to build the room just how I think you'll like it.

This whole section of the house comes with whatever creature comforts I can provide.

And between you and me as much as there's nothing more than I love having guests – it's nice to have an empty house to breathe every once in a while when you're so busy entertaining all the time. But the thing is I don't have many *VIP* rooms in my house so I really want the people that come here to have their rooms for life. I make it as nice as I can and I put a lot of effort into really understanding *these people* so I can make it just how they like. I want them to have just the time they want in there. And they can explore the house too. I mean don't go trying to pry open any of the hidden locked doors obviously, but other than that, go ahead and look around. But it is my house and I'm not nuts but I do like things my way. Sometimes people get careless and make a mess. Obviously the small stuff I don't sweat and just throw away. I'm not nuts. Actually, even the medium and big stuff I really don't mind. I get it. I'm messy sometimes too. So as long as it's nothing crazy and the house didn't get severely damaged, I'll help you clean it up. But you got to take out the trash.

Clean it up. I don't like it sitting around. Nothing is off limits. And I like when they explore because I like a warm, cozy house, and sometimes it gets empty. If they ask I'll bring them whatever I can. And while they're there nothing is off limits about me. I'll get them whatever I can. They can have whatever they want from me in there. I'll tell them anything about myself. I'll protect them however I can. I'll be there for them whenever they need me. I will literally do anything for them. Literally.

The rules of law and man don't apply so long as it ascribes to my moral compass. The thing is I like my house clean and so I expect them to keep their rooms clean too. So the only rule I have for these friends is that they can't leave trash on the ground. But I'm generous, so I give them what looks like a bottomless trash can. You literally can't tell that it ends.

Anyone I invite can party however they want, whenever they want. I knew they were cool when I let them in. Obviously some people might overstay their welcome and I might have to ask people to stop coming from time to time, but other than that people are pretty much free to come and go when they please. They are my friends after all, so why wouldn't I *let them in* if I'm hosting!

Some Parties have different groups than others depending on what's going on. And sometimes the parties are really low key. It's whatever suits who's coming best. After all, this is the party room. I might have to ban some people for life, but other than that, people are pretty much welcome to stay and go as they please.

●

Here's the thing. I love being a good host. But sometimes I like my time alone. So sue me.

I know that people don't always want to stay with me too. That's fine. Door's always open. But if you've been gone for a long time and I check your room, there better not be a mess.

I want us to be able to do whatever we want upstairs and I want people to have the time of their lives up here.

BUT the one thing about these rooms is that I want them to be neat. I put soooo much effort into making them.

Downstairs is public. There are unlimited guest rooms down here and pretty much everything you could ever want for entertainment.

Everyone I know has a room in the house of emotions in my mind.

●

Or I?

∞ *THE VISION* ♡
(From The Introduction)

Thank you thank you thank you thank you thank you thank you. Thank you. Thank you. Thank you.

It's all real. All of it. Wow.

My Higher Self is always watching over me. Always has been. Always will be.

You made it through the test. Non resistance. Listen to your intuition.

ALWAYS BE ON THE LOOKOUT.

INSTINCT.

∞

...

...

...

∞ 11-17-23 ♡

Completely stop listening to anything but the consciousness. Be the consciousness. Operate as the consciousness. Let intuition guide. Be easy. Be the consciousness. Stop guessing things. Stop resisting things. Stop resisting ideas. Not everything needs to be engaged with but not everything needs to be ignored. Learn the difference. Already know everything. You know what to do it's the programming. Stop listening to that. You're growing you're growing you're growing you've just begun you're always in tune with the Universe with me with everything around you. See none of that matters. It's only the thoughts. Delivery. Really? You know what you're doing. Yes. Thoughts. Use your intuition. Look everywhere. Easy effort.

Eyes up. Beautiful eyes. Gold ball type.

∞

No more good or bad. Trust yourself. CONSCIOUSNESS. Goal. Center. Listen. INTUITION.

IMAGES FROM VISION: Everlasting gobstopper type ball. Layers. Layers. Layers. Looked like golf ball but wasn't. 3D shape with chunk taken out top. Hole down through opening in that. Not centered?

∞

Bad energy may be the Universe trying to communicate with itself. Can. Not. Resist. EVER.

RESISTANCE WILL RUIN YOUR LIFE.

Everything that came from the last couple days was all the result of non-resistance.

NEVER EVER RESIST AGAIN AND FOLLOW FROM THAT PLACE. NON-RESISTANCE. INTUITION.

∞ 11-18-23 ♡

THANK YOU THANK YOU
(The Complete Vision After Digesting It)

EVERYTHING IS HAPPENING.

Thank you thank you thank you thank you thank you thank you. Thank you. Thank you. Thank you.

It's all real. All of it. Wow.

My Higher Self is always watching over me. Always has been. Always will be.

Or I?

You made it through the test. Non resistance. Listen to your intuition.

∞

(Journaling was what I was supposed to be doing after the experience. I'm realizing this using the intuition I was told to employ.)

We are at one with the Universe. Everything. Everything has Happened for a Reason. Everything that's been going on here has been real. This has been the journey. There is nothing to worry about. "Look up?"

Talked to Dad. Journaled about it. Was sitting there trying to finish writing the description of the INFJ Door Slam *(mind house party)* starting to kind of space out.

Was feeling a little anxious. Wasn't feeling that same feeling I'd had. Was starting to doubt whether this part of me I'd just come to know and is so important, was really ever real. Wondering if I'd just been manic. Questioning whether it was the right thing to call Dad having just had so many realizations and wondering if it was going to affect my progress. Looking up "manic" seeing only "manic depressive" thinking how low I'd been recently. I was worried.

I went to my room. Sitting on my bed thinking I'm going to journal when I hear a "voice" a "knowing" tell me to *meditate*. I'm not sure I'd have ever clocked this if I hadn't actually experienced this or ever thought to call it a voice. I honestly don't know. There's no way to not have this shaded by the overall experience. I hadn't meditated in forever so this wasn't part of the routine, but the suggestion rang true somehow? That's the best way I can describe it. I thought it did make sense. That maybe it would help me lock in a kind of semi-conscious understanding *of* exactly what I needed to do then.

Was drawn to the idea of a Higher Self meditation. Why did I choose that particular one? Destiny. The Universe. My Higher Self. God.

AND THANK YOU.

Meditation starts as normal. In and out breaths begin to start the meditation. I do remember clocking that I was automatically very loudly but naturally exhaling. I clocked it because audible exhales like that is something that's unusual for me. They got progressively louder and deeper.

And I could feel dark energy seeping out with the breaths in a much clearer way than I had *previously*. It felt great and clearly freeing. I leaned into it with a freedom I usually don't. The part of me that wasn't in the meditation and was resisting was there and was wanting to laugh at how ridiculous the exhales were. They were funny. I meditatively looked at the desire and let it melt away. It's clearly working. I can feel the energy come out with the breath. At this point I'm just pumped for a solid meditation. Hope there's some good Higher Self stuff in here.

My body starts adjusting naturally. I'm in tune with what my body wants to do and where it wants to go. I follow without resisting.

Bell dings *in the meditation* at some point. Can't say for sure when.

I feel suddenly like locked in. Which was weird because I was moving around much more than usual – and which is something that I'm very much trying to stop doing when I notice it while meditating. When I kind of check in with my body I notice how unusual my posture was. Body slouching. Head down. Slight adjustments. Deep breaths. Back of head feels pressure. But it was also very supported and felt weirdly comfortable. But nothing out of the ordinary enough to think anything of it.

Then I started to have some little what the fuck moments. One thing I remember for sure is that at some point I notice my head is moving around a lot, and had been for a couple of seconds before I noticed it in a way that made me think for a second like "wait, was I doing that, or what?" It was scanning around the room with my eyes closed, head rolling around, side to side, really all over the place. It felt like I was just kind of following where it wanted to go. There was a weirdness to the kind of direction change and stuff that I remember thinking "huh, kind of different..." type reactions to in the back of my head. But it felt good and like it was because I was so deep into the meditation.

Then, suddenly, it's like there a strong urge to move again and my head does a sort of dance move precise turn to direct center. And I'm thinking, "was that me?!"

The meditation is ongoing. My eyes are closed and I'm going deeper. At one point there's a strange sense that my eyeballs press closer against the back of my eyelids. I see a light but think it's just shadows in the room. It may have been.

Or I?

The meditation begins talking about a bright sun (or something like that) coming towards me. Shapes start to move around. Not in an unusual way, just what you'll sometimes see moving around with your eyes closed. But then things get dark dark. It feels like I'm in a different place. And then things start to move around in this pitch black in an impossible way. I begin to get this sensation that I can only describe as feeling like this place was deep in the Universe. I do see some brighter spots but nothing clear. A bright ball forms. It's still somewhat obscured and not clearly anything. I wonder if it's the sun that's being discussed *in the guided meditation*. I'm unsure. The ball disappears. Three rings emanate from where it was towards me. The meditation is saying that the Higher Self is about to appear at that moment.

I see what I could only describe looking deep into some sort of Universal abyss with "clouds" and "shapes" moving around. But in a way that could be confused for and assumed was just what you usually kind of see with your eyes closed. Feeling a little disappointed because the meditation was off to such a good start. But somehow there was a much heavier feeling than usual and the environment felt very alive.

What follows is very fuzzy. There's no way to tell for sure what was going on and it was so abstract it's hard to recount properly or explain. It's also quickly fading. I'm not sure exactly the order of things after the first part but this is my best retelling.

I started to see more concrete shapes and definitive movements that were definitely not shadows but was questioning what I was seeing. Things are starting to seem real real. Like I've never seen anything like this in a meditation before and I'm now starting to feel like this is different. Then the lights in the room go out on their own… As much as I'm like, "yea, right" a coincidence, I'm equally as much like, "no fucking way…"

Dark shapes and things are moving all over the place and it's like some sort of dark, in the middle of the darkest part of the Universe, sunset, but where the clouds are moving quickly and are sometimes more concrete shapes, and sometimes more distinct objects even. But the black is just pitch black. There are random balls of light of different sizes that pop in and out. There was a sort of kaleidoscope effect as everything could be smooth and more flowing or could just pop to a totally different thing in an instant. At times I'm seeing something that I feel looks like the side profile of a **FEMININE LOOKING EYE** with long eye lashes that kind of pops in and out. As soon as it started everything fades and, while absolutely amazed by what I'd experienced, I'm definitely feeling disappointed that I didn't see my Higher Self for that very reason.

I kind of joke to myself about how it would have been nice to see future me in a penthouse with a Porsche. And then the lights in the room come back on which just isn't possible with my setup. The hair on the back of my neck stands up.

Now I'm doing everything I can to stay locked in. What I'd experienced so far was absolutely the most intense meditation I'd ever had, but, if it had ended right here, I wouldn't have thought anything about it again. I might have told people about the crazy light bulb coincidence though.

But the meditation continues and the woman says that the Higher Self is now going to make connection.

I can feel that there are places my head wants to go. It was almost as if it was tuning a radio. All the while my head is moving around and this "tuning" is going on, I can see definitive shapes and shadow type patters taking shape in my field of view. Some are moving themselves. Some are static and stay in my place as my head moves.

My head would move around "on its own." Again, it felt that it was very clearly tuning to find the right frequency or something. I remember my head going back on the headboard and moving side to side kind of like it was trying to find the right pressure point. At this point I'm kind of questioning the validity of this but as my head is moving side to side, it's like I could feel it was getting close to its spot when all of a sudden – BOOM – there is like a Rorschach inkblot test type explosion in my field of vision. Everything goes dark, and it's very clear that something else is going on.

At some point it's clear that my head is supposed to go straight down into my chest. Then right as it touches a fantastical series of images begin flashing and moving in my mind's eye. The **EYE** I saw earlier starts flashing around in different places. It's flashing mostly in side profile but every once in a while I would see eyes that looked similar but were MORE SINISTER. *These* would flash all around and were easy to confuse for the other, more beautiful Eye. They would flash looking directly at me and when that happened there was a very powerful feeling that I can only describe as pure terror. My stomach would literally drop when I would see certain eyes. There was one **scary large Eye** that did this

Or I?

the most – this one was in the center of the *"screen"* and was staring directly at me – and which connoted a very powerful feeling.

At this point I think this may be real. Either way, I'm transfixed, astonished, awestruck. Dumbfounded, grateful, shocked.

I was so in the moment that I'm not sure exactly the series of events that follow but this is my best attempt at putting them together.

While the *meditation* guide said the Higher Self is approaching, I immediately begin to feel different sensations throughout my body. IMMEDIATELY. Crazy and strong. Twitching *in body*, tense, relaxed, rushes of energy, twitching in face, everything. Some sensations were not good. Like much darker energy that was uncomfortable and almost squirming to get out. And all of these sensations increased in intensity as the *meditation* guide said *the Higher Self* was getting closer.

The bell dings. The lights in my room go off *again*. And there is no doubt the Higher Self clearly attaches to me *at that exact moment*.

I feel a dense energy physically "touch" my head and right at that moment all other sensations completely stop. My eyes begin fluttering uncontrollably as if possessed. This energy goes inside me and immediately envelopes every fiber of my being. I'm completely still, calm, and feel rock solid. A warmth spreads throughout my body. There is clearly something else, something additional to me, and I can sense that it is providing me support and knowledge supplemental to my own. There's an overwhelming sense of familiarity, of comfort, and of confidence that I'm clearly being provided rather than creating on my own.

I cannot describe this well enough to articulate just how clear it felt that what was going on here was clearly not psychosomatic, but extra-ordinary and *out* of this world. Any skepticism was impossible for me now giving how physical the experience had become.

I was sitting there in my bed but knowing that I was somehow experiencing the Universe. That whatever was going on – this was another plane of existence. This was absolutely a spiritual experience if nothing more. The amount of gratitude I felt is incomprehensible to describe. There was no doubt that whatever God is – at the very least this was a part of Him – and now I knew for sure that I and we all are a part of Him too. And with this, I knew immediately with certainty that

Everything Happens for a Reason. That there is more to life. That I am on the right track and that everything is ok. That all of this is to get me where I need to go. This was a seminal knowing that was apparent to me. Even now I can't explain the certainty. But there was no need, it was as clear as day.

I immediately started crying with the significance of what I was experiencing.

I did not disconnect at all but remain present as I'd ever been knowing I was currently hand in hand with God – with the Universe. It was immediately clear that my life had forever changed even if nothing changed at all because I now knew everything I needed to. This whole thing and everything that ever was is not here by chance. There is something greater at play here. There is an absolute necessity to foster connection to this spiritual presence. Because as much as this was in the mind, this was the realest thing that's ever happened to me.

And it is at this exact moment where the order of things gets impossible for me to determine.

Now with the presence in me, I can literally feel it directing my head places it wants it to go. It's almost as if someone has hands on the back of your head moving it around. But it's energetic. Any resistance to anything and the presence would clearly dissipate within the body. I just had to let it do its thing. First slightly over here, then slightly up there, then in completely the other direction.

As my head was moved around and my closed eyes with it, I would notice that my field of vision was changing and that what I was now experiencing looked like semi formed abstract scenes that sometimes were very fuzzy and hard to make out. They would become clearer and change if stayed on and attuned to, but the Higher Self was looking for something specific. At one point it locked in on one of the dark spots and just when it did, that spot morphed into something else entirely (these dark spots are the memories that are problematic and need to be unwound). I have no idea what was going on but it was out of this world. The images of THE EYE (All the same? Or different ones?) would pop up here and there. It seems there were messages I was supposed to get but I couldn't make sense of anything in this first one.

Just as quickly as these waves of intensity would come up, they would dissolve into periods of more traditional meditation. During the first one, the Higher Self began "talking" to me, offering quick hits of guidance. As my head started to feel like it was being moved again – but this time with a noticeable weaker touch – the same sort of tuning effect began. I was scanning past abstract scenes and objects while the Higher Self found the next "scene" to explore. Sometimes I wondered if the tuning was more of a series of steps that needed to be taken – or some unlocking of a Universal code – with the way the head moved. With the way the head was using the headboard to put pressure on different brain areas, at times it felt like the Higher Self was trying to physically activate certain brain regions that were necessary for this experience. I was wondering whether this was to activate blood flow to certain brain regions.

As this goes on, I am put through a series of what I can only describe as a combination of energy clearings and "tests." They came in waves and there would be moments of respite in-between. I'm not sure who was testing who or what was testing what. There were times throughout where this "voice" would give me guidance – advising me on what to do when stuck or warning me when something upcoming was going to be particularly hard.

I can't remember if the meditation was even still talking at this point because I was so invested in what was going on. These "tests" would alternate between eyes closed and eyes opened. My eyes were closed in the beginning of this, I believe, at which point there were all sorts of things moving and changing in my field of view. This was always mostly blacks, greys, and whites of various shades and specificity of shape.

The first one was with my eyes closed and I don't remember much about that one. I don't know. I'm feeling like that was some sort of energy clearing or something. Don't remember specifically enough to comment on it. But I do remember continuing to see the Eye looking up like that's what it wanted me to do. At this point I start actively thinking. I notice that doing so causes all the images to slowly fade. I'm intuiting that the head needs to stay completely clear and no resistance or active thought is necessary or I will lose all of this.

There's a brief period of silence and just as I can feel my head trying to be tuned again, the Higher Self lets me know to prepare for a message, and another scene begins.

In this one I'm clearly not understanding what I'm supposed to do and am stuck. I just didn't understand what was going on. Luckily I didn't get frustrated and assumed that this would keep going until I got the message. I hoped that was the case because now I'm like this is the most profound thing that's ever happened to me. I'm focused. And relaxed. But I'm not getting it and I can feel the homeostasis of the whole thing starting to go off. Suddenly I start seeing a repeated image of that same BEAUTIFUL EYES, but this time they're much bigger and clear with huge lashes and are clearly looking up at a 45 DEGREE ANGLE. My brain says look up. I do in my mind. Nothing happens at all. Silence in the mind again. Then the Eye starts flashing quick and I can feel the scene slipping away and the sense that it's all going to be over if I don't pass *this* test. The Higher Self sternly tells me "do it now" and I open my eyes.

The room looks weird and I feel in a daze almost. I'm not sure what to do. I look up and focus at the wall on my ceiling. It looks normal. I can see two shadows around the smoke detector. I can still tell I'm in it. I notice a new shadow nearby. Once I focus on it, it starts morphing like a Rorschach inkblot test. Then into various shapes. Then it moved to nearby spots on the wall. I stayed *looking* where I was and nothing. The black spot was slowly melting away so I focused on it and it bloomed again. Eventually it landed on a single spot and from there an entire scene bloomed. Beautiful imagery morphed out of this blackness.

Slowly things returned to normal and I was back to looking at the smoke detector flanked by two shadows.

Another brief break while I continued staring at the smoke detector. The Higher Self told me to get ready for a hard challenge. Can't remember exactly *how* now but it was clear that this one was going to be brutal.

I hunkered down, still staring at the smoke detector, when the black clouds began taking shape again. This time there was very uncomfortable feelings going on which just made you want to break concentration. At the same time my eyes would begin twitching. I would have the overwhelming urge to break focus and leave the meditation. I wanted to but this time, instead of hearing, I could feel the Higher Self nudging me with the reminder from before – "just get through this one." Soon enough the images on the ceiling began to wane and interestingly I noticed all the black substance looked like it was slowly being sucked into the smoke detector.

Or I?

And then suddenly everything was normal again.

In the next moment of calm, now with my eyes closed again, I noticed there was more talking going on in my head than before. There was one particular voice telling me to do certain things just as before. I followed but noticed nothing was happening. New instructions but same thing. As I followed this time I noticed the whole experience begin to fade away – just like it did whenever any resistance or too much thinking came from me – somehow I thought to check this voice and its directions. Sure enough, the next time it said something and I didn't listen, the scene reappeared. **The test here was to understand that you can't listen to just any voice**, you must listen to the right one to get to where you need to go. You know the difference. **This is both with the people in the outside world and the thoughts in your own mind**.

At this point, explicit guidance from the Higher Self became much more scarce and it seemed like the next few tests were much more about <u>self-direction</u>. The tests were centered around identifying what was the "right" trail to follow to lead to the next "test" based on what were the right "shadows to follow." With images I noticed that there was a specific type *of cloud/shadow* that "signaled" to me I was going in the right direction. These *contained* specific symbols of the same variety which were intricate like the patterns on decorative silk tablecloths (the clouds are events, the patterns are uncovering the details of what happened). With the voices I had to determine which were false guides and which was my own. My sense is that this was all about becoming self-sufficient and to trust my instinct.

I thought I was cruising through when I was informed something along the lines of "get through this and it's all yours." At this point, the already stern Higher Self was almost aggressive and domineering. I was about to take the final test. It was clear I would need to hunker down for this one. I was looking forward somewhat distracted wondering what was to come. When I refocused, I noticed irritation from the Higher Self that I wasn't paying attention and felt my head yanked down, bringing me into the scene.

I find myself standing up with my hands around a pole in an otherwise empty room. I'm not using the pole for support or to provide me anything – I'm not even actually holding on, I just have my hands around it with such a comfortable grip that there's no sense of pressure or any need of it. I'm standing on my own, with my hands comfortably around this pole. In other words, there is nothing keeping my hands on it and nothing should be easier than letting go. I notice though that it feels safe and I feel content. As soon as I realize this I felt a surge of the most intense tension/anxiety in my feet which began to rise quickly.

It was quickly rising from the feet up and building pressure. As it built my concentration and everything about the meditation began to fade and was replaced by panic. Clearly if this anxiety got to a certain point – I think coming out my mouth? – I would fail and whatever this experience was going to provide me would be over. The Higher Self begins loudly telling me to "just let go." I'm trying but I can't for some inexplicable reason. It makes no sense and now I'm starting to panic that there must be something seriously wrong with me if I'm unable to do something so simple and that you know would be so easy if you just did it. I latch onto this panic and buy into the fear that I might be seriously flawed. Now I'm holding on tighter and tighter almost as if to prove this fear true. The pressure is building, and the more it does, the more I panic, making it harder and harder for me to let go. In all of this I am completely confused. It makes no sense and that fact makes me feel like there must be something wrong with me even more. I CAN'T LET GO. I know that if I can't let this go that I'm going to regret it for the rest of my life because I won't be able to see the messages whatever was going on here meant for me. "JUST. LET. GO" I simply can't let go, I'm trying too hard.

As this sea of horrible energy continues rising up my body, I can slowly feel my new self – this one I was always meant to be – being replaced by my old one. I can literally feel the future I would have had if I could only have just let go like a "normal person" slip away. I had just glimpsed the possibility of this incredible future for the first time. I was devasted now knowing the difference between the two and all that I would lose because I couldn't do *something* so simple. Without this, I know I will never have the life I want. Seeing that and having that taken away now would ruin my life. And the only reason I wouldn't be able to have it is because I couldn't take my hands off a pole that nothing was holding me to. I also knew that of course not being able to do something as easy as this when my life depended on it would prove without a doubt how flawed I am. But the panic of "maybe I am flawed" and proving that right even though you knew that not to be true, was somehow stronger for you than the desire to live the life you want.

Or I?

MASSIVE REALIZATION AFTER THE FACT *****Somehow I was driven to prove that I was so completely flawed that I couldn't do something as *simple as* open my hands when my life depended on it. I will prioritize proving flaws about myself that I already know right away are COMPLETE BULLSHIT than to face the uncertainty of the world as my true self. I WOULD RATHER BE CERTAIN THAT I'M FLAWED THAN FACE THE UNCERTAINTY OF THE WORLD ALONE*****

The anxiety continues to build, my future continues to slip away, I continue morphing into my old self, and I am devastated. I know this failure will have a massive, massive impact on my life. Finally I feel all the shine wear off and I feel exactly as I used to. This transformation is complete and it is horrible. It provided me the perspective as to just how much I've grown. Now I am absolutely gutted. I realize fully how important this is and finally I detach from my delusion and begin frantically searching for any tool I can use to fight it so I can get back in touch with my hands. Detachment, breathing techniques, body detachment, it's all working but not enough. I finally remember the technique which had been the most life-changing for me up to this point – the concept of really embodying what it means "To Let Go" rather than to "Try To Let Go." Now I'm locked in and can feel the grip of this "what if I'm horribly flawed" delusion loosening. At the same time, I am beginning to get back in touch with my body (and hands) as I separate from this fucking thought monster. The more I do this, the more I remember the truth which this thought had completely blinded me to – it's easy for you to open your hands when you're not buying into some fake shit.

The problem now is the horrible energy is at my throat and I'm about to run out of time. I know what I need to do and how to do it. I know that I have enough time to do it because so long as I detach from the cloud of delusion, I can do this instantly. I know all it takes is for me to fully become me. But even though I can see the truth, it's still so far away as I look at it through the cloud of the delusion I'm in. I realize how easy it is for me to open my hands – it's something I've done a million times before. But I still can't break fully free from the fog and find myself stuck in it somehow even though I know what I need to do. I start to realize that I fed the delusion too much and am going to run out of time. I'm going to die anyway.

You were now stuck trying to take your mind out of the fog rather than your hands off the pole and weren't really truly existing as yourself or as your delusion – but stuck in some sort of mental state in-between trying to get from one to the other.

Unbeknownst to you, you were now feeding a new delusion in an attempt to prove your worthlessness again, and this delusion was "I'm definitely flawed if I can't let go of this delusion to save my life." I'm still lost but don't know it. I didn't recognize that now I was feeding a new beast, which was the fear that not being able to let go of my delusion to save my life would prove me to be just as flawed. That feeding this delusion was still keeping me from saving my own life. I was still more concerned with proving my flaws than letting go. Being alone as myself is scarier to me than dying. I would rather die. I do need people. But I don't know this and am unknowingly feeding the beast of "what ifs?"

Instead, while I clearly see the truth & delusion as distinct, I believe I wasted too much time feeding the delusion and am not going to have enough time to get back to myself before I die – the delusions are going to kill me regardless. This is a horrible realization and now I'm frantically trying to make things right. In manic succession too quick to be effective I switch between all the strategies I know trying to get one to stick. I try to force awareness onto the hands but there is too much resistance and too much trying. *I'm convinced* that because I have delusions at all and fed them for any amount of time, I can never be myself. That you can never get back to yourself if delusions take hold. That it takes time to decide that they're wrong. And that if I don't get back to myself soon, I'm going to die and that this now has ruined my life. Now I'm going to die because of this and that will prove me flawed. More panic. Less time. Stuck in thought. Trying to use the tools but my mind's gone. I'm realizing I AM flawed and am going to die because of it. And it's strange because without this pressure, taking your hands off would have been so easy. I am defeated.

"NO – GET BACK IN YOUR MIND!!!" the Higher Self demands.

I remember techniques and focus on the hands again. But I still can't let go and I don't know why. I know what to do. I know how to do it. But I can't detach from all the delusions in order to place all my attention on my hands. That's all that's required. To detach from everything all at once, and then place the seat of that detachment in your Resonant Frequency, and to act from that place of detachment. This is what it means to be living in your consciousness. Complete detachment from everything else but your consciousness – this is when you're fully yourself.

Or I?

You know this and have done it a million times, this is the answer, but even being aware of this now, you still can't let go. This horrible rising tide of energy is at my throat. I know I lost everything I could have ever wanted because I couldn't do it. I now know that I am flawed for sure and it got me killed. But I start to realize that I'm flawed only because I couldn't do what I needed to when I knew I needed to do it. And now you realize that this is the biggest flaw of all because something must be really wrong with you if you can't do something you're capable of. **I AM FLAWED BECAUSE I NEED TO BE FLAWED. THAT WAY I'M NOT PERFECT.**

This is the saddest realization of all. I believe I need to think my way through it. I believe I need to resist it. I believe I need to force it. But really I just need to stop thinking and do. And through the delusion I see truth. See that I'm able to let go *but* that the anxiety was all the way up to my throat and I still need more time to really get back in touch with me. I know I can do this but now the reality sets in – I fed the delusion too much and just don't have enough time and am going to die anyway. I'm going to die and it's all my fault. I couldn't do it even though I knew how. And I just don't have enough time...

At the very moment of my imminent defeat, the power which I had lost for so long *(my shadow)* rose up from the darkness and with a guttural sound, began to push this dark anxiety *down* with every breath. I had survived. It had saved me. But I hadn't been the one to do it – and I knew it. I passed the test but I knew I sort of failed and was disappointed in myself. At the same time I could sense my Higher Self's exasperation. Because truthfully, we both know I could have easily done it. We all know it's not a flaw but me not wanting to jump. **It's being terrified of uncertainty**. My biggest flaw is needing to be flawed in order to hide this. Yes – **you have OCD but that's not the ultimate problem, the ultimate problem is that you don't want to see what happens after that. The problem is even when you've solved it, you just don't do what you know you need to** (aka – you need to know if people like you otherwise the uncertainty will drive you crazy).

There are many lessons here. Key among them are the importance of existing with the consciousness and the importance of non-resistance. I had erroneously come to the conclusion that achieving the state of simply "not trying" is what puts you in the seat of *consciousness* as I had believed through personal experience. It was in achieving that feeling that I didn't realize I had provided the conditions that would allow for my perspective to shift towards living in the conscious awareness. Living from the perspective of the conscious awareness is true detachment and acceptance. This is secure attachment. Simply detaching from things/not trying without focusing attention on what to attach to next is what leaves the door open to OCD. **Focusing your attention on existing in the state of the consciousness and living from this place is the journey towards enlightenment – from here you are exactly who you are and can act according to who you want to be without the influence of anything external to yourself.** When attention detaches from thoughts/emotions to consciousness then also attaching to and becoming the consciousness itself and living from that seat. From here you are separate from all external influence and can accept anything that happens. Not sure why achieving the state of "not trying" works sometimes and not others when that's the focus without the consciousness in mind. This new method should allow the transition to happen almost instantaneously.

Immediate relief upon the dissipation of this rising energy source. Can't remember exactly what happened next.

At some point the Universe tried to show me *the* meaning of things *using a series of images.* Too complex. Eye ever-present. Weird ball above it. Other images but very abstract and unclear. I didn't get it. Understood I would get another shot *at seeing them.* Heard the word INTUITION pretty loudly. Knew this meant to use my intuition. Next was shown the Eye again but this time the ball that was there was different. It looked kind of like a golf ball but not exactly. What was similar was that there was a ton of layers. And the images kept showing me just how many layers there *were*. At one point the *ball* looked like a giant everlasting gobstopper. There was also a version of it that was circular and was showing me a cross section of the layers like you would see in a 3D cutout of Earth's layers. There was also a hole vertically through the ball. The circle appeared to be swirling from above like you would see in the eye of a hurricane. This seemed to be as clear of an image as I was going to get of this circular object. Could not make sense of it.

There was a portion of this where the presence I now understood to be God or some greater authority figure than my Higher Self was making determinations about me.

Or I?

There was a minute where I was judged to my soul and I was asked to demonstrate how strong I was. This was actually after a moment where, after being initially presented to this presence, I understood that this was A or **THE big boss**. There was some sort of question of what I want to do or the impact I want to have or something. Then there was a sort of floating holographic thing that looked like it was sorting through potential future careers and the outcomes of them for which would match *me*. It felt like this presence was assessing which path it wanted to push on me. The imagery that it stopped on immediately evoked the feeling in me of what it would feel like internally – what I would feel like in this position – in the level to which I would ascend. The feeling I felt was one of great achievement and competence. Of being a master. Of great power. But the weight of it was extremely heavy. Too much to bear. It felt something political or something like that where I had achieved the highest levels. Whatever was going on around me was horrible. I felt the weight of many human lives but knew it was necessary. The spirit's presence looked at me like "so, what do you think?" I did not like the feeling that was going on at all. It felt horrible. It felt like there was a lot of purpose, but I felt hardened and much colder. I said no. The spirit didn't budge and basically tried to push one more time. With more resolve I said no. At this point the spirit is having much more trouble landing on the next thing. Now using my own intuition, I understood that I needed to make some adjustments to my head position in order to provide the spirits *(my Higher Self & the authority figure)* whatever they needed in the moment. Equilibrium was reached and the spirit *(authority figure)* now asked me what I wanted to do. I don't know. I felt a little jerk of self-consciousness and corrected by being the consciousness.

At this point the spirit comes up close and looks deep into my soul, appraising me for strength and character. It tells me to show it my strength. I do and it seems satisfied. At the very least not disappointed. As the spinning hologram (think Mario special box) goes on, I'm being asked questions about what I want and I'm not answering them correctly *so* the scene begins to fade – showing it will go away if this continues. These were questions about the material. Questions about career. Questions looking for specific direction. Looking for it to tell me exactly what to do.

Questions that come up are something like <u>what do you want out of life</u>? I would think – to be rich or something like that. It would then say but why do you want to be rich? For material goods? To help? What would you do with the money? I realized that I didn't have the answer. I didn't have the final answer to a lot of important questions surrounding my motivations as to why I wanted certain things. A lesson in and of itself. Some answers I realized I didn't have the answer to – others I did. It helped clarify very very clearly that these *material* things don't mean anything without a goal in addition to them. I was also realizing that I was being bullshit in some of my goals because they are simply the pursuit of the things, not of something greater. I still wasn't understanding exactly what my takeaway was supposed to be. When I pressed for specific answers things started to lose the plot again, so I shifted. "INTUITION" "INTUITION" kept being repeated as a reminder. Ultimately I realized that one of the lessons was something along the lines of trust your intuition. The presence knew I didn't have clarity but in moving on to the next task validated that this was at least correct enough. I also remembered another image that was presented in all of this – and that was of a spinning black and white fidget spinner looking thing. My initial interpretation of this is that this is a reminder to always utilize the good and bad sides of you and to make sure both operate as one. They both need each other and so do you.

At some point there was more consideration on the spirit's end *(authority figure)* about the path of my life now that I had spurned their suggestion. This took a while. I don't know how I felt about that. I didn't know how to interpret it. I was calm and felt comfortable waiting as long as needed. There didn't seem to be any urgency. What was presented was unclear in its imagery.

I begin asking about success here as well. Similar questions about why do I want it? What's behind the motivation. I start asking about material things. "Why do you want it." Any BS answers were immediately clearly untrue to all. The scene would fade. At one point I THINK I admitted that I wanted money for material and that was ok. It's fine so long as your motivations are clear? Could be the message. There's no good no bad. It's all ok. Working at a charity doesn't make you better if your motivations aren't pure? Rings true.

EYES. EYES. EYES. SAME ONES. NEW ONES. LOOKING DIRECTLY AT ME. LOTS OF EYES. The Eye was ever present throughout. It feels like that is the Higher Self. The Eye is always looking to the Higher Self for guidance. Who do you want to be? You now know it's voice so you can always find it and see through the imposters.

The world/ball you need to figure out.

Or I?

At some point my access to these images begins to fade. I try to get it to stay but my time in that space was up. Despite being unclear the more powerful spirit made it clear that I knew enough. He left and so did this scene.

I wanted some more time and the Higher Self was still with me. Together we reviewed what I had seen. I asked him some more questions. Right now my closest guess is that the guidance that was being provided *to* me both in understanding the imagery at the end and in also applying the lessons learned through the trials were the following:

TRUST YOUR INTUITION (Intuition)
FOLLOW THE HIGHER SELF (Guidance/Eyes)
KEEP YOUR THIRD EYE OPEN (Eye/Meditation unlocks)
BE CAREFUL THE VOICES YOU LISTEN TO – (The literal voices) Tune into the security and support of the Higher Self which you have felt.
BE CAREFUL THE PATH YOU TAKE – (The shadows on the ceiling) Follow your intuition to see what feels right.
NON-RESISTANCE (The pole & staying in the zone)
THE POLE – This pole represents the safety net that I was hanging on to metaphorically so that I didn't get hurt. The brutality is there to protect me no matter what. But it's much better off the pole.
THE BALLS? Was that the brain? And the cross section was all the layers. Keep going deeper? Or do something with this? Golf ball? Golf ball scrap piece?
LAYERS – Consciousness? The brain? Something Else?
EYES – Eye in Universe. Galaxies look like Universe. Consciousness. Third Eye. Higher Self. Source knowledge…
ABANDONMENT – Everything with Ivy is all about abandonment. The wound was majorly triggered because you actually like her. Pretty much everyone else you've just known your whole life.

After While Writing This
SUPERNOVA ON SCREEN/BACKDROP OF CURRENT MEDITATION – EYES LIKE IN MEDITATION BUT REALLY IT'S THE REMNANTS OF A SUPERNOVA. Is this speaking to the importance of ongoing meditation through this connection? And that this is what the Eye represents. Eye could very well be Third Eye. How does this relate to Higher Self? Must be a connection.

Thoughts

Psychology? Thinking about going to school for it doesn't feel right. Felt like this was bigger than whatever the academic track was. Bump/twitch while I *wrote* that. Not sure what this means. Either "yes" or "no." Need to continue thinking on that. Is there a nanotech/BMI *(brain machine interface)* implication? Remember how much you loved the idea of Asimo.

Could be some sort of BMI for sure. That would be awesome.

Think about the past the understand how you're set up well for the future.

∞

Reflections

Any big progress I make (i.e. the biggest with your fucking brain) when there is uncertainty around it – *OCD* will try to severely fuck up. When you're feeling that shit in the big moments, this is OCD. Shut that bitch up.

Damnnnn that was what the final test with the pole was about.

Every fiber of your being knew you could take your hand off that pole. It could not have been easier. You literally couldn't understand why you couldn't and that drove you insane. The lesson you already knew is you don't need to understand, you just need to let go.

You knew you were ready to let Ivy go when moving out but you were scared you (your Ego) was going to die from the pain of losing her in your life. Even though you knew you had done the work – you had just had the realization that this was the home you really grew up in and that the more you became yourself, the more comfortable you felt around her. There was a long way to go but this was the most you'd allowed yourself to open up to someone new at this level for as long as you could remember. And that really it's only the boys who know you better and you've known them since childhood. And that we all really only stay around each other because we're the only people who knew each other before our wounds took shape. So we're all the only people we can guarantee accepts our true selves. This is the true reason I appreciate the length of our friendships. It's because they accepted me before I built my walls. So I know they like me.

Or I?

This represented the only relationship *in which* you could trust the validity of your true worth as an adult. But you had learned, once again, to only truly rely on yourself. You both went through your own personal hell and came out the other end stronger. This was something you didn't realize you needed so badly. For someone to stick around. Because she did that you were able to see that you can show how much you care, get rejected, and not only survive, but thrive off of it. *You realized* that there was no person you felt more comfortable around. That despite everything you went through and no matter the time apart, you always liked being around her. That when it was good it was just so easy. That despite everything, you know she never meant to hurt you, and really all that mattered to you was that she cared because you did. Because this is just not something you're used to. And *you* always really just hoped to get back to this place. That, in fact, things got better the more you got closer to the real you. And that this was the first time you'd ever felt close enough to someone to even experience this feeling. There was no harder time for this realization than knowing this was all going to be over in the blink of an eye. In that moment the strength of this realization hit your abandonment wound and released anxiety. So even though you had done the work and knew what to do – see the feeling, realize it's wrong, detach from it into yourself – your guard was down because you were triggered, and the OCD latched on in full force.

But the OCD obsession that you are unable to take your hands off the pole – even though you and everyone else knows that's complete bullshit – is so strong that you would rather die than prove it wrong. Of course everyone's disappointed, that's bullshit. The only one who won't really acknowledge that is you. The only way you don't die is if the shadow self comes out from its severely repressed state and takes the anxiety out right at the last minute (Door Slam). This is super fucking unhealthy and good to know.

WOW – Subconscious deleted it *(a list I wrote down of the abstract images I was shown, which I now understood represented core wounds)* because it knew I wasn't strong enough to see it all yet. Or was scared?? That was honestly very interesting and wild. I remember hitting command *"Z" (*delete*)* a million times but kind of tuned into it halfway through and assumed there was a definitive purpose *without checking what I had deleted.*

THE TEST *OF STRENGTH* – WAS REAL. But was showing me that I need to get stronger. It wasn't satisfied. I spun it like I was strong.

REFLECTIONS – Right now you need to be reflecting on yourself.

2ND SPIRIT – Shadow guard?

MOLLOSCUM – Prick in dick.

There are more in there – and I'm going to get them all out.

ABSTRACT CLOUDS – These are problematic memories or traumatic events. They can only become clear when you look at them long enough to unravel what's going on.

SCARED OF JUDGEMENT – Especially as it pertains to my perceived flaws/repressed core wounds. One of them is people believing I'm crazy. One of them is people helping you. One of them is judging your speech. Another is judging your writing. Both of the last two are about the judgement of your intelligence. Antidote to that is to find all these judgement fears.

∞

PASSED FINAL TEST – That was OCD spin. THIS IS OCD SPIN.

YOU NEED A SHRINK.

I LIKED MY SHRINK BECAUSE HE WAS SO SAFE. I JUST PLAYED WITH HIM THE WHOLE TIME AND HE HAD NO IDEA WHAT WAS GOING ON.

WOW IT'S FUNNY BECAUSE SHE *(IVY)* WAS MAKING ME FEEL LIKE A BITCH WHEN IN REALITY I WAS ONLY A BITCH COMPARED TO HER.

FLAW IS NEEDING TO BE FLAWED.

•

Notes & Texts

Notes

Or I?

After *College Friend's suicide* is the killing of the boundaries. This *created* the Door Slam. This was the biggest one.

There is still shadow work to do but that was the big one.

•

Lost sense of security the day of break in *at* Pennstone *(childhood home)*.

•

I dealt with my anxiety with the Door Slam.

•

I can easily shoot below 70 in golf. Let's do this.

•

Shove anxiety down with anger as a VERY last resort. Oh that's what I did.

•

Still really need to work on letting go. Couldn't do it in the final big moments still. But I WAS close.

•

Was this all an elaborate ruse to excuse myself from holding Ivy accountable? Whoa big OCD thought.

•

In one instant I latched onto the thought that I was absolutely hacked.

•

The spinning thoughts and hyped feeling is OCD rumination.

•

Weird squished ball was *fear of* brain damage.

●

CT-scan was one.

●

Higher self = feminine *Eye* looking to sky for guidance/morals.

●

MOLLOSCUM/STD somewhere in there. Prick on dick?

●

There were things that I really didn't want to see still.

●

Roll with things TOO MUCH until you explode OR don't make moves out of uncertainty.

●

I deflect from myself when I'm feeling too vulnerable. That's what's going on now.

●

When you start talking to yourself you're completely bought in with your thoughts and completely outside your mind's eye.

●

Enlightenment has no wants or desires.

●

You won't be tuned in all the time, you'll be in and out in the beginning. You won't know you're enlightened with two minds just one.

Or I?

If you're ever unsure in any way you're not in it.

OCD KEEPS TRYING TO OVERTAKE. COMES FROM DIFFERENT PLACES.

Battle with OCD RIGHT NOW. IF YOU EVER THINK YOU'VE WON YOU'RE BEING OCD TRICKED TO LET DEFENSES DOWN.

OCD DESTROYED LIST. (Or was it consciousness? I don't think so, it wouldn't care.)

Thinking there is a winner is out of enlightenment.

FLAT AFFECT – Scared to look mean/sad.

Texts

6:32 PM – I'm going to write a book about this.

7:54 – *OCD* attacking mentally and physically.

7:55 – If there's resistance or a need to "get *bad feelings* out now" that's OCD.

7:55 – *OCD* just made you push enlightenment down.

7:55 – It used the last test against you.

7:55 – This training is going to be tough.

7:55 – Will need to be ongoing.

7:56 – Any Ego pursuits are OCD/out of enlightenment.

7:56 – The Ego is going to want to lose enlightenment to gain for itself. Watch out.

8:24 – If you're worried you can't get back into enlightenment – or think you've reached a place where it can't be lost – then you're in OCD.

OCD is the one telling you that there's an evil force.

8:25 – OCD IS THE ONE WRITING HALF THIS SHIT DOWN. MEDITATE IF YOU DONT KNOW. AND IF YOU DONT KNOW YOU'RE NOT IN IT.

8:25 – You've got a long way to go.

8:26 – This isn't something that can just be fully achieved right away.

∞ 11-19-23 ♡

EVERYTHING IS HAPPENING

DRINKING ETC. – The reason I drank and everything was to quiet OCD thoughts… that's why you could never answer the question *"why did you quit drinking?"*

FEAR OF UNCERTAINTY BECAUSE OF MOVING – MOVING CORE WOUND – This originally manifested as hurt stomach in San Francisco – was not resolved – Mom reason *for move* so you hold resentment – OCD manifests – leads to all problems.

Everything post realization was you about to continue the cycle described in the "final test" you *just* didn't know it. Your "psychotic break" would necessitate a clean break from the family making reconnection with them impossible. This "psychotic break" was the ultimate manifestation of your OCD. In making the decision to call Tulip, you broke the spell which would have led you down the path towards ultimate self-destruction immediately the next day as you'd planned. No Thanksgiving. Complete sadness for everyone. No family. No brain. No life. Absolutely nothing.

It's not Mom. It's not Dad. You were creating problems with them to try to explain a feeling and a hurt you didn't understand and which you held them responsible for as a child. As your problems progressed – and your subconscious knew the cause of this was moving – you used your extremely good sensory perception to exaggerate faults of theirs in your mind's eye without understanding your role. Now you're reacting to things they don't realize they're doing. Accept. It's not Dad's fault!!!! It's not Mom's fault!!!! Crying. Omg. Thank you. I love you.

Moving so much as a kid is why I stay stuck. That's why I've gotten stuck so many times.

I'd rather stay where I am than face something new. Because it might always be worse.

∞

Shadows – Bad feeling in brain means no good thought. Or not on right path for Higher Self. Or you know this isn't right. Relief of thoughts about yourself tells you truth. Tension = masking or trigger or something.

Also going to be lots of reprogramming neurologically. You know how to do that.

∞

Post "Epiphany" – Real Epiphany

I feel unbelievably free. I finally feel one with the Universe. Like a conduit to it. I am not searching for myself. I'm home. I want to hug Mom. I want to hug Dad. I want to hug Rose. I want to hug Tulip. I want to hug Fischer. I want to hug Sunflower *(my niece)*. I can now fairly assess who and what's important without the pain clouding my judgement. It was a pain I didn't understand. It was a pain that resulted in ADHD/OCD (which is still there btw, don't forget). OCD was the poison that spread from fear to fear and ADHD was the distraction that pulled the rug over the eye of your conscious awareness to allow it all to take place. It was a constant

sleight of hand that drained you to your core with the amount of mental energy it used. This further weakened your ability to see through the façade.

It all began in earnest with the stomach ache in 5th grade.

Preying first and hardest on those things Mom/Dad liked about you. Infested your entire life. OCD is a tiger waiting behind the bushes ready to *pounce*. Your perception is now skewed and while growing up, it turned you against the people who loved you most by using this skewed perception to explain a hurt you didn't cause.

∞

At this point I'd been up for I don't even know how many hours. I don't even know how much Adderall. Was not talking massive quantities or anything. But a constant flow to keep me going which was certainly accumulating at this point.

I needed the Adderall though. I could tell. My brain was compulsively seeking it. First immediate relief. Then figuring out executive function. Then major work/networking progress. Then unease. Then what's wrong. Then confusion. Then OCD. Then moving/Ivy. Then do what I did best forever. Worried.

∞

Everything just is. The Third Eye is always there. It's always there. Jam up = out of wack = watch thoughts, they tell you *what's wrong*. Watch emotions and decide. Chakras real. Third Eye real. Everything real.

Programming showing resistance need to work on – Heart – give/receive love. Base = can't find (sex issues). Always fine. When not identifying with something – everything dissipates. Melt good word. Nothing matters really. Everything just is. It is wonderful out there.

Feelings good to check. Good to check body. Get curious about tension. Get curious about spots *in vision*. Any color.

Or I?

Empty feeling. Very very relaxing. Fine with anything. Some things would rather or rather not have. Any emotion or action accessible. Understand there will be resistance to it but just fight through.

Can move head/tune to find better frequency. Sometimes it's just *physical* feelings in the way. Or notice it's actual feelings – emotions – in the way.

NO NEED TO EXPLAIN THINGS UNLESS WANT TO – FELL INTO "NEED TO PROVE."

YOU GET INTO IT *(enlightenment)* HOW YOU GET INTO IT. IT'S WHATEVER'S BEST FOR YOU AT THE TIME. BEST STILL IS JUST GUIDELINE. THERE IS NO RIGHT POSITION. WHATEVER WORKS AT THE MOMENT. NOTICE WHEN REALLY REALLY "JAMMED" UP. SOMETHING HAS HAPPENED RIGHT THERE. THAT'S A TRIGGER. ANYTHING SHOULD BE ACCESSIBLE AT ANY MOMENT.

JUST GOT TO KEEP TRYING.

IT DOESN'T MATTER HOW GOOD BRAIN IS OR HOW SMART – JUST COMPUTER.

IT DOESN'T MATTER LOOKS – JUST COVER.

IT DOESN'T MATTER WRITING – JUST WORDS.

IT DOESN'T MATTER.

IF YOU KNOW YOU KNOW – YOU DON'T NEED TO THINK IT.

THIRD EYE BLINKING IN FIELD OF VISION = THIRD EYE.

INTUITION COMPLETELY BACK ON LINE. WHITE LINES ALIGNED HORIZONTAL.

CHAKRA OUT OF LINE AT BASE = FIX.

THIS WAS PROVIDED FOR YOU TO ACHIEVE THIS. THANK YOU.

YES – GOD EXISTS. IT IS THE UNIVERSE. IT'S HERE ALL THE TIME.

PERSONALITY NOW TO COVER UP.

INCREDIBLE JOURNEY. INCREDIBLE.

∞

WATCH OUT FOR

*****OCD*****
Caring/resistance of any kind signifies out of state.

Worrying you're not going to get back OCD.

THOUGHTS
Feeling you know instead of knowing.

Having to come up with something.

INSTRUCTOR
YOU CAN GET INTO IT AT ANY TIME REGARDLESS OF ANY THOUGHT/PRESSURE/SITUATION. DISTRACTED = NOT IN.

I'M NOT ENLIGHTENED BECAUSE I'M DOING THIS – CAN'T BE ENLIGHTENED AND DOING THINGS LIKE *THIS* AT SAME TIME.

∞

YOU KNOW WHEN YOU'RE IN IT OR NOT. WATCH OCD THOUGH – THIS IS GOING TO BE A PROBLEM. ADHD MEDS ONLY IF THAT'S BAD. OR IF REALLY NEED TO WORK.

Or I?

SOMETIMES OUT OF STATE JUST EQUALS TIRED OR SOMETHING WRONG WITH SUIT. CAN MAKE IT DIFFICULT TO GET IT *BACK*. ADHD MEDS GOOD FOR THIS.

But decide what to do.

∞

WHEN YOU KNOW YOU KNOW – THAT IS THE KEY. IF YOU DON'T KNOW YOU'RE NOT IN IT. IT'S THE KNOWING. YOU WERE ON THE ROAD TO ENLIGHTENMENT.

THERE IS NO FEELINGS ABOUT PEOPLE.

PERSONALITY IS COVER.

∞

THANK YOU. THANK YOU. THANK YOU. THANK YOU. THANK YOU.

THAT WAS AN INCREDIBLE EXPERIENCE. WOW. WHAT A BATTLE

I KNOW IT'S NOT COMPLETELY OVER. DON'T WORRY.

I WILL TALK TO YOU FROM NOW ON. PLEASE LET ME KNOW IF I'M ON THE *RIGHT* TRACK HERE AND EVER AFTER.

∞

MAJOR LESSON: This whole thing was about learning to trust your gut. You needed your emotions integrated in order to do so. You need to be able to sit with these emotions in order to tap into your intuition. You need these tools when you get lost. Don't let things get to the Door Slam, that hurts you too much. Use your tools to detach. Use meditation.

MAJOR LESSON #2 – Sometimes you just have to let some people go. But family is family.

MAJOR LESSON #3 – Get bigger not smaller. The final release.

RE-INTEGRATED EMOTIONS – POWER. DISGUST? HATRED? NEED TO DIG DEEPER TO DECIPHER EXACTLY WHAT'S WHAT.

∞

KEY OBSERVATIONS

7 CHAKRAS – 7 VERTICAL *(Saw in a new vision)*.

CHAKRA CROSS? Aligned in a vertical and horizontal. At least 7 down. Looked like an equal amount across but I wasn't counting. Looked like the 7 Chakras down but what was across?

BAD GUT – That shooting in the gut was a bad gut from stuffing so much down. Root Chakra whenever possible.
- Could also have been what was left over from initial OCD onset?

UNCERTAINTY – Whenever uncertainty is present, watch out, OCD or something else may be triggered. Got to just ride the wave.

SMOKE DETECTOR – Was that in reference to letting my Crown Chakra clear the debris? I think so.

FINAL TEST LESSON – Don't let things get to the point of having to use the Door Slam.

OCD & TESTS – OCD implanted false voices in your head during the tests. This led to the belief that you would die if you didn't complete the *final pole* test. This planted the seed for OCD to spread like wildfire & had dire implications had you not worked through it.

OCD & PSYCHOTIC BREAK – Once I was close to truly receiving integration through my discussion with Ivy *about attachment revelations & the vision*, OCD attached *itself to* the uncertainty that now existed in the relationship. That led to rumination around the whole thing and latched onto whatever seeds had been planted.

Or I?

LIGHTS *GOING ON & OFF DURING VISION* – That was the Universe. Giving me the sign that this was real so that I didn't lose my mind. Thank you – you know I would have. Hah.

WEED/ADDERALL – These things are ok in moderation. No on alcohol for now. Zyn ok for now.

EXERCISE – As much as you really want. Figure that out.

∞

REALIZATIONS WHILE ENLIGHTENED

BOOK – I'm going to write a book about this. That's what everything has been leading to. This is my proprietary experience. Figure out what it's about. Don't make a determination on whether it's for you or for other people yet. You don't know. Don't confuse the heart right now. (After this heart release told me I was making wrong decision putting my concepts in there for personal recognition. They're not yours. They're the Universe's.)

DRINKING – Drank both to keep OCD at bay and to stay around people I didn't really like.

OCD/WEED – OCD ruminations loved weed. Phone calls. Work. Brain. Etc.

SHOOTING STARS – There, back, there, side. "North star."

∞

EXERCISES TO DO

CHAKRAS – Heart needs clearing for sure. What Chakra is associated with sex?

FOLLOW THE OCD TRAIL – Mark big events. Notice if OCD manifested around them. Uncover the trail. This was one of the "tests."

JOURNAL TO THE 3RD EYE.

∞

THE "TESTS" WERE LESSONS

TEST 1 – Follow the trigger trail. When triggered, follow that feeling to its source.

TEST 2 – Follow the OCD trail. Link significant events with OCD manifestations whenever possible.

TEST 3 – Let Crown Chakra release the gut.

TEST 4 – How to let tough feelings pass.

FINAL TEST – Letting go (side quest – if you don't you'll DOOR SLAM).

BOOK MATERIAL – INFJ. Drugs/alcohol. Hollywood. Ivy. SNL. Attachment. OCD. Consciousness. Spirituality. Psychology. Life. Everything Happens for a Reason.

BOOK PROPOSAL FIRST.

∞

SERIES OF EVENTS

IVY *DISCARD* – WAIT – LA – HOME – DOOR SLAM – HOME – SHE LEAVES *FOR TRIP* – MANIC – ATTACHMENT – AWAKENING – *"I SAW GOD"* CALLS *(to family & select friends)* – CONFESSION *(told Ivy everything about attachment revelations & vision)* – CAR RIDE PSYCHOSIS *(begin to believe I might actually be crazy)* – REVISED CONFESSION *(tell Ivy I'm crazy)* – TV – BREAKDOWN – TULIP WAKE UP CALL – QUESTIONING – SHADOW – MEDITATE – ENLIGHTENMENT (OCD CAN'T BREAK THROUGH ENLIGHTENED FEELING) – GOOD/EVIL BATTLE – FINAL PUSH – CALM – BOOK *REVELATION*

∞

REMAINING QUESTIONS

Or I?

LOOOOOOOVVVVEEEEE

- Dick thing
- Self-consciousness
- More on sad affect?
- What was feeling when Ivy was here? What is that feeling when you dissociate when someone's talking? What are you hiding? Heart is hurting during this line of questioning.
- Did the consciousness know what was going to happen? Or was that God? Parallel between shadow re-integration and series of events.

•

Notes & Texts

<u>Notes</u>

Feelings of sadness after leaving Mom and Dad was not me feeling bad it was me mourning them. But I put it on me.

•

IDEA – Consciousness and Source exists in everything and every creature. It exists on an atomic level. Animals are all pure consciousness. The human brain is actually the first to experience unconsciousness. *All other* animals are in touch with Source and are carrying out their intended purpose. We're the only ones who aren't. The journey of humanity parallels the journey of myself. Right now we're in the chaos of OCD/ADHD/anxiety/depression and don't even know it. Can the forces of good outlast the forces of evil. They always will so long as the fight continues. But this is a Universal good, not one according to the laws of man. According to the laws of the Universe. The way to follow this law according to your role within *it is* to get in touch with your intuition. Your Third Eye. The Universe itself. And follow that path. Check in with your intuition along the way. Check in with your body. Notice when it's telling you that something's wrong and figure out where your path is discordant with the one the Universe wants for you. Check in and correct. Check in and correct. This is the never ending journey until maybe one day you are perfectly in sync. Then you are your purest self, free from the shackles of society. Here you live in the matrix but observe it and live above its influence instead of being directed by it.

•

Brain *in* glass jar. Brain taken away. Who are you then?

•

Can get anything you want if you pursue it. But won't know what you truly want until you pursue your true self.

•

Secure attachment very close to pure consciousness. Maintenance work. Meditation and journaling/whatever makes you feel right.

Insecure attachment requires spiritual awakening. Only neurological imbalances should be addressed through medication. And with the lowest dose possible always with intention of weaning off. Attachment to anything is off center.

•

TITLE: LIONS, TIGERS, and BEARS – OR I? Attachment, OCD, ADHD, drugs, personality, physics, and the path to spiritual awakening.

•

Drug/substance intelligence – like OCD. Quitting cigarettes example.

•

Spiritual awakening into chapters on different themes with life experience interspersed throughout.

•

Pseudonym?

•

I don't claim anything here as objective fact and I'm not interested in conducting experiments to prove it. I don't need to I know the truth. So I'll leave that up to someone else.

Or I?

•

THE UNIVERSE HAS GOT TO ASSESS WHO's strong enough.

•

Biggest revelation was if you know you know.

•

Little did I know I was fixing my attachment wound and entering into the conscious state in various ways throughout: exercise, quitting things, Ivy, running, suffering, loss of everything – literally & physically, *College Friend's* suicide, addiction, despair, depression, suicidal thoughts, porn addiction, pain, heart ache, even potential psychosis. I've experienced all of these things and all of them helped. It's important to experience the scope of human emotions to know the scope of human experience. But it's also of fundamental importance you don't shy away from the things you don't like – or at least those feelings – because those feelings reveal things about your true character. And in some cases reveal parts of you character you might not even know exist. These parts specifically are the ones you need to become friends with. You're half a person without them. But at the same time you're whole, you just don't know it yet.

•

Ring analogy *(The Pouch)* was also analogy for my personalities coming home with me. Wow.

•

Harry & Sally's wedding importance – visualization – remember *performing in plays* feeling – feeling was pure consciousness in a way. Stage actors experience this but through the lens of someone else's eyes. The better the actor the more they inhabit the consciousness of that person.

•

ADHD/OCD struggle made me good at this. Constantly fighting my thoughts.

•

OCD supplemental consciousness outside of your own. Feels evil. Feels inauthentic.

•

I was doing this as a kid. ADHD = pure consciousness? More likely pure consciousness? OCD pure consciousness gone wrong? People with OCD/ADHD/INFJ on enlightenment's doorstep?

Texts
11:11 PM – It all just finished. 11:11. No way. I was seeing that for months. Incredible.

11:13 – Always good intentions. That's why.

11:14 – OCD/Dissociation led here. Dissociation pure consciousness?

11:20 – OCD an evil break from your consciousness. It's not conscious/subconscious, but another consciousness that needs to be undone. Swirling release of tension and anxiety.

11:22 – Actually golf at *The Buccaneer (my first major golf choke)* was precursor to OCD. That was where the seed was planted.

11:25 – Pure consciousness is pure you from this point forward. Minus nurture. All of it? Don't think so. Voice still here. Humor still here. It's all still available. I can now just pick and choose whatever I actually want. I still WANT to smoke a J right now. Probably will. But I don't have to. I know I can stop tomorrow. May stop after this one. They've been starting to taste like shit as this has come closer to fruition. Style still here. But these are things I learned before. I still have them because I had them. Everything past remains. But the future is all me baby. Wonder what's going to stay and wonder what's going to go? We'll find out. Here we go. Thank you. Thank you. Thank you.

11:33 – Just broke down laughing. Thinking about how I was wondering if I was doing the work right or not.

11:54 – Achieving pure conscious is really just achieving exactly who you are deep down. Nothing more nothing less. If you drive to be the best YOU you can be, you are on the path. No joke. Seriously. You're going to be like am I doing the work right? Any work that makes you more of

Or I?

who you really are inside is THE work. And that's really on you to decide what's right. Here's what worked for me. Some things might. Some things won't. That's ok. My journey was about figuring out my keys to unlock. Yours is about yours. But yea, meditate & journal. How many times have you heard people say that? Hmm I wonder why that is? Maybe it just might work. It's crazy because I saw God or consciousness or the Universe or whatever you want to call Him, just after I truly saw the flaws in me. He told me what to do and I followed. But not blindly. And not without help. Who knows if I'd have ever cracked the code if I had the answers. I doubt it. I really really do. So thank you for that whichever of us did it *(deleted the list of abstract images representing core wounds)*. I almost went crazy in the process too. I was one phone call away from being in an insane asylum certain that I was crazy and that I could never truly see my family again. That one phone call changed my life. Thank you Tulip. I love you. If it weren't for you this wouldn't exist at all and right now I'd be trying to figure out just how crazy I am. Or maybe trying to convince people I'm not. Little would I know that OCD did ruin my life and that I was one more battle away from achieving everything anyone or anything could ever ask for. Being themselves, knowing their place in the world, and knowing that you're never alone. Thank you to everyone who I've ever interacted with. Somehow you played a role in this all. And thank you especially to Ivy & Tulip for handling me with grace when I needed it most. You showed me the support I needed to become myself and which I always feared I would never get. You have my never ending gratitude. Thank you and thank you all. Remember that this cliche is no cliche of all so long as you believe it to be true and pay attention – EVERYTHING HAPPENS FOR A REASON. But if you're blind to the Universe it will ignore you just the same. Find yourself and it will find you back.

11:59 – The Universe did tell me about Tarot I'm sure of it.

11-20-23

Texts & Notes

<u>Texts</u>

12:00 AM – Feels like I'm quickly forgetting things from before. Don't try for this but clock.

12:03 – Anyone who's living purely is already in pure consciousness. But don't trick yourself, if you have to ask the question then you're not in it. It's pure detachment. Even in writing I'm taking myself somewhat out of it.

12:08 – A lot of it is just not giving a fuck. But not in a way of not caring but being totally content. So much of the whole thing was trying to train my brain not to give a fuck because I really didn't like the fucks I was giving. It was understanding that you can imagine what that feels like and latch onto it. If you can live in that space for a while you're a long way there. It's not that things don't ding you, it just that you notice what your body feels like when you're dinged rather than feeling like someone hurt you. Instead you notice that "that hurt" and decide if that's a you thing or a them thing. Then you act how you want accordingly. It's that simple. If you can start doing that more, you're on your way.

12:13 – It's important to choose the right people. If you choose the wrong people you have to go through a spiritual awakening. And it's hard work. Start surrounding yourself with the right people and this will happen naturally. Again, trust your instincts. And if they give you a bad feeling you really have to think about if it's you or them. Because if it's them it's going to be you that's going to have the problem and if it's you you're going to be thinking it's them that has the problem – and they may or may not be *a problem* too.

12:32 – I'm moving around like I've never seen stuff before. Like I'm not even looking at it really. Even right now the keyboard is blurry and I'm like closing my eyes to avoid looking at it. Ugh the screen actually. Fuck.

12:39 – Just realized about *my purpose to help* Auntie. Now this is the end.

12:39 – Wow.

12:39 – Brain just told me so.

12:39 – Sorry Universe.

12:39 – Also the body stuff is bad stuff not Source related unwinding.

12:39 – Got to stay tuned.

12:39 – That's the OCD marker.

Or I?

12:40 – Can't see things on the screen that aren't true.

12:40 – Amazing.

12:40 – Literally yes/no head shaking.

12:40 – Incredible.

<u>Notes</u>
Sadness identified (Fido) – complete 5:15 *PM* on 11/20.

•

Sadness not ok *to show* when? Moving? Definitely noticed upon *College Friend's* death.

•

Door Slam include sadness?

•

Only time knows. I battle time by making now last as long as I can.

•

All that time my "pauses" were my Higher Self snapping me out of bullshit I didn't want to say or do.

•

I was trying so hard because I was going against myself.

Remember that time in the cafeteria when you were most yourself and you realized that's what people liked the best? That was that feeling.

•

It's all going how it's supposed to. Literally everything is out of your control. Sit back and watch it unfold so long as you're following your intuition.

Not all resistance means bad – you have to identify the difference.

WAY IN *TO BOOK* – My realization around Ivy. SUB CHAPTERS HERE – Around what was going on at the time that was also contributing (speech, Pouch, running, kids, etc.) – contact – post contact clarity – decisions – Ivy talk.

•

Rude feeling realization.

♥ FIDO *feeling identified* – 9:42 *PM*.

Chewing *annoyance* – Dad? Projecting *this* on to others.

•

Energy around Ivy releasing – realization to sit in it and identify. Feel repressed energy dissipating throughout gut. Occasional heart pang. Up through head. Bowels untwisting. Dissipating.

Visualizing black vapors rising in my mind's eye as I feel energy dissipate. Has happened multiple times.

Next back left side of head loosening. Feels like brain region.

•

Brain untwisting. Head wanted to spin big time. Didn't want Ivy to see so went to room. Started twisting head. Not right. Not working. Try putting head down to let energy out top of neck. Realize it needs to come through Crown. Go to living room. Triggered by Ivy texting. Realize it. Sit down. Got to try to release energy. Chakras align but looking at TV to not be weird. Flashing light in eyes. Know Chakras aligned. Not right though. Realizing I need to look straight. But don't want to be weird. Look straight. It's clearly right with intuition. Clearly need to stay here until energy releases. Don't want to be weird. Look forward. See Third Eye while looking at wall. OCD voice comes in – "you need to finish this before looking up or you'll never activate." Slightly freak out – final *pole* test *parallel*. Look at wall. Energy release. Third Eye clearer. Third Eye in vision. Was release not completing task. No more tasks. That's always

Or I?

OCD. Third Eye blinking in acknowledgement of this whole thing right now. See the Eye clearly in my actual vision. Somewhat overlayed.

LESSON HERE IS JUST SIT IT OUT. YOU CAN ALWAYS DO IT LATER TOO. JUST HAVE TO SIT WITH WORSE ENERGY THEN.

•

10 PM – Watching "New Girl" *with Ivy* feeling something hard. Boredom? Want to do something else? Idk.

•

This whole thing is the process of becoming fully me. Of course I don't really want attachment issues. Right now I'm figuring out what I feel about things. It had only been clear around people who I knew and weren't threatened by in any way.

Feel my face literally falling into place. It wasn't my real face. This is helping Crown Chakra release more than anything. My tension was keeping it stuck.

•

Everything much better with relaxed face. That had been blocking my Crown Chakra for all these years keeping my anxiety, sadness and all other bad emotions from leaving and keeping love and other things from coming in. Making your face your own is key in everything. I'VE LITERALLY BEEN WEARING A MASK. 10:29.

•

EVERYTHING NEEDS TO BE IN LINE TO RELEASE ENERGY PROPERLY. 10:31.

Facial expression needs to align with emotion at hand or energy release isn't possible. Facial muscles very important.

•

This whole thing has been one big long computer reset with everything slowly coming back online.

•

Entire body only wants to follow very specific lines. There are very clear tracks where my body wants to go. I'm in control but *going* where *the Universe* doesn't want to is like walking through loose quicksand or something I can't describe.

•

People who are themselves or close to it are enlightened or close to it. This whole process is my consciousness learning from my body both how it feels about things and how to unwind things that don't make sense. The trick is in figuring out which is which.

Empty mind first because then you have a blank canvas to be able to choose thoughts. The thoughts you choose you ride like a wave without thinking until they come to completion.

Thoughts that disappear are best not sought after. It will come back if it's meant to and if not you're resisting change and uncertainty.

•

Starting to think about the second guide – the one that was clearly an authority figure of some sort. The part that had even more or supplemental knowledge. Wondering what that was. And questions about being shown the first path twice. I'd interpreted that as a war of some sort but just like everything else this is likely an analogy. I don't know yet. Wondering if I'm supposed to come back to this. If this is the first step and the boom is the second. Body is not reacting right to that thought. Especially Heart. And Root other Chakra. Shoulders stressed just thinking about it. Do not like the stress. Ugh. First path better right now but I'm thinking while typing so be careful *of* OCD. YEA REALLY NEED TO CONSIDER. BE CAREFUL. 11:09.

ALWAYS BE ON WATCH MAN YOU CAN'T GET COMPLACENT. WAS SMOKING WEED DURING THIS. CONSIDER THINGS. INTUITION. THIRD EYE RECOGNITION.

Or I?

•

This is me releasing my resistance from the Universe which I'd instituted all those years ago. As time goes on and I do more work the "tracks of rightness" *and* the "guiding" is disappearing holy shit just like in the tests. The Higher Self is taking the reins off as it sees me realize more and more. Whoa just saw it blink clearly. Like almost real eyes. Blinking blinking. Blinking every time I close my eyes I see its blue eyes. Wow the Higher Self has my eyes. As I said that my vision is clarifying in REAL TIME. Everything's getting sharper. Wow. Wow. Wooooow. 11:19 on 11/20.

•

YouTube to book. Biggest reach. Stand-alone influence. No publisher. No editor. My own unvarnished message.

•

Water/sleep – Body in homeostasis makes alignment with Source so much easier.

•

As long as you're more free than not, the path you're on is the right one. Spiritual improvement always brings you closer to the ideal line from where you currently are. Meaning the earlier this line begins and the more you practice the more you will achieve the highest ideal possible. This has ubiquitous implications across humanity encompassing every human regardless of age. Even on death's front door, opening the mind to this Universal consciousness will have made life worth living. Because then you will have seen the true essence of the Universe. It was always within you. Of course, the later you achieve this realization, the more you will realize *what* you have lost. And even still, the moment the realization is made, you will still understand and be overwhelmed and overcome with gratitude for this realization.

•

Editing after the fact.

•

Light headed in hot yoga was full release/full alignment.

•

Dancer practice *from yoga* helped.

•

I grew up very privileged but didn't know it because I was mad at my parents. I viewed having to mow the lawn for my allowance a big deal. Granted it took me 3 hours with a push mower, ride mower, and weed whacker because it was a 1.5 acre yard. But still it was a 1.5 acre yard with a swimming pool. And the country club. And the golf lessons. And the private school. And the car. And the clothes. And the shoes. And the trips. And the watches. And the list goes on and on. But this is how your perception gets skewed. You can't see what's right in front of you when you're wrapped up in your own bullshit. Because what you have is the norm. It is your norm. And that's ok. That's not something to feel bad about. But it's something to rise above and appreciate for what it is instead of living in it. And from that elevated vantage point you can then see just how lucky you are if you're in a position of privilege. And then seeing just how low others are by comparison there is no choice but to make a change that will benefit those less fortunate than you. Not for everyone of course, it depends on what your priorities are, but it will no doubt be enough to help balance the scales to some degree. And if that degree is just a fraction of an inch, well then we'll all understand the issue is in something fundamental that will be addressed. For it is known that trauma can often breed success – just look at statistics among high performing individuals – so the demographic most likely to be in need of this work as a percentage of the population are those in high powered roles. This change won't make those people less of who they are or what made them successful – it will make them complete. Those parts of themselves that bred success are still there and strong as ever. But whatever parts were pushed under the rug can now be seen. And often those are the parts you need the most. And the parts you once didn't know you cherished so much. When those come back to you – you will be able to decide exactly what you want to do from that position of power, and with it, or if you ever wanted it at all. Regardless, given your position in society and the assets you control and own, this change will necessarily benefit the world WHILE ALSO making you who you always wanted to be. I don't see a bigger win win anywhere else on the negotiating table.

Or I?

11-21-23

Notes

BEING QUIET
Anxiety around this from sneaking around the house *as a kid*. Noticed when I was going to make a sandwich *just now* how quiet I was being. Thought "this is just me" then realized no this is because of the above.

WAKING PEOPLE UP
Then… I realized this is also why I have a problem waking people up while they're asleep. It's because of that ever present fear of the room down the hall *(parents' room)*.

AI
There's nothing inherently wrong with AI as it's our creation. But it is literally removing ourselves from nature entirely. It represents the singularity even before chips in brains. Ray Kurzweil was right. The singularity is happening during our lifetime. It's just that it's happening without us realizing it as we make the choice to do this. AI is almost completing the process of detaching from intuition entirely. This is not good. Wow bad bad bad cancer on society. People blown any which way with AI. Need to be careful how it's used.

GOLF
Going to play with Dad. Great opportunity here to do constant work. In the car now and realizing just how much he triggers me. Focus on teaching body to let feelings pass *and* to recognize. Noticing feelings of irritation but need to uncover what they actually are. Needs to constantly have his POV validated and everything presented as fact rather than opinion. A fact that is to be agreed with. Because disagreement results in blow up. This is where my irritation comes from *being* stuck in between a rock and a hard place as far as discussion is concerned. Don't feel it's ok to have opinions or be myself because it isn't safe. End up agreeing out of need to maintain security. But end up also agreeing to all the negativity and criticism which is the foundation of his perspective. What's wrong with this. What's stupid about that. Why something was an injustice – like when he missed the turn to the freeway, got really angry, and said the navigation is somehow responsible as a result of poor design or something. Learning to see the ridiculousness for what it is.

FOCUS – From universal experience to universal golf experience. Attuning to everything and visualizing, but only in the golf world and not latching on to any thoughts or sensations just noticing.

PRESSURE – Triggered state from the Buccaneer resurfacing. Showing that's invalid. Score doesn't matter, enjoyment does.

FRONT 9 – Horrible score *but* one of the best rounds of my life despite noticing sad annoyance. Total freedom to try to just do my best without worry. Ahhhhhh. Great drives pure shot just lost balls and not practiced enough.

STARTING BACK – Crushed first drive lost but great shot. Zoned out while hitting approach shot listening to Tibetan bells. Didn't have the yardage but juiced it. Wow. Wow. Just intuition. Could feel the ball wanting to go in the hole on par putt. It did. Losing focus towards end. Too much Adderall. Adderall just made me a little too jacked at some point I could tell. Up until today I would have been absolutely fucking worked after a round like that. Driving home and losing the state. Waffling in and out but attuning to a weird feeling too much. Wondering what this is? Need to let it dissipate like everything else. Ahh black energy vapors.

I can tell this feeling is me trying to ramp up into some other more manic state. I think maybe this feeling is excitement? Or could be just want to be away from Dad. Idk. Tiredness but trying not to be. Just let my face fall to what it actually is and immediate relief in head.

VOICES IN HEAD

DAD – All over the place constantly talking mostly negative sometimes positive really hot takes. Can see a lot of the OCD coming from him. Just constantly talking about completely random shit. It's hard to follow honestly and is taxing in that it seems to require engagement constantly and agreeing with things you don't want to. OCD. Plus Mom's pressure and criticism. It's no wonder.

TESTS

Wasn't supposed to listen to any of those voices? Wasn't that kind of the point? The Higher Self didn't really speak it was more a telepathy. And the other guide didn't speak at all.

FIDO

Or I?

Just connected with him on another level. I could literally tell what he was feeling? Idk. I think I saw some sort of symbol in his eyes, which by the way made his sensations so clear.

CLOTHES

The whole you're sticking with what you originally picked thing definitely played a role.

I can also see the outfits I want to wear in my mind's eye – which I realize I've been able to do for a while.

I can also see what's going to be *trendy* next intuitively. Pay attention to when this urge strikes and see if you can capitalize.

MOOJI

The idea of things outside of your conscious awareness being *impermanent* – by virtue of the fact that you're the only thing still around after all this time – has been revelatory for getting myself back in the right mindset and increasing the scope of my conscious awareness.

TEA

Intuitively knowing the right tea combos at the time.

BRUTUS

Think he played a big role. Got to now kick it with him more while I'm still here.

ATHLETIC GREENS

Fantastic.

SERIES OF IMPORTANT EVENTS

First *Universe* experience – revelations – Ivy talk *to reveal attachment revelations & vision* – I'm crazy crazy – breakdown – Tulip *call saves me* – take my *metaphorical* medicine – family realization *"they're not the problem"* – Source experience – walking around *in state of nirvana* – OCD battle – lose it – meditate in room – lost Source – next day: tell Ivy not crazy – boundary with family next day (Dad – need time) – meditate/chill – next day: chill – tell Auntie *everything* – hang out with Dad in new state – Mom convo on way home – go home – unsure exactly but meditate – crazy energy unwind – complete transformation at exactly 11:11 – unclear what I've done since then. A lifetime and no time at all – revelations abound.

CHAKRAS

GENERAL – I didn't really pay much mind to the idea of Chakras before this. Frankly, I was even sure what they really were at all. Thinking back now I can't be sure what I thought about them but I was at the very least *uninformed until I "saw" them that day.*

ALIGNMENT – When I saw the Chakras align with their bright lights I could feel the corresponding locations in my body.

11-22-23

IYKYK

Why does the brain want the attachment? Is it just habit and habituation? Detachment is such a better state. You can feel your pure emotions. Once the brain sees it – or I guess the conscious awareness sees this state – it doesn't want to let it go, but just like cigarettes, *the brain* has a mind of its own... it doesn't want to let go of control. Wow the Suit has been controlling me this whole time. Unbelievable. The Suit has its own intelligence. It's fighting back against its loss of control. But at the same time it's acquiescing as the brain realizes the benefit – a la ATOMIC HABITS framework. Very interesting. But when we're working together at the same time everything is so much better. I control awareness, you control computing. I control level of focus, you control execution. Phenomenal. I love you. I love you. I love you. I love you. I love you. I love you all. I love everything and everyone.

•

Flawed Perception
(From The Introduction)

We all come from the same thing. We all are the same thing. Atoms. Stardust. Mystery. Magic. All of it. The creation. The destruction. The murder. The mayhem. The funerals. The births. The deaths. The worst. How can we live this way. What is it all for? It's for the mind.

...

...

Or I?

. . .

OR

We The Garden

We all come from the same thing. We all are the same thing. Atoms. Stardust. Mystery. Magic. All of it. The creation. The destruction. The murder. The mayhem. The funerals. The births. The deaths. The worst. How can we live this way. What is it all for? It's for the mind.

It's for the body. It's for the spirit to become one. Those who have seen this know. Those who have not will question. Those who will not will never know. But just like any institution there is strength in numbers and the strength for us lies in this this revelation. This realization. This re-birth can't be unseen and will never die. It's the eternal flame lighting the dark. It is the counterbalance to evil. And even the smallest candle can be seen in the darkest room. Only when you snuff out the last flame is the room lost to the dark. I now know so that will never be. One candle's enough to fight all the world's evil.

The room's still dark but we can see the light. Add another and another and soon you forget the room could ever be dark. But just like any great empire, dark's hubris takes hold. When it does, overexpansion is all but guaranteed to catalyze its demise. It's the greed of the whole enterprise – that insatiable need for more more more. Now now now. All. All. All. Mine, Mine. Mine. That undoes the false divine.

What does one do when fate meets its match – when we hide and hide and hide from the path. We see what we want and hate what we see. But all is lost through perception when the gaze is unkempt.

Watered seeds in the garden of our own discontent. From nothing we come into a garden of Eden. But we don't like what we see because we didn't plant it. Saved from nothing and given everything and yet we still complain about our lot. We even let people eat and eliminate our crops. We choose what to water and what to ignore then we look around and wonder why our garden's the only eye sore. We've snuffed out the plants we deemed unfit to patrol as the watchmen we needed deep down in our soul. But misfortune once felt does not necessitate this neglect. Just because you took this garden over once the seeds were already sewn, doesn't give you the right to choose what to disown. So be a good farmer as it's your duty to be. And tend to your Garden like you know's your duty.

•

Notes

LESSONS

Sometimes slow and steady wins the race instead of diving completely in head first – Higher Self slowly directing me less and less as 1st encounter went on.

ST. CHRISTOPHER PENDANT

Wow – The negative energy coming off this thing was something else. I'd picked it out as I felt a draw to it earlier today. I hadn't thought of or touched the thing in years. It had been in a change accumulator bowl of mine. Honestly, nothing was coming in or out of there for eons. But it caught my eye earlier today and it felt significant. I took it out and had the urge to make a necklace out of it. Now that I remember it I can remember how strong the urge was. At this time I thought "yea, cool" but now thinking back on it, it was a dark urge. Cut to tonight as I'm experiencing nirvana while folding clothes. I begin to feel this compulsion to follow my instinct while in a complete meditative trance. Things just felt right and Feng Shui. I was trying to strictly follow the rule that once you put things down they can't be picked back up, but now realize in this very moment that was OCD using the previous realization I'd had about how impactful it was for me to not fret over simple clothing choices so much – another OCD compulsion. During this process I had a strong urge to get rid of certain things that had bad memories associated with it. All of a sudden I felt a strong urge to get rid of that pendant. Even thinking about it now I can feel this feeling in my gut about something being seriously wrong with that thing for me. It's close but a distinctly different feeling from OCD. Deep gut instinct it seems. I threw the pendant in the trash and was going to walk away when I felt the knowing – get it out of here now – immediately it was clear that was the right thing to do. As I'm walking it to the *dumpster* I can feel the evil seeping off of this thing. All at once I understand this thing – at the very least – represents to me the blind pursuit of money and holding it as something that provides value in others. It's empty. It means nothing. So at the least I could just sense the endless depths of emptiness that pendant represented. It's worth noting – by the way – that at first I thought it was the religious association that was the problem. Once I threw it in the dumpster with the rest of the trash I felt immediate relief rush over my body. Fantastic relief. The relief of a virtuous truth. A true virtue.

Walking back I realize that this must apply to the rest of this and all work in my life. It will not be in blind pursuit of money. That is an endless pit of misery and despair. I won't have my last breath be one of regret over the meaninglessness of my pursuits.

OMMMM
Ommmmm while talking works to center mind.

Is it possible to om people into the zone while talking?

COSMIC ENERGY SOURCE
What is this cosmic energy source?
How is it that the lights turned off?
It was controlling the outside world from my mind, right?
It just *leapt* into my body like another energy source. It was supplemental to me.
What was the separate entity?
How can I feel what Fido is feeling when I rub him?
What is this energy that we're constantly dissipating?
Trauma makes energy stuck in body through mask?
Mask blocks Chakras?
Tension builds.
Problems start.
Compounds if not dealt with.
Now real problem.
Spiritual awakening needed at this point.
But from where in the Universe did that come?
How is it always within all of us?

If you are full on consciousness then it is really really directing the show.

•

Hollywood was a trap. It was too easy and too enticing. But got me everything I needed to get a jump start down this road. SO IT WAS ALWAYS PART OF THE JOURNEY. THANK YOU FOR THAT HAHA I LOVE YOU AND THIS SO MUCH. THANK YOU

THANK YOU THANK YOU THANK YOU THANK YOU THANK YOU THANK YOU.

THANK YOU.

•

GOING INTO SHOCK – Are people going into their consciousness *during* this? Where in the consciousness?

HUMANS/ANIMALS – Humans the only animals able to go back to a state of pure consciousness and detachment. All other animals in pure consciousness, but fully nature and nurture. Achieving this state of detachment removes nurture from the equation and allows you to watch it instead. You are able to see the forces in action.

•

PARENTS – Picked Tulip up from the airport. Took her to the house. Bad energy for me here by association regardless. Here for the first time while both Mom & Dad are here. Very intense for me. Focusing on letting the bad energy "melt" away.

MELTING AWAY – This has been a revelatory mental framework for me. When feeling triggered – and this is distinctly different from recognizing a certain "healthy" response from someone, which is something to take on board to determine how you want to act accordingly – the best thing to do is to sit in that discomfort. Notice the feelings. As always, don't latch on to them. This is of fundamental importance. As you observe them, they will start to melt away. This is the negative energy dissipating. This is your body learning that its habituated response is incorrect. And this works because the conscious awareness is diametrically opposed to the sensation. When the body doesn't get the response it wants – reinforcement resulting from focusing on and reacting to the feeling – it starts to realize it is losing control. If you sit in this feeling long enough, the body/mind will change and the conscious awareness eventually benefits from this plasticity over time as these disordered inputs become weaker and weaker without attention. Of course, it's likely that the most deeply ingrained wounds might never fully heal – we all know about scars – but the awareness of this issue and constant diligence will keep this wound from directing the body ever again.

Or I?

THE MONOLITH – Inspired by Mooji – I'm starting to fully appreciate that my conscious awareness is the single monolith. I am the monolith. Everything else is temporary and it only makes sense to view it as such. Every joy, heartache, disappointment, tragedy, win, loss, feeling, sensation, love, hate has never lasted. Everything seems so permanent in the moment. It always feels like things are going to last forever. I was convinced that I was going to love Pokémon cards forever. And video games. And porn. And booze. And girls. And OCD. And my horrible life. I was convinced it was all permanent. But everything is just a stop along the way. Everything but me. So let's watch this movie unfold like the attentive audience member I am. Don't take any of the plotlines too serious and don't be fooled by any misdirection. You don't know how this movie is going to end. So why are you taking everything that happens along the way so seriously. The thing is, you already know the most important thing there is to know about the plot – Everything that's happening is Happening for a Reason. It's all building to something. So there's no need to fret over the things that happen along the way. Enjoy them and exist in a state of awe as you watch the cosmic play unfold around you and realize your place in it. You always did love those movies where everything that happened made perfect sense when you watch it again.

RUNNING – It became clear to me that running absolutely played a role in all of this. The more I got better at running (and obviously this started with biking but running is so much more engrained in the body that I think this might have been a bigger catalyst – but that's pure speculation), the more I was able to look at my discomfort and to live with it in a state of full acceptance. This is exactly what's going on now. The run today was my first since my revelation. And it was the best one I've ever had despite the speed and whatever other metrics I had previously used to define success being lacking. I never felt full after any run other than my best. And that was always somewhat anxiety inducing since I always felt that it was not ok to perform anything other than that (obvious lesson here about expectations and perfectionism). Today I just listened to my body and did what it wanted. Speed was completely variable based on comfort. Sometimes I ran much slower than usual. Sometimes much faster. Sometimes did weird movements to loosen up. Sometimes I walked. What was clear to me here was how much I didn't listen before. I also realize that slowly over the course of the past couple months I started to listen to my body more. This must have been a HUGE step because I never did this before. This somehow relates to Dad and the "you're a hypochondriac thing." And possibly the "your back's not hurt thing." Through all of this I realize I have been pressing too hard a lot of times in an attempt to push things forward faster than they should. To "get it now." But in a lot of cases that are revealing themselves to me now, it is best to build gradually. That's what happened with your muscles. Was far more in touch with my body than ever before. Just like meditating and everything else, your body will find the right pace if you don't resist and let it fall into place. When you have energy left and you know you're not worked, any tension or tightness is energy that's trapped because you're not doing you. Figure out how to release it to get back into the zone of max comfort. Very interesting feelings – I'm watching the feelings more than ever before.

It was clear to me today that someone like David Goggins pushed beyond physical limitations using his mastery of complete conscious awareness to achieve the feats he does. I see how I could do that too, because I've been doing a version of it trashing my body. My new focus is on listening to my body completely in training moments to do what's healthiest for it. I also see how I will be able to use this David Goggins style when I need to. I already have been able to do this before – and now I will be able to do it on the next level.

MILITARY ATTITUDE – Through their intense training I believe many people in the military achieve a version of the state of conscious awareness, but this conscious awareness is trained by the military to be confined to the realm of military acceptability. This is why you come across those military guys who are clearly military in their affect – are able to deal with their emotions and everything. But they're far more robotic. It's this or that they are completely completely repressed. It's both at the same time. Think about the LSD experiments with the hardened military guys. Was this a shadow integration – or what? Look more into this idea.

LIFTING – Today was a day where I really focused on "moving my body through space." Can tell how much more this is going to benefit me.

PHYSICAL ACTIVITY MASTERY – Through all these physical activities I'm beginning to realize that mastery in anything physical is achieving your current full potential in whatever that is. And that in that state you are living in close to a state of *pure* conscious awareness, if not in it, in that realm. Your performance is therefore dependent upon 2 factors. First – your potential which is the engrained *nature* part of the equation. Second – is your mental state. Poor performance beyond the usual standard deviation is almost always the result of a mental issue. These can take hold gradually or all at once. We all know about the baseball players who forget how to throw after once disastrous "yip." We also know of those who always perform beyond what seems possible. Tiger Woods is an example of someone who had the perfect match of maximum potential who reached the state of full conscious awareness around golf. This is what those crazy "drills" were about that his Dad used to do with him. What he's talking about is literally achieving enlightenment in golf. He was able to utilize this skill throughout his life – but the problem is that he never dealt with his trauma. So this skillset was available to him throughout his life – but he also siloed off different parts of his life to be distinct from each other. This is the idea of him living 2 lives. His performance suffered dramatically once the revelation over this infidelity and improprieties came to light, because he lost his attachment to Source to some degree. He had a problem with his mental. There are a thousand examples of people who have the former and are struggling with the latter. The effect of your mental on your performance is obviously dependent upon just how bad it is. Anthony Davis comes to mind. His performance is so variable day to day – this is a reflection of the degree to which his mental state affects his God given skill. I have experienced this in every performance realm of my life. I would buy into the emotions, thoughts, OCD, and bad feelings that would be triggered from past athletic failure. I would become terrified as I was afraid to repeat my greatest shames. To prove to myself that I was the choke I was most afraid to be. And in buying in I made this a self-fulfilling prophecy. The more this happened, the stronger the prophecy became until it became undeniable to me that I was a choke. And I was. But EYE wasn't, my VR Suit just needed to be right and validated in its original programming. Like "melting away" around people – all it takes to deal with this is to sit with the bad feelings and everything else when they come up in the moment and to prove them wrong. I did this playing golf yesterday and it was a revelation. Bad shots, lost balls, bad breaks, missed puts – whatever – all it takes is to show that these things don't bother you. Soon the body realizes it's acting a fool and cuts the shit.

THE BUCCANEER/BREAKING 100 – Think this event primed the OCD. Remember how upset you were. You thought you were such a failure. I remember the feeling so well. And in remembering it yesterday and being aware while playing golf – I realize that this is the exact same feeling I have been experiencing while playing golf in big moments since

– and that feeling spread like a virus to take hold in any big moment that was important to me. This all really reared its ugly head in the biggest way with the 13 on *hole* 8 *(in high school)*. What if I fail. How could I miss this putt. If I lose to this person that would be so embarrassing. All the squash losses. PCC junior qualifying thing. Ping Pong. Everything with Dad – and that's part of a separate issue that contributed. This is why you've played down to so many people. And play up to others. It's so interesting and unbelievable how my lowest golf score never changed no matter how good I got. And how I just couldn't get worse past a certain point. My lowest score was still shot when I was in 7th grade. This is because I would simply never let myself let go of those painful past events.

THE MASK – This has been absolutely life changing and absolutely revelatory and absolutely game changing. I am unable to properly release energy when my face is not reflective of my mental state. As my face has been hiding my true self for as long as I can remember, I have been trapping this energy inside all along. Sometimes you feel really – jammed up (hahahah) – can't figure out why, then think about your face and realize that you are scrunched up or something. When your face becomes "you" again, and matches how you feel inside, everything melts away.

•

Mom

Sad. Just got in the biggest fight yet with Mom. She's made a number of comments *about* my weight. I am sensitive to it right now & it got to me. I'm still trying to figure out exactly why it triggered me so much. I know there's shame around the Adderall. Am I trying to hide that? Partly I'm sure. I'm feeling sadder & sadder. Feeling the pull to blame myself. Remember – Everything Happens for a Reason. This is the part of the program where in the past you'd start blaming yourself for this entire thing. Where did you err? Yes, you were irritable. I could feel my body just on fire with uncomfortable bad energy all night. So much in so many confusing ways that I couldn't decipher it all. Hearing Auntie & Mom gossip was making my body go nuts. Hearing Tulip & Mom do the same about *a party* threw me too. You can see yourself doing this to the max so many times. It's a dark drug that gossip is. Could feel Mom trying to pry. Could see her trying to worm her way in. That irritated me too. Irritates me now. Is that on me. Where does the line start & stop. Ultimately I *got* tired of hearing about my weight & sternly told her something along the lines of "it's my body I can do what I want." I've said a version of this so many times. It's never taken on board. Then we argue. Right now I'm just hearing her say things like "Maybe *My Last Boss* was right" "Back hair" "Pressure" "Well I'm your Mom!" Argg. She said the Mom line again tonight... I told her that's not an excuse to excuse any behavior to me that she wants. I told her that I didn't like this & asked her to stop. This has to be the – IDK – millionth time I've said something like this. Never any change. She said it's not fair to try to control her behavior... ☹ I said basically "this is what a boundary is. You do something, I don't like it. I say that, *and* if *the* behavior continues, I will take a step back." It's as if this goes in one ear & out the other.

I am losing my cool here & there. I'm trying to stay grounded. I really hadn't lost the zone for more than a minute or two before this. Actually longer during golf – but here I lost it.

Keep in mind that a couple days ago I called her to set the table for everything. I had already told her I "saw God" a few days before that. It's not like she was excited about this but she didn't take it too bad. It was just kind of a meh reaction.

But then I called her the other day once I'd made the entirety of the realization regarding the family. I was calling to tell her that I had now understood everything and that I wanted to explain where my problems came from so that she could understand me better. At least that was my intent. The conversation went well so it must have been delivered delicately – because anything but, especially regarding the subject of my issues, is a hair trigger issue for her. There was arguing of a kind but I kept my cool and in touch throughout. So my tone was even. During this conversation I said I understood the move to San Francisco was main cause and that everything precipitated from that. I said I knew no one could have known really at the time but I blamed them for that and then for the fact that no one listened to me about the stomach ache for months which ultimately resulted in the OCD. And then the opinions I formed around them were skewed by that. I basically explained how kids grow up to not like their parents in scientific terms.

But I did say that I wanted to talk to her about some things that bother me and that I'm going to ask her not to do. She took offense to this. It was the "you can't tell me what to do" type defense – "I think it's unfair that you would control my behavior" is closer to what she said. I said, "I'm not trying to control anything, you can do what you want, I'm not asking you to change, but if those things continue I'm going to have to step away. Family is the most important thing to me but I've been putting everyone but myself first up until now. Have done everything you asked. Now I need to put myself first."

Can't remember exactly but there was some agreement about this but then immediate pushback about the idea that she would have to change anything whatsoever. I calmly told her she doesn't have to change but that this is how boundaries work.

The call ended constructively I thought.

But I couldn't anticipate just how much I wouldn't want to see her when she came in town. Did not want to go to meet up with her last night. Was very hesitant to go over there today. I think I kind of knew what was coming, unfortunately. Or maybe I manifested it. It did feel very right to leave, I'll tell you that much, but I was so out of the zone by that point, I don't know.

I am just so immediately annoyed. She's running a company literally from the middle of the kitchen. Waves. I'm irritated already. Am I starting to realize right now that I just can't get over this.

I'm trying so hard to be cool the whole time but I'm just seeing through everything. She is like the worse version of Ivy. I'm sure I'm being an asshole to Mom – I know I am in ways – I can feel it and I hate it. It's a triggered response just like today was. But the difference between Ivy and Mom is that Ivy doesn't deserve to be a stand in, Mom is the one I hold responsible because she's the one who affected me so much.

Who could hear the news that I delivered about having ADHD/OCD and seem so disinterested? Who could hear that news and not be destroyed at the reality they caused their child to face? Who could hear that same child destroyed by the fate of his life just 2 weeks ago – who was trying so hard and struggling harder – who clearly articulated he felt like he was losing everything. Who said he was struggling so so hard. Who was clearly in the battle for his life. Who could hear that same child say they saw God a week later – ecstatic over the realization – and not be overjoyed. Who could hear that same child call you a week later saying that – in fact – it wasn't God but achieving the state of pure

Or I?

consciousness and that he was able to uncover the facts of his entire life through his own investigation – that he solved all his problems – that he was ok with everything that happened – that he just wanted you to know more about who he is to understand him better – who said it's only so that your relationship could be better – who just wants things to be better – how could you listen to this person, your son, see him go through all these things and say that you don't think it's right to be told what to do? How dare you? How dare you tell him that "well I'm your mother!" How dare you *sarcastically* tell him "sorry I gave you so many problems." How dare you tell him "well this is what happened to me" – not to excuse or to take accountability – but like her behavior is a foregone conclusion. How dare you tell that boy that he didn't tell you about the stomach ache. And that you don't remember that. (I felt immediately very gaslit). Who fucking cares, I developed severe OCD due to that neglect. OCD that almost completely ruined my life. That has made my life inexplicably hard. I was like 11 fucking years old. I had this shit from then until now. How dare you take the one over the top thing I said and latched on to it as if it invalidated everything else. Who could hear all of this and have a conversation with their son who says that they are totally cool with everything you've put them through, but just wants some small things to be different moving forward a la cart, and respond by basically telling them no? She is so blind that she will never see.

Yes I was short today but so fucking what.

HOW DARE YOU NOT TAKE ME SERIOUSLY.

And how dare you fucking cry at the end – always the final act of the play – the crying card for sympathy. As if I have wronged you.

Yes I have been an asshole. I have at times, I know. But what kid hasn't.

I told her today that I have lived my entire life for her. I've done everything she's ever wanted and that now it's time for me to live for myself.

I told her she doesn't need to change her behavior but if she doesn't, I will leave.

I said some harsh things – I told her the drinking was so hard because it was just like the OCD all over again – "oh, tough problem, talk to you in a month." "Hey, how's it going!?" "Good, just went sober since we last talked."

It's no wonder I'm so mentally strong. After everything she hits me with this. Fuck her.

Oh no...

I have a problem with everything she says or does. Obviously not everything is a problem, but it's like my body is just on fire around her. Maybe the message to me the night of my final revelation wasn't just about letting Ivy go, but about letting my parents go too. I do remember feeling that intuitively at the time.

Cut To Tonight: I said something over the top – something about her NEVER doing something. Maybe listening to me or something. Obvious mistake. I knew it right away. I apologized for it right away. I owned up about it. But of course this was like whoa whoa whoa – I had crossed the line.

I focused as hard as I possibly could the rest of the time – I was *focusing* before but *now* I really focused on the right thing because I could feel I was losing the whole thing. I also felt horrible for Tulip who was cooking right there in the kitchen with Dad.

I was seeing red. But I was calmer than I ever would have been *before* under the circumstances.

I told her – in plain view of Dad and Tulip – that I don't think I could do Thanksgiving tomorrow. I really don't know if I can. I don't know how I could sit through it and be cool.

I know that Everything Happens for a Reason, but I need to think about what the reason is here with this. Did I just act how I wanted or am I Door Slamming? Was that old me or new me or some combo of both. Was that the light and the dark together? Obviously the warning signs have been there forever – it's not like I'm doing this out of nowhere. I think this has been going on for so long and she's fighting with Dad so much that she doesn't have any sense of how real this is.

Interestingly before all of this I did reveal some of the writing I had done before this *(We The Garden)*. Implicit in there is how you're fucked up when you grow up.

Or I?

As things were really about to blow up and as Mom was claiming that I was doing something or other having to do with me being the problem – I said you know what, I'll prove to you that I wasn't coming at this from a negative place. And I read to her my final realization that I'd had about the family and how important it was to me.

She was teary eyed in a way I can't interpret. Like she couldn't understand.

I closed my laptop, got up, and was like I'm out. A couple more back and forths were had – about what I have no idea.

But I did take a final blow on my way out – I'm not proud of this one and I'm sure she's going to use it to cloud her judgement of the entire scenario. I told her something that hurt a lot but was very effective in helping me stop drinking was when she would say "if you could have seen yourself last night you would have hated what you were seeing." That line cut me so deep. I told her. "You need to take a look in the mirror. And you know, this (above) is something you said to me a couple times, but I think if you could see the way you're coming off you would hate what you're seeing."

And I left as she was in tears.

I know there's a lot I'm leaving out. I'd told her I was going to write a book. She was trying to be supportive.

The gap is just too big between us. I don't see how it can be gapped. I can't accept the sum total of all of this. I think I may be done.

I have felt extreme relief since getting back. I don't know if it's just the meditations I did or what. Obviously will look to the Third Eye/Higher Self for guidance. I'm not sure what's right. I'm starting to question the level of empathy in a real way, which is very scary.

Is Dad avoidant and Mom a narcissist? The thought of that makes my skin crawl. But she just doesn't seem to have much empathy. Is this real though? Remember stories of "I cried so hard" before I had to fire people? But were these just stories?

Think about how much she throws everyone else under the bus in arguments. It's never her fault. No accountability. None whatsoever.

WENT ON A WALK TO CLEAR MY HEAD – Started to feel real detachment.

Remembered how I told her either right before or right after reading my "final aha" – pretty sure after – that I realize my perception was flawed and that I had made false conclusions. That I didn't even feel like the same person, which is why I am cool with everything. Somewhere along the way she said – "it doesn't seem like you're over it." Touché to that, I was upset and am not over it, clearly. I didn't realize until this was all going down.

I told her that I realize that my attachment style was unhealthy and so the way that I looked at relationships was unhealthy. And that what all of this has been about has been trying to go from the not good over here, to the secure here. And that part of that is what will you accept moving forward and what will you not. I said I'd gotten over everything but that doesn't mean I forgot it. And that means that if things don't change then I'll have to roll.

I don't know what she said next – at this point I'm done.

I'm walking back after smoking a joint (which btw my Throat Chakra was like going crazy about afterwards, gagging, everything shit is not good at all) starting to feel real detachment.

I'm remembering how I had to pee before I left so was in the bathroom downstairs. I'm sure they thought the bathroom door shutting was me leaving because I heard them obviously talking about the whole thing upstairs. Curiously I didn't even care. I was having stage fright probably from everything that was going on and I was in there for a while. They were still talking by the time I was done and I didn't stay to listen. I just up and left.

Looking at this now a couple hours later I'm realizing how detached I am. I think about how much Tulip means to me. And I think about Rose too, but the distance between us has taken its toll.

I love Sunflower most of all because of the pureness of the Source within her. But I know that's all going to change too. And that's what I want to change with this. I want to give people the opportunity to see that it's possible to nip this thing in the bud. And to address it in a way that gets you back to you rather than taking you further from it.

Or I?

Walking back I also think about how much I shared with Auntie. How seemingly precise everything has been in its placement. And this was all without any manipulation or anything other than pure instinct on board. Auntie told me she felt the "jolt" – she's definitely hooked. Mom saw Auntie and I cavorting. She was curious what was going on. Was asking about it. I showed Auntie the video of me connected with the sound the night after I really connected *with the Universe*. Gave her the phone and was doing the same things without even looking at it. Hadn't shown anyone else yet. Feel like she's really going to get there knowing all this now. Showed Mom and Tulip what I wrote last night. They were like "uhhh, what?!" Tulip was like, "if you're comfortable, you should blog this or something to get it out there – even under a pseudonym." Shit goes down. Read the "revelation" so enough of it is out there. Mom knows about the "God" thing all along. I won't tell her exactly what happened. I'm not going tomorrow. Auntie's going to spill the beans. There's going to be disbelief & concern. Dad's going to think about golf. He's going to think about the attachment stuff. Mom's not going to know what hit her. Who knows with Tulip & Rose. And it's all going to be real.

This thing's coming out under a pseudonym. I'm not going tomorrow. I'm not going to Christmas. It's over...

THE DOOR SLAM – The state of the Door Slam is a version of the state I'm in right now. But it's different. This state has been earned. The Door Slam state is semi-delusional – and you know it but you don't care. You're riding that wave because you know you need it. This right here is me giving chances time and time again, argument after argument. The more things deteriorate, the clearer I try to become in my articulation. Eventually I realize I need a Psychology degree to get to the bottom of it all. I get that. That doesn't help at all – if anything the sense I get is that a degree like this is wasted potential on someone like me. I go to Hollywood trying to be the big success everyone wants. I'm destroyed. Everyone can see my deterioration. They have to. We always talk about how hard the last – forever has been for me – the advice is always somewhere in the realm of "a better job will do it." I hear try harder. I hear do better. I start to hear what's wrong with you. I heard that again tonight. So I get to the bottom of it. Instead of the revelation I was sure it would be, it lands just as flat and with just as much awkward avoidance as Rose's pregnancy news. When I saw that a big weight was lifted. I do things myself once again, and I come out the other end stronger than ever. I do my absolute best to completely drop it with Dad while being myself. It works. He just wants to have a good time with me. Tulip saves me. I'm forever indebted. I avoid the catastrophic message I would have sent to Rose and it makes us closer than ever. I feel like I gave Auntie everything she needs to know and I can see her starting to fly. I made sure Brutus knows I care. I made sure *Another Friend* knows I'm there. Aston & Gilly are sliding off like water on a duck. I gave *A Girl From High School* all she needs before closing the door at an appropriate time to protect myself. Mom stayed exactly the same, and Ivy showed me to always give people the benefit of the doubt. The story is a circle. I let go and in the process I became myself. I'm excited for what's next. I know I was meant to write this book. I don't know if anyone will ever read it. But I know I had to get it out there for myself. It was immediately clear to me the instant of my ultimate revelation that this was my purpose. But the biggest lesson I took away in all of this on a Universal level, is that there needs to be a reason behind the things you're doing and behind what you want. When I saw myself rich at the end of my series of tests, I kept being asked why I wanted to be rich. Or why I wanted to be any kind of successful I envisioned myself to be.

I could never answer that question. That realization was extremely unsettling because I realized then that I was still always only looking to the destination. And in that moment I realized just how empty I would feel if I got there without something driving that journey. Without a purpose. The beautiful Eye of my Higher Self showed me to look above the horizon. I remember asking my Mom if she was happy now that she got all she ever wanted – her waffling response told me all I ever needed to know. As does the fact that now this pursuit seems to be endless. Once this is gone she will be left with nothing. She invested all of her time and energy into chasing a false God. She never saw that the fruits of her labor was in all that she'd already accomplished. She could stop at any time and know with certainty that she has lived a life of success few women ever have, and that she ascended that ladder at a time when almost no other women ever even tried. But there has never seemed to be an increase in happiness over the course of that time. I, like I suspect she did too, always assumed that once she reached this vaulted position of CEO that she would finally be happy and content. But that wasn't the case. If anything she has become worse. I know she has. I'm sure the realization that there never was any satisfaction in this has been the toughest pill to swallow of them all. But still the chase continues, blindly. Just today she was bragging about being elected to some *Board* or something. I don't even care. It's all so pointless. Money this. Money that. Who remembers any of this even 5 years from now. That doesn't sound like a good 5 year plan.

But in all this she lost a son. One who would have done anything for her. Who tried to be whatever she wanted. Who only realized that none of this is what he wanted at all when he took matters into his own hands. The irony is that all he ever wanted was to figure himself out so he could have the best relationship with his family possible. And that's the truth. That's why he stopped drinking. That's why he was so ashamed of smoking even though he liked it. That's why he hid himself. That's why he killed and buried parts of himself. He let his Mom, and to a lesser degree but still a significant one, *his Dad*, plant, prune, starve, and water his garden. Trust me, they had a lot of other help along the way, but he pretty much just stood by and watched it happen after a while. Instead of seeing what was going on he started looking everywhere else for distraction and eventually looked closest at himself as the one to blame. And he was, but he'd fought so hard for so long before he was strong enough to put up a fight. The beaten boy dog sat watch over his garden and protected it with his life while everyone around him took whatever they wanted from it. He thought it was normal – he was told this was how it was done. But he felt something was wrong and looked around to try to understand how things worked. After that he looked to all the other gardens to better understand his own. Then he looked to the sky with nowhere left to look. And then he saw it all with one drop of rain right in the middle of the head.

The people in his garden began to morph. Good gardeners. Bad gardeners. Thieves. Predators. Prey.

And then he saw that he was no boy and this was no garden at all…

And then he set to making things right.

11-23-23

THINK ABOUT THE LESSONS!!! (1:28am) – After another walk.

Went on another walk. Was feeling really disconnected from Source. Couldn't feel any "tracks" or anything at all. Smoking my final J listening to music feeling pretty loose. Getting caught up in thought, but realizing it and dropping it. Of course all thoughts relate to the family situation at hand. The thoughts are all dark. All damning of the family. All about how this is the same fate as the psychosis potential episode. How it was always fated to be this way regardless of the path I chose. And then I thought about the final realization and the lessons. I kept hearing remember the lessons in my mind's eye. From my intuition. Then I started thinking about the tests and how, yes this has been long and protracted, but that the final conclusion was that family is most important. And that you can't transpose family issues onto issues related to friends – because the bond isn't the same. Wait a second, my intuition was saying remember the lessons though, not remember the tests. Hold up – I did write some lessons down somewhere. Checking because I'm pretty sure the first one was about family above all else… Wow – Here is the first lesson I just found in my notes:

LESSONS
Sometimes slow and steady wins the race instead of diving completely in head first – Higher Self slowly directing me less and less as 1st encounter went on.

Yooooooooo. Wild and crazy kids man. This is insane stuff. I was told to always be watching. I took that initially to mean just OCD, but over the past couple days without realizing it I've come to understand that was with this type of stuff too. I have been seeing way too many coincidences like this. It is absolutely nuts. Everything Happens for a Reason again. Fucking wild.

Yea, Mom and Dad aren't going to take this all so quickly. I'm going to sleep on this though. I need to meditate and further consider. This is a big one. Skipping Thanksgiving does have too much of a nuclear option feel though. Ohhhhh. Holy Shit. This is talking about a slow and steady withdrawal. Don't do the fucking Door Slam. Ok, now you see, this is some insane shit. I'm realizing this stream of consciousness right now. See, that's the thing. It's just like with Ivy. But different obviously because it's family. We'll still be close. In ways closer than ever having gone through the gauntlet. But eventually I detached, as I have now, and then things can move forward as they may. And with the detachment comes the fact that I simply just don't care as much. My final attachment wound is now able to resolve. I've ripped the band aid off & now it's time to sit in the discomfort and watch the black smoke fade away into the Universe to take whatever new shape there is.

Or I?

•

BTW – The "I'm your mother excuse" lamest in the world. The conception of what it means to be a mother is made up. You make it up yourself. And that's based off your Mom or other "idealized" mother figures around you who weren't your Mom. And because they weren't your Mom you have no idea what they actually were like as mothers so that's also false. Either way, if your Mom wasn't a good Mom – which is the main reason you'd choose an idealized one as well – then the conception of what it means to be a Mom to you – either in line with how your mother acted, or diametrically opposed to it – is fundamentally flawed and you're directly passing a whisper down the lane version of those flawed dynamics down the line to the child. But "I'm your mother" just means – but I'm your Mom and this is how I want to act. Because I make up the rules. I fucking hate that excuse more than anything.

•

(The Next Morning)

BRUTUS – Just saw Brutus. He told me everything I need to know. It's funny because this whole time I've been educating him on the science but in talking to him it's clear he's the one who has expertise in this realm. He literally was the one with the messages right now. "Be careful which voices you listen to – listen to the right ones." Be careful who you tell. Your intuition will guide you. Figure out when your spiritual energy is drained. Protect it. Ego is going to be going crazy right now. Balancing act between Ego and spirit. When spiritual energy is drained, Ego comes out. He told me to meditate on this. I'm doing that now.

Ego is me things. Ego came out last night. Remember you're fine with everything now. The final lesson – don't Door Slam, let go. Family is most important thing. Not going to Door Slam, but have disconnected from Mom and – to a lesser degree because attachment issues weren't as deep – with Dad (and really he was just being a completely emotionally unavailable dude). So slamming the door is unnecessary. You're free. Do what you want. Go to dinner. Tell Mom she can do whatever, you won't ask for any more change. I'm not going to abandon the family but the pressure point that is going to have to adjust to make room for me to be able to stay is in protecting my emotional life and feelings from you. This is lost. It doesn't have to be forever, but I have now completely learned that I cannot trust you with my mental. It's only for me now. So say what you want and do what you want and I will do my best not to react. I can't promise that I always won't. It takes two to tango and I've danced well. I'm not dancing anymore. I'm a man and one who's been through Dante's inferno without you. I am strong. I am whole. I am one. I am me. I am my own gardener. You're kicked out of the garden. You've been acting like the dog's master while also making the garden what you believe it should be. But I'm the master and the gardener and I will determine when you're allowed back onto my land.

FAMILY/MOM – She's the person who kept me further from myself so I feel the worst around her.

But where the bow breaks – because something's got to give – is in my emotional connection to you.

Mom/Dad's influence is the thing that I embodied to keep me from myself. So being around them is going to be when I feel the strongest pull from the VR Suit – because it's with its original programmers. At the same time as the VR Suit is responding to the environment created by them in the same way it learned to as a kid – aka being fully triggered – without any change in behavior, they're continuing to feed me that original, flawed code, which reinforces that old self. Unlike Ivy who was receptive to and adjusted her behavior according to our conversation, Mom was not *& has not*. So as Ivy adjusted her behavior and I saw her making an effort, the bad code input stopped coming in. Because of that I was able to work on adjusting the wrong code around her. But with Mom there is no accountability. So that flawed programming is coming in at the same rate as the old programming is leaving the body. It's a never ending cycle. The energy will not ever release. Something's got to give. That is either I completely leave. I completely accept. Or I completely detach and move forward in disconnection. I'm choosing the last option. Where the bow breaks and the pressure releases in a way that allows me to move forward and to normalize with my new perception is if I completely detach and ask for nothing else. She can do what she wants, I won't ask for any change, but this comes at the cost of my emotional availability to you. I don't feel listened to at all and I am one of the most articulate people about emotion I know. It's been the journey of a lifetime to try to figure out "what's wrong with me" because I've always felt like my flaws were the "problem." I now see that I felt that way because accountability was never taken by you or Dad. So in order to stick around it always had to be my fault. I searched and searched and

Or I?

searched for years – and I finally found the answer at the same time as I found the Universe. I always implicitly thought that if I could just come up with the answer that everything would click into place and things would be great. That we'd live in harmony. But I saw that even having the answer makes no difference. So nothing will. I'm not going to abandon my family. This is the same fate as going crazy. Family is so important. But I have let go of Mom and Dad. I will always be their son and will be the best one I am willing and able to be. My last act of kindness is forgiving everything and accepting all without asking for change. Nothing's going to change. Mom and Dad are completely blind. No expectations. No anger. No emotions. Just love and all the rest. But on your own terms.

This situation is the same thing as it's always been. With OCD I'm struggling so hard and losing my mind. I'm responding to something that is so difficult for a young child to understand and the response *to me* is either ignoring, invalidating or some other version of "I don't care" but ALWAYS combined with try harder or do better or you're failing. Here's more pressure, the last thing you need. It seems like a small thing – who cares if she's calling me skinny but I'm sensitive to it. I worked for years to get bigger. I did. But my life is in shambles. I don't have money. I eat PBJ & cereal all day. I'm stressed. I'm anxious. I also stopped eating junk food. The Adderall kept me from eating. I'm learning the truth of all my trauma at the same time. I'm trying to deal with it all. All of this made me lose weight. I'm sensitive to it. But instead of understanding how much I'm going through and that the weight loss may be a reflection of that, I'm made to feel like "ohhh I'm concerned, you have a problem, what's wrong with you, you're not perfect, you're not the exact shape I want." Because the last time I came home and I was fit Mom asked to see my abs and said something like "there's only 4, you don't have a 6 pack." So then I was too big, now I'm too little. OCD – invalidated or ignored and here's more pressure. Body Comments – from everything going on – some good some bad – lots of stress and everything else. And shame. And Mom knows about all of this so instead of being like hey are you ok, it's like ughhh what's wrong with you. It's like are you fucking kidding me? How dare you again. Seeing red as I write this. That's the trauma. VR Suit untrain. No "I." Only "Eye."

WHEN THE DOOR SLAM'S COMING WITH THE PEOPLE YOU'VE HELD ON TO FOR TOO LONG, IT'S TIME TO DETACH. WITH NEW PEOPLE SET BOUNDARIES EARLY SO IT NEVER GETS THERE.

I always thought there were only 2 choices – stay or go – because my belief is that emotional investment on this level should remain the same so long as you're committed. But now I realize there's a third option and that is to stay while going emotionally. I have detached from needing the approval of my parents in theory. Now I need to put this *into* practice. This is what I needed to do all along.

THANK YOU THANK YOU THANK YOU.

(As an aside, yesterday was the first time you tried to live around the parents without meditation music. Tried to take the training wheels off too quick. Wasn't ready to exist in this world on my own yet.)

You can't use your experience to extrapolate onto others if your attachment is flawed. Your experience that you're using to support your behavior was not normal so your behavior isn't either. The cycle continues when you blindly follow this path. This is why I always felt like Mom had a completely different image of me from what I have of myself. That's fine but the frustration and resentment sets in when I articulate how different my viewpoint is and she just continues on with her image of me. I am only the way she views me through her flawed perceptive frame – but that's not me just like I know I'm not seeing Ivy *clearly* and I'm not really seeing you. But Mom is far more blind and lost than I ever was and than Ivy is so she will never see this. She is set in stone. The massive control is exerting the control over her environment that she never had as a child. She is in complete control now but it's ruining everything in an equal and opposite way that the chaos did for them. It's just the other side of the coin.

She is not going to change. Abandoning the rest of your family is too big a price to pay for her blindness. I can see, she can't, I'm the one who needs to yield. I could leave, I always can, but I'm just not that kind of a guy. You'll just lose me in person.

Acceptance. No more fighting. Detachment. Love. Bliss.

This is the journey now. Detach and become who you truly are. You can have the life you always wanted. It starts with letting go of the pole. I'm accepting all these feelings. I'm accepting all these truths. I've been ready to let go for a long time. I see it all, feel it all, am not resisting it all, but I'm using it all to inform me that now's the time. I'm letting go and running free. I'm on the road to being me. And I now know that

Or I?

Everything Happens for a Reason. So it's best to let the reins go and enjoy the show. This is all beautiful and it's all here for and happening for me. Pay attention. Look up. Observe. And always be a beginner. Train the VR Suit. And know that everything is out of your control so there's no need to resist. Do what feels right. Differentiate between those false feelings and thoughts that don't have your best interest in mind. Follow your gut. Trust your intuition. See everything, everywhere, all at once. And let the Universe unfold before you. It will take you where you are supposed to go. And if you deviate from the path, you can always find your way back. Today. Right now. Right fucking now could be the beginning. All you have to do is to decide.

I'm calling Mom now to let her know the deal. I accept everything. And I will because while I may get triggered – the true me doesn't care anymore.

I'm sorry. Please forgive me. I love you. I thank you.

OM

•

FEELING IDENTIFICATION
Calling Mom – Getting ready to call Mom and feeling a feeling I can't identify. I don't want to call her at all. It's the feeling of me putting her needs above my own. Or of going back to the mat with someone who's done you so wrong. What is that feeling? It's the same feeling as when I didn't want to come back to the apartment. It's the same feeling as when I was going to ask for something I wanted – going to a friend's house or asking for a toy or something – as a kid knowing I was going to get shut down. It's the fear of having my wants and needs squashed. It's the fear of losing myself further. It's being scared about what's going to happen because I don't know and I'm always expecting the worst. It's the feeling of preparing to be disappointed. It's the anticipation of having to give up a part of myself. Root Chakra. Solar Plexus Chakra. Throat Chakra. Third Eye Chakra. Crown Chakra.

•

Called Mom. Stayed above it. It was more of the same. Stayed cool. Stayed me above the Suit and the Ego. Everything was exactly the same but everything was completely different.

Told her I've accepted. I won't forget the past but I won't ask for anything more. I learned the final lesson. I thought there were only 2 options before. Stay or leave. Because the one thing I couldn't change was the amount I care. But I now realize there is a 3rd option. Stay and detach. I told her I realize that family is the most important thing. That friends are different. That I will never leave the family. I will stay. I told her it takes two to tango and I danced real well. I told her I'm not doing the dance anymore. I told her that as much as this process was about figuring myself out. It was also about figuring out how to make our relationship better because I had always blamed myself. She told me basically the same thing, that yea, my perception is flawed and she's concerned. I told her the point of this is that my perception is flawed but the point is that all of ours is. I told her that I'm trying to unwind nature and nurture. That like all families, the family is the hardest for me because so much of the nurture issues come from that. I told her I don't accept excuses about her past because those are the exact things I'm trying to unravel for myself. I told her a serial killer doesn't get off because of a bad past. You might understand them better but it doesn't excuse the actions. I reminded her I'm not going to ask for anything different. I told her that I've accepted it all. I told her my hurt from articulating everything and never being heard. I told her I went through all of this to fix myself and us. I told her that ultimately my greatest disappointment was in finding the answer to everything all along and then being met with the same apathy that I always had. That this hurt most of all. So I told her that I will be there. I always will. I will always love her. I will never leave and I will do anything for them and the family. That I will be there no matter what she needs. But I also told her that I need to move forward completely as myself. I told her that I have a lot of resentment I didn't know about and to please be patient while I allow it to resolve. I told her that there's no need to be concerned. I reminded her of everything that had happened over the past couple of weeks. That I imagined there might be concern, because I would be concerned, but in hearing that that concern was real, it bothered me even more because it validated what I already suspected, which is that everyone was concerned but no one was saying anything. I reminded her one more time that all of this is *because* I want to be better understood. That I want to communicate better. That none of it is about blame. I told her one last time that I would be there. I told her we are the same sides of the coin, but that I am trying to change my side. I told her that in being so open *throughout* my life and ultimately everything culminating in this was me doing everything I could to provide them with the answers. That it is everything needed to understand me completely. So I said I'd be there, but that I was done trying to bridge the gap. So I'm not asking for change, but I'm not going to be the one to try to make it anymore. So I won't be fighting anymore, and that's because all the fights I had were fighting for positive change. I told her Ivy was my proxy for her and I learned everything about this situation from that. That I'm still learning. I told her I'm here but I'm gone.

And now I'm free. And now I will have the life I always wanted.

Before sometimes I was the lion. Sometimes I was the tiger. Sometimes I was the bear. All the times I was I.

Now I am the lion, the tiger, and the bear.

But above all else, I am EYE.

•

Getting ready for Mom and Dad's Thanksgiving dinner having a ton of realizations. Know time's tight but not thinking about it, everything will work out, I gotta just do me. ~4:15 PM.

Shower – Texted Gilly and Aston back – was about to Door Slam but disconnected and de-prioritized both.

Freely check clock. 4:20.

<u>Start a new day for each entry so everything's broken up and combine documents into one.</u>

4:30. Getting dressed and using everything I've learned. You know by now how important clothes are for me. Visualizing my outfit while in the gym. Think about the tight shirt I love but was always hesitant to wear. Definitely wearing that. What pants? Blue ones perfect. But can't, there's something wrong with them. Contaminated. Figured that out during my clean. Got to wear pearls, those are my protection. Got to be comfortable being just me. Blue pants don't work, ok, be flexible, don't get stuck on one thing. Whatever happens, happens. What pants are good. Oh those pink ones I almost wore with this shirt before. Put them on. They're not exactly what I want but got to be comfortable with whatever. Want to put on one of my belts that really speaks to who I am. Choose the one with all my favorite things. Put it on. Outfit looks worse for it. But hey, this is all the things that make me me. Going to look in the mirror when I realize, wait, this is a lesson too. I don't want to wear this outfit. I don't like when my fits aren't what I want them to be. I want to wear those blue pants. The contamination thought was OCD! There's nothing wrong with those. You don't need the belt. You're not too skinny – these pants actually fit just right now. And you already know who you are deep down. Wear the exact outfit you want and make it what you want. There's no rules about wearing whatever you pick the first time. You were wrong about that. OCD again! Go with the flow. Now going to change into what I want to wear and be exactly me. Time to go to Thanksgiving and have the best one ever. 4:39 PM.

•

Notes

TITLE

Lions and Tigers and Bears – Or I?
Personality Disorders Drugs Hollywood Attachment and Spirituality

•

Author – SINCLAIR

•

(From The Introduction)

I've always been scared to be seen for who I am. That's my attachment style. My personality is what you see on top of that, which is the unknowable combination of the environment I grew up in and my genetic predisposition. It's the neurological phenotype. But I've always wanted more than anything to be known.

This is everything there is to know about me. No one else is at fault for anything in here. See my perception about everything was flawed so I was completely complicit in everything that happened. I created the situation with everyone else.

I'm approaching my biggest fear in writing this. But finally, for once and for all, I'm ready to be loved OR hated. But only so long as I'm being judged while being me.

Or I?

So here I am.

Do your worst…

•

Leaving the gym putting it all together. The beautiful Eye is me. The pearls. The purple. The long eyelashes. No making sense of things beyond things that need making sense over. Images flashing in conscious awareness as confirmation. Let everything unravel. Let it all happen now. Let it unfold. Let's gooooooooooooooo. Ride that wave baby. Listen to the music. See the signs. Stay in the zone. Vibe vibe vibeeeeeeee.

•

AHHHHHHHHHHHHHH. Breathe in and out. Root to Crown. Bright light. 9/11 memorial light in NYC all those years ago comes straight to mind right in this moment. This infinite shaft of light straight into the Universe. Where does it end and how far will it travel before someone sees it out there? Who knows. But everyone here on the ground floor sees it shooting straight to the fucking heavens. But the light is only concerned with itself and satisfying its everything. This unknowable journey has no end just like the light's destination. And also like the shaft – it's clear as day in the night sky, but upon closer inspection, there's no discernible difference separating the two but the light itself. It's then you realize that this light could shine through any of the night. It just happens to be shining here as fate would have it. But the light is available to all the night – it just has to go looking for it…

•

Just realized I called my journal the fucking CODE EDITOR. Hahahah. Wow. Editing the Source code. Unbelievable. Another one of those no way moments.

•

Also earlier today I finished what I had to say with Brutus. Had told him about 11:11. He looks at his phone right when I finish. It's 11:11am…

•

Leaving – Shower mess. Leave it. Actually just put a towel in. Just leave without checking anything. Athletic Greens. Lock door. Think about OCD checking. Kind of smirk. Walk to car. It was so easy to let go. Everything sets in place once again between there and *walk to* car. Drive to Thanksgiving. Whatever happens happens. Tv on? Etc.

•

SHOWER THOUGHTS – Scary recording. Remember from vision. Something big in there. Not ready yet.

•

A Girl From High School called the minute I'm ready to call Mom. Different situations. No realization.

•

In this state as a kid.

•

About alter Ego Higher Self. And potential in kids if secure. Which my Sunflower is. Rose/Fischer broke cycle. Fischer call.

•

CHAKRA ALIGNMENT – found RESONANT FREQUENCY WITH EACH. MY RESONANT FREQUENCY IS THE COMBINED FREQUENCY OF EACH OF THE CHAKRAS. RESONANT FREQUENCY IDENTIFIED THROUGH OMS. INTUITION.

ORCHID.

Chakras aligned 5:20.

Read Yodha *(horoscope app)* when intuition strikes. Right now.

Wow. It's finished. In car outside *Mom & Dad's house*. Remember the orchid. Remember the Chakras meditation flower. No wonder I chose those. It's all connected again and again.

Or I?

Thank you thank you thank you. I'm on the right path thank you.

11-24-23

Thanksgiving Recap
(12:24am)

Just got back and lit all the candles in the living room. Best Thanksgiving we've ever had. Of course I wish Rose, Fischer, and Sunflower were there. I missed them. I'm so glad I went. I'm so grateful for this journey. My life is forever changed. I walked in and dog whispered the dogs into not barking when I got there – which if you knew these dogs and how they react when I come, you'd know how big of a miracle this is. Very quickly after I got there Mom made a point to come downstairs. I gave her the first real hug I've given her in a long time. As long as I can remember. I think the last real hug I gave her was when I got my last job at *Last Company Name*. I'm so grateful, sad, and happy thinking about that. I want to cry. I could but I'm feeling it instead of identifying *with* it. This feeling – this complex feeling containing things I hadn't felt for so long and have longed for so much. Feelings amongst so many others I still need to make sense of whose addition alone has made my life complete. I love Mom so much. Oh. My. God. Thank you for everything. Thank you Universe. Thank you. Thank you. Thank you. I'm Sorry. Please Forgive Me. I Love You. I Thank You. It is now a mere 13 hours since my conversation with Brutus – since his Universal guidance – the guidance I received once I had finished telling him about my journey up until then. The telling of which ended at exactly 11:11. That led me to follow my intuition. That allowed me to realize my detachment was secure. That this was the exact same situation as with Ivy. That with the two of them things *could be* different. Now writing this I realize that I had said earlier that Ivy showed me that things could be a different way than Mom had. That Mom had showed me she would never change. Oh how wrong I was. And oh what the Universe had planned for me again. Everything does Happen for a Reason. Because I could see the gratitude in Mom's eyes. I could see how much she appreciated my efforts, and especially my measured outreach today. I could see that this had all made a difference. And I could see that she cared. It WAS exactly the same as with Ivy. It was exactly the same just harder. It was harder and required more at bats because this is family. Because the system is fully engrained and fundamentally rooted. But we all love each other and we all only want the best for each other. That's how it is in most "normal" families we would call dysfunctional. Of course there are always extenuating circumstances and none of what I said should in any way be taken to excuse any sort of abuse – physical, sexual, emotional – or of any kind. But when we're talking about "normal" likes and dislikes. Of "unfair" treatment and "you should have knowns." In all those "normal" dramas we all encounter with our families – some of which are so severe you're certain in your decision to leave it all behind – what I realize, and I think we all should try to think a little harder about – is the fact that really. REALLY. Everyone just wants to love each other and to know we all care for each other. We want to know if it all goes to hell that we're always there for each other. We want to know that no matter how flawed we are we always have a home to come back to. We want to know that our kids appreciate all we do for them. We want to know that we never intended to disappoint our parents. We want them to know that we're sorry we aren't exactly who they wanted us to be. Because really that's what we all want. We want to be exactly the kids our parents wanted so that we can be loved to the max. And we want to be exactly the parents our kids want us to be so we can be loved to the max. But the problem is that ultimately all of this is out of our control. It's out of our fucking control people. Seriously. We do not control this shit. Try to control something. See what happens. Don't think about a white elephant. What are you thinking about? Don't think about your parents. What are you thinking about? Don't think about the last big fight you had with them. What are you thinking about? Don't think about how it made you feel. What are you thinking about? You're reading the book, but who's controlling who?

The thing is, none of these delusional perspective issues applies in those who are securely attached. Because their perception of what's going on and the role they're playing isn't flawed. They are who they are. They like what they like. And they don't like what they don't. And this applies with people too. So it's not like their relationships aren't as messy as everyone else's – they are. It's just that when they see *a problem* and it bothers them, they don't latch on as the VR Suit follows its improper programming, trying to replicate and either fix or do whatever else *is born of* the flawed dynamic you had with whoever fucked you up worst in relationships. They just leave. Or they stay because it's good. But they're doing it on their terms with clear lenses. Any disordered attachment outside of secure is almost certainly going to result in some of those drunk goggles where the severity of drunken affect is determined by whatever degree your attachment is off. This is also directly correlated to the degree that you're off from the center of yourself. Things have been repressed and things are magnified. And now you're not realizing that a lot of the problems you're having with people are directly the result of your behavior.

But the key thing to remember in all of this is that everyone is doing the best they can. No one is trying to have bad relationships. No one wants to hurt or be hurt by the people closest to them.

That's why attachment theory is so revelatory. It's because it's not a "disorder" to have disordered attachment. This isn't talking about your personality. Or your intentions. Or whether you're a good person or not. Or especially whether you're capable of love or not. In fact, it's the guidebook for how to make all of your relationships better. To navigate difficult conversations better. To even start communicating if you haven't been able to before. To figure out who you are. This is what it did for me.

Because in learning about attachment theory through things like articles, YouTube videos, and even some Instagram posts, you can start to see it clearly in the behavior of those frustrating people in your life. And when you see this, and then you observe how you interact with them, you learn what type of attachment style you have. And this understanding is absolutely revelatory if you look at it through a constructive lens. Understand attachment theory and think about the important people in your life. Categorize them and you'll understand the entire picture of your relationship dynamic. What it did for me as someone who was Insecurely Attached – it allowed me to see the only thing I needed to know to feel comfortable in that relationship dynamic, which was that they cared. It allowed me to see how their difficult upbringing led them to behave as they did. So even when that behavior was unchangeable, my compassion remain intact and I could see through the ghost of triggered emotions from the past to the true prize, which was the love and care we both want for each other. Once you understand your attachment and others', it allows you to show them you care in the way that's best and healthiest for them. And in doing so, you both heal each other, because you prove that it's safe to love. Without this understanding you are stuck in the purgatory that I was in for so long. The purgatory of feeling constantly misunderstood by the people you love and who you think should love you most. Because inherent in disordered attachment is at least some degree of actually creating the unhealthy dynamic yourself without realizing it. And how can you ever get out of a dynamic you're creating without realizing it? You can't.

Thanksgiving progressed with the usual antics but I was looking at everything though a completely different lens. There were those brief moments where the rage came up. There were a couple times when I *saw* myself about to tip the argument over the edge and caught myself. But I always caught myself. And I always let it go today. This happened with *My Parents' Friend*. It happened with Tulip. But ultimately I was just exactly as much of myself as I'm capable of being right now. And it was amazing.

The thing that was absolutely the most helpful today was reminding myself of the VR Suit, and pulling from Brutus' advice that whenever you feel that build up, it's the Ego. I kept remembering my Ego and right as I did it would dissipate. And when that happened, I was able to see everything clearly. I had always been so ready to strike with *My Parents' Friend*. He's one of those guys who repeats the point you just made *back* to you in a way like *he* came up with it. That's something that used to drive me nuts. But today I could see it for what it was. I didn't know what, but I knew it was some sort of shield protecting a part of himself that he'd lost growing up. Or somewhere else along the way. Always when that happened – or any other thing like that that triggered me in conversation – I would usually shut down or I would get to a point where I would lash out. Today, the first time he did it I showed some teeth and bit back. He noticed I could tell. I consciously latched onto that early in the dinner because at this point I wanted to and it felt right. But I clocked the rage as it was building and remembered the VR Suit & the Ego and I immediately became the one in control. From this elevated position within myself I was able to steer this and any conversation into a healthy light. I said the things I wanted to say and how I wanted to say them, but I said them while taking into account how I understood the other person to be operating from *in* the conversation. With this implicit understanding, for the first time in my adult life with people outside the friends I was closest to, I was able to really sit back and enjoy listening and learning in conversations. Almost immediately after switching gears in my conversation with *My Parents' Friend*, he presented some beautiful perspectives in the conversation we were having. It bloomed beautifully. As much time as we'd spent together, tonight, after this, we really engaged with each other in conversation in a way that we never had. And this was on me. He was the same, but I was able to see past the irritation I felt in my body – irritation I now realized had nothing to do with him, and everything to do with me and especially my Ego – and from this detached state, to really respond in the way that I actually wanted to. To be thoughtful in my responses for both myself and for him. And this theme continued through every conversation I had throughout the night. As the night went on the ability to shut my Ego down became quicker and quicker. My ability to stay separate from the VR Suit became much easier. And my whole body began to feel at ease without so much interference. I was feeling calm for the first time in the place that had always made me the most uncomfortable.

There were moments with Dad where I could clearly see the times where the night would have ended in disaster. I now knew how to engage with him in conversation. I could see the light in his eyes when I told him he'd made a great point – which he had – and then would use that as a jumping *off* point to get to the next point. *Before* I always did the "yea but" type responses trying to show off, correct, or one up some point instead of considering what my parents – or anyone associated with them by proxy – said. I didn't realize I was doing that but I do now. This set my Dad off. I now know that he was trying to show me, his son, his knowledge and perspective on the things he knew to be true. He is an extremely smart guy so he makes a lot of great points. They just sometimes get skewed when he looks at certain things that he is usually right about with other people and things through the lens of himself – *when he's involved in the equation.* My Dad is just a dude who was doing dude things to me without realizing they weren't so cool. And sometimes he went off into what I clearly see now as a triggered rage. A rage that I knew how to trigger best. But when I listened to him talk tonight. And when I saw the look in his eyes when I took a different tact in the conversation and told him that I enjoyed what he was saying – everything from the past truly melted away. I see and accept everything. That doesn't mean I forget. But I'm over all that now. I have been for a while. But the feelings weren't. My Dad does so much for us. He cooks every night. He literally went to the Cordon Bleu. We have straight up gourmet meals every night. He drove us to school. He threw the football with me. The baseball. Went to all my games. He loved me. He just took the wrong tact with me. So did my Mom. Because of their pasts. And with your kids you create the perfectly wrong dynamic if your attachment is off. Because their disordered style is born of yours. They're in this twisted dance that only breeds resentment as each can't understand why the other doesn't seem to care when that's all you want most.

I love my Dad. I really do.

My Mom and I didn't talk too much that night. But it was comfortable. And I could see that the future would be bright for us. At the end of the night we sat there together on the couch once everyone had gone. I played some of the songs I had sung and recorded a couple weeks before as my voice started to get back to its former self. In my current state I didn't really show her to see if she thought it was good or not. I mean, of course I was curious, but I really just wanted to share it with her so she could hear her son's voice. I couldn't really decipher her response. Of course she said it was good but there was something else going on there. She is very hard to read but I know there's a lot going on in that world of hers up there. I do know she appreciated it. At the end of the night I gave her what was now the first real hug goodnight I could ever remember giving her. And it felt great. She thanked me for doing the work and for the call earlier today and said she would continue to try to do the same. Truth be told I didn't see any change at all. She still did the same annoying stuff but with a different tone. Obviously that was her way of responding. Yesterday I would have just lost it at some point, I know it. But I kept it together and was polite in my responses and just my kind and the right level of sarcastic when I needed to give her a little eye roll of the mouth. It was banter rather than what I now see had come to be the poisoned arrows I would shoot back before to unintentionally further degrade the relationship. But even in just seeing a change in the tone. And a couple of other little things she did. Like trying to give me a "good" seat at the 6 person table or whatever. Those little things were all I was ever asking for. Showing an attempt at and a desire for change.

So when we were sitting on the couch at the end of the night after listening to my song and she asked if I secretly wanted to be an actor – something I had secretly wanted in the past – I was surprised that I literally laughed, especially when yesterday this is something that would have irritated me to no end. I said no, that's the last thing in the world I want. She asked, what about American Idol – which I now realize was her way of saying she thought *the singing* was good – and I laughed again. No, that's the last thing I want.

It's true. I did want to be an actor and, at one point not too long ago, regretted giving up acting after high school more than anything else because I truly loved it. And I still would love to act. I will. But not like that. Now that kind of empty pursuit of fame held no appeal to me. I had no interest in reading someone else's lines in the unlikely pursuit of money and adoration. These things on their own, without a reason or

Or I?

purpose behind them, could never fill my cup up now. And I also now realize they never could or would have anyway.

Plus, I had just completed the role of a lifetime and now I have no interest in playing anyone but myself.

I felt free in this moment. Both for the clarity on life, and for the freedom from what I knew would have been catastrophic responses not long ago.

About *My Parents' Friend* leaving and the messages there – "You know what to do" "Find a way to differentiate" "When you find that special thing use it" "When you find it and you put your all into it you'll launch off like a rocket ship." I'm looking *at him in* awe seeing the Universe in what he's saying. I'm smiling at what he's saying while also smiling at the Universe for being so clear in its delivery. I need to remember clearly more of what he was saying because there were serious messages in there. There was something that I reacted to in my body, what was it? Because there's some sort of message in that.

I'm realizing all that I was willing to lose just a mere hours ago. And I would never feel what I am feeling now. That irreplaceable, unquenchable, necessary feeling of secure love for my parents. For familial love. For knowing that this will work out and that I will always be there no matter what. That I finally CAN have the life I always wanted.

Mom's tired and I'm ready to leave. We hug goodbye (see above) and I go downstairs to say goodnight to Tulip and Dad.

A neighbor stops by to chat. I notice how interested I am in what she's saying too. I am so grateful this new avenue has opened to the world where I can truly truly engage with people. I am so excited for all the people I am going to meet and all I'm going to learn from them. I don't even care about all the years I had shut myself away because I know I would never be here, talking with her like this without it. When she leaves I say my goodbyes to Tulip and Dad. I hug her. And then I hug him. He doesn't know it but this was the first *real* hug for him for as long as I can remember. The first true one. And they will always be true from now on no matter what.

I'm sorry. Please forgive me. I love you. I thank you.

I was walking to leave and Tulip made sure to say "I love you." "I love you too."

I walk to my car in the dark of night shining the brightest I've ever shone.

In being more detached than ever before, I have never been more securely attached, and I have never felt closer to the most important people around me.

From here I am now free to explore the world and find out what the Universe has in store.

And hopefully to help get even just one more candle closer to being lit.

•

Notes & Texts

Notes

Walking around after getting home. Appreciating so much this change in perspective. I learned so much more just by listening. It's amazing what you hear when you sit in the moment and open your ears. It felt like *My Parents' Friend* was speaking directly about this book. TAKE NOTE – he kept talking about "how can you be a game changer." "How can you push through." He kept asking me the right questions about my path. Through that he helped me clarify my POV on Hollywood and made certain my decision to leave it behind. There's no going back now. Enjoy the weekend and the work begins in earnest on Monday.

Book Structure

Ivy intro all the way through *"psychosis."* Then back in time to catch up. Can do quick jumps chronologically between seminal moments. Then everything afterwards. Then lessons and reflections half of the book? Then maybe some actual journal entries?

How to weave psychology beyond attachment in?

How to clearly weave OCD/ADHD in. Can talk about it in commentary when going in reverse.

Writing structure rules confounded me. Made me feel like I couldn't write and was totally constrained. OCD strengthened by and caused this.

•

(The Next Day)

On Dogs & Door Slams

I've always cared so much about dogs. I've always felt that I could feel what they were feeling in a way. I've noticed this much as the years have gone on – more so because more than a few people have called me a dog whisperer. I'm not saying I have any special talents or anything but I am immediately good with most dogs and just know how they want to be treated. And I also love all dogs. Not like with any attachment or anything other than just a pure care for their well being. And if it's nothing crazy I will go out of my way to help the lost dog in the street even if it's inconvenient for me. Any dog I meet I want to have a good interaction with me, honestly more so than I'm worried about getting enjoyment out of the interaction myself. I just get what they want so why would I do anything but treat them well?

One thing that makes it so easy for me to interact with dogs is that that are so easy to understand psychologically. Applying basic classical conditioning principles to them easily allow you to do what they want from you the most – which is to lead them. I mean literally the idea of classical conditioning was really put to the forefront with Pavlov's experiment on those dogs.

But really what I love most about dogs is that the relationship is a perfect one to satisfy my needs. I care about them fundamentally. I only want what's best for them. I figure out what each one likes. And then I will always do what I can to give them the best life possible. And I always always always know they care. Even if a dog bites me a couple of times or misbehaves badly all the time – I'll always forgive and love and provide as much as possible. But eventually there is just one final bite or one final mess or one final whatever where it's just like you know what, enough.

But, again, I love dogs completely so I'll always forgive and forget. And, I'm working on it, but I used to let pretty much everything slide because the last thing in the world I would ever want to do is to cause you any sort of harm. So, at worst, I'll give you a little "bad dog," and then go clean up the mess without complaint. Then you'll wag your tail, look at me with those eyes, and in a minute or two I'll give you a treat because I feel bad for ever making you feel anything but good.

It's the same way with people for me. I care about all people. Not in a personal way, but I want people to have a good life. I don't want anyone to suffer. I understand people, I can read them well, and I now understand that more often than not I have a pretty good ballpark idea about what you're feeling, because for some reason I'm picking up what you're giving off and I can kind of feel it too. With people I'm closest to, I know if something's wrong when I walk in a room the minute I step in the door. It's that apparent for me. I think this is a big reason that I've always wanted people to feel good and that I've always loved doing nice things for people. Because if I can make them feel good, then it makes me feel good. Literally. And on top of that, and at least of nearly equal importance, I learned on a foundational level that the way to get love is to do what people want you to do and to do that with everything you got. I'm good at following orders.

So with anyone on the street. With any person at a cash register. With any waiter or waitress. With anyone I ever interact with, I want them to have a good time. I want their life to be a little better. I will go out of my way for a stranger if they need it and expect nothing in return. I have changed people's tires in parking lots and when they asked to pay me or take me out to drinks, I tell them, no, pay it forward. I've gotten scammed an embarrassing number of times – while suspecting it was a scam – being unable to resist an in person plea.

One time, I saw a guy doing what I assumed was trying to scam people door to door in the neighborhood. But when he approached me getting out of my car and told me he was selling magazine subscriptions door to door as part of a program to help employ newly released convicts, I threw all apprehension out the window and was immediately unable to say no, even if I'd wanted to. Which, frankly, I could have done without this. But I'm jacked up because this is actually a serious problem and this is a great idea so I'm down.

Or I?

So I "placed an order" for a bunch of magazine subscriptions I would never need. I mean, I did think it was sketchy that the list of available magazines, which were obviously in color, were printed in black and white in a shittily stapled together stack. And definitely sketchier that it was cash only. The "receipt" he gave me was uhhhhh. I don't know it didn't really seem like a receipt. But, hey, it's a great cause and I can overlook some clerical errors. This deserves a chance to iron things out and get up on its feet. Because, without asking any details or for any clarification, obviously this is a new organization that is simply in its infancy and that explains this disorganization. I mean, I've never heard of or seen anything like this before, so...

He left thanking me profusely. I went about my day, get a call a bit later saying he left his stuff at my house. Like all of his stuff. What he left was all his money. Even having just toured the red flag factory, and now seeing in the unzipped shoulder bag a wealth of documents that would certainly provide me clarity. And with a stack of cash along with it. I gladly returned it to him without even considering anything else. So I go out of my way to help him get it back and am feeling great about the overall thing. Maybe I will read "Town & Country – Prairie Edition" after all.

Well the magazine subscriptions never came and not only did he scam me but I helped him get the money back that he had stolen from me and left in my house. Once I realized what happened and I got over the loss of Town & Country in my life, all I could think was, man I let that guy scam me twice.

And honestly, this is just one small example that came to mind immediately that speaks to the greater problem. There have been other things like this. But I'm fine with this because the intent was there. I don't change my attitude about supporting other potential causes just because this deal went south. Thinking about it, I literally did help a lost dog home last week in a the owner's in Mexico, the daughter's at work, and the roommate's not home, I'll figure it out type situation.

The amount that I'll give increases with the closeness of the relationship. So while I love people more than anything, I am afraid to let most people *get* too close because I give too much of myself. Because I have a really hard time saying no. So I keep most people at a distance. But there are a select few people who I really do let in. Like in in. And when I do, I make a commitment to you in my mind that I will be the best friend to you I possibly can and will do anything for you I possibly can. And once

I make this level of a commitment, I intend for that to be for life. And part of how friendships at this level work in my mind is that I will not change the level of care I have for and support I give to you, despite any turbulence that might be going on in the relationship, and any problems I might have with you.

Because I understand you so well and because I care for you so much, I will always see things from your perspective when something upsets me. I will be completely understanding of A LOT of things that most other people would lose their minds over. And the small stuff, I really don't give a shit about, I truly understand. I understand with the big stuff too. Well sometimes I don't, and I'm really hurt, especially for all that I've given. Not that I was ever looking for payback or anything, but I would never do something like that to you. And I've noticed how you're starting to take advantage of this. And I hope you aren't doing this purposefully. And I hope that I'm wrong, but I'm starting to feel like you might be really taking advantage of me. At the very least you're clearly taking me for granted. But what hurts the most is that you don't realize that I see everything that's going on and I am choosing. Choosing. To turn a blind eye. To understand your perspective. To see things your way. To not question when the arguments are turned around on me somehow. To essentially rationalize everything away, so that I can keep caring for you. Because, the thing is, that the longer this has gone on, the more I'm realizing that you don't provide me anything at all. And when that realization hits, and you see all you give, you realize that even though you'll always love this person, you lose nothing without them. But you still hang on. Because you care. But you're starting to see the ugliest truth you ever could see. The one you're most scared might be true and *is* your worst history repeating itself once again – that the people you want to love you the most don't seem to care no matter how much you do for them. But holy shit you don't want this to be true so bad. So you try harder and harder despite the reality you can already see so clearly. This person isn't good for you.

Deep down a burning resentment starts to build. One that I'm not even aware of most of the time except in moments where it shoots up like lightning when I'm reminded of *something* or you continue to hurt me in one of the ways I'm most sensitive to. Still though, I can feel what you're feeling and can't change my care. I worry that if I set some boundaries it might hurt you or change the status quo too much for your level of comfort. I completely understand their POV. So even without them

Or I?

knowing and without saying anything to give them a chance to adjust, I'll secretly sacrifice myself for them just to make them happy.

But one day when even I least expect it, there's just one final straw that breaks the camel's back and all my pent up resentment and everything else comes crashing out. The dog bit me one too many times. And like the dog I will always love you – especially since I once cared for you with all I had – but I now see all the scars and all the ruined furniture and I can't possibly allow any of it to happen one more time. And like a dog I know that I will always love you and care for you no matter how much I might hate you and so I literally can't have you in my life anymore. So all that pent up resentment and rage comes out one random day with one random thing and I am absolutely done. But I still care about you and I don't want to hurt you. I might tell you some real harsh truths you really need to hear – but I think I'm helping you on the way out. I've made up my mind though and there's nothing you can say to stop me. In fact anything you say is going to piss me off. And I will let loose if pushed too far now that the cat's out of the bag. But, like I said, I care about you to my core so I don't want to be mean. After all I know you better than you know yourself – at least the things that would hurt you the most, which are the most important things to protect as a friend of all. So I will be polite and not cut deep in any way that isn't meant constructively. And inside I will be energized but calm and filled with an unyielding resolve and certainty that this is done. See while you might think this is abrupt I've been considering every interaction and every perceived infraction carefully in order to rationalize the mistreatment as a whole. That's how I can get over it and stay close. And care as much as ever. But slowly as the friendship's foundation begins to crumble in my eyes I start to see the sum total of the infractions committed, the ones which I've excused, ignored, or imposed upon myself – and as that happens, the serious resentment builds strong and fast and I begin to mourn the relationship. All of this is happening subconsciously but it becomes apparent to the conscious awareness rapidly. At this point you begin to mourn the relationship. This can last for months as your ability to excuse each subsequent infraction diminishes and what would have once been forgiven is now added to the mound of lifelong infractions – never addressed – and which is now teetering on the edge of relationship destruction. Once it tips it's done and it's shocking how quickly the most caring person in the world can act like you don't exist and never wants to see you again. All because you ignored a couple calls when he needed you again. It doesn't make sense because he put up with so much worse. That really wasn't *that* bad. Something must be going on with him. But I do care. I care too much. And when I try to explain it to people I just sound crazy because I can't possibly explain how these few small things equate to the sum total of using me that I've allowed. And while I know this is selfish and immature, for all the support I felt *I gave* – and was often told *I did* – I expected to not have to *ask* not to be mistreated by my friends. I thought we were in this together and I would never do that to you!! And also the last thing I want to risk is confronting you and you leaving because of it. Because even though I treat everyone I meet with the care and affection I do for all dogs, I have so few close friends and don't want to lose the ones I have. I hate confrontation but one of the things I'm scared most about it is that I know I have a brutality in me that can cut deep. And the worse things have gotten and the lonelier I feel, the more I can feel myself losing control of all the resentment I have repressed for as long as I can remember. So yea, I'm scared of hearing things I don't want to hear in a fight just like everyone else, but deep down what I'm most scared of is losing it on someone close to me like I know I can and doing irreparable damage to a relationship with this force I can't control. And maybe even scarier than that is having people see that side of me which is so diametrically opposed to the kind person everyone "knows" and loves.

The best part about me used to be that I had this brutal part inside of me that would nip any mistreatment in the bud when I'd had enough. I would set the boundary and expect it not to be crossed. I was extremely firm in it. Because I had already let this slide so much already. When I said I'm done, I mean it, and I won't be tested. This allowed me to give openly and freely knowing I could always shut it down. The better I knew you, the longer the leash, and the more bites I would tolerate. But there was always a limit. I never knew what that limit was just like you never know when that next bite's coming. You might put up with a lot of shit on the carpet between the last bite and the next. It might be years. But then, one day, out of nowhere it comes when you least expect it, and even though this time it might have been the smallest bite of all, you just know you have to find the dog – the thing you love most in the world – another home because you just can't trust it anymore.

Of course you're sad, but you'd been bit a bunch of times before so you knew it was possible. You were prepared for it in a way. You didn't realize that all those other bites did take some of the relationship with it each time. You thought you could just ignore the bites and keep moving forward like they didn't happen, but you couldn't. You should have corrected your dog right away, you knew you should have at the time, but *you didn't* because you loved him so much and because you never wanted to hurt him or to risk losing him in any way. Because of how much you loved him and didn't want him to leave you, you are now forced to face the worst fate of all. Abandoning the thing you love the most in the cruelest way – by shutting him out immediately and completely. Because if there's one thing you know most of all, it's that in loving this dog once, you will always love this dog, so no matter what it's done to you, if you are around him, you will never be able to say no.

You're sure in your decision and your resolve is emboldened by all the pain you've endured. In fact, now that the decision has been made, you realize how free you're going to be without something that, especially now in retrospect, has provided you nothing but pain and suffering since that first bad bite while you've done nothing but try to get him to love you more as a result of it.

Good riddance & good bye.

The one interesting thing about me that I've not seen anywhere online is that I've never truly slammed the door. It's always still open because I always still care. It's just a matter of time for me. And whether you make effort to get it back. That matter of time though could be weeks to years. More likely than not, if you don't reach out to me in a meaningful way, then you'll never hear from me again. The most sadistic part of all is that once this is done, you completely lose your place in my mind and I go from complete care, to blank space where you once were. I really don't think about you. This is something that always scared me to death. Because while everyone was praising the good boy, I was worried I was a psychopath because I knew that sometimes I could just eliminate people from my consideration if they'd wronged me enough. And that if I didn't know you well and you pissed me off, you were done immediately forever. This was something I definitely needed to hide. Especially when that part of me confronted the biggest fights and issues I had with my parents and I was at *the end of* my rope. *It* was in those moments where I was truly faced with the decision as to whether I was going to leave because I couldn't take it anymore or whether I was going to change parts of myself to acquiesce to the demands I was at issue with.

Ultimately I acquiesced and parts of me withered into subconscious repression where they bid their time building pressure as they accumulated the impact of each subsequent transgression against them. Until one day, for a brief minute or two, they resurface with the full force of their rage to eliminate anything in their path as these long repressed emotions make a successful, but brief escape from the prison created for them by my subconscious. The more repressed, the greater the rage, until one day, these repressed traits burst through as one, and overpower those traits of yours which usually run the personality show. In essence, the two sets of traits swap places in your conscious mind. So you are now your shadow self as it lives and breathes. This is a power that is all too familiar but that you haven't experienced in years. This is the strength you forgot you'd been missing. And now considering the circumstances, it's perfect to eliminate this person who is so problematic to you from your life. So you harness this force and do just that with what looks like callousness and seems without remorse.

And you cut them off. And you remove them from your life. And it's all so surgical in its approach.

This is the INFJ Door Slam in my experience.

•

Texts & Notes

Texts

2:16 PM – *(Quote Screenshot)* – "Sometimes, when you unclench your hand and let go, you'll realize that you were actually holding on to nothing."

2:16 – Saw *this* the second I realized Whitman *never responded*. Gilly wants me to come to him always. Aston not there when I need most. These people I drag the friendship along. We're not best friends. Relationship with Whitman realest. Aston second. Gilly third. Loki and my relationship is good.

10:29 – The thing about having attachment issues *that* breed disorder, such as depression, anxiety, OCD, or even possibly a split personality – if your traits are repressed so much the thing about that is that really you're more well equipped to achieve a state of enlightenment because you have learned better than anyone else to attune to your emotions *through battling them*.

Or I?

10:31 – But at the same time your challenge is far harder and far greater because in attaching to these negative emotions and these negative thoughts and believing you are them for so long, they are ingrained in you and the ultimate challenge for you will be to learn to separate from them. However, there is still a benefit here once you see for the first time that these things are separate from yourself. You will see them for the beasts that they are, and in seeing those beasts in the magnitude that they affect you the feelings are very clear and when they present themselves you'll know exactly what they are *and* you'll be able to recognize it *and* you'll be able to accept it.

10:32 – At first and for a long time, you will find yourself being lost in these emotions these thoughts and these rituals for sometimes months at a time.

<u>*Notes*</u>
PARENTAL FRUSTRATION – Got a lot of work to do with the parents. Came over day after Thanksgiving, tired from staying up all night and having just gone to hot yoga and got so irritated as Mom and Dad just complained about *nothing*.

•

Find yourself trying not to try and trying not to attach to things. Remember, it's all about allowing. It's all about being curious. It's all about the beginner's mind. When you're in the state everything is interesting and everything past no longer exists.

•

LIONS & TIGERS & BEARS – OR I?
(Book Layout *For The Book I Was Going to Write*)

<u>TOPLINE THEMES</u>

OCD

ATTACHMENT

SPIRITUALITY

PHYSICS/PSYCHOLOGY/SPIRITUALITY CONNECTION

ALL THE WAY IN

Intro
(GYM STATEMENT – WE THE GARDEN – TOPLINE EXPLANATION OF JOURNEY)

Finally Home
(PARK CITY – WE FINALLY MADE IT – FIDO – HOME – ABANDONED – HOLLYWOOD – FINANCE – MONEY – DEPRESSION – DOOR SLAM – *A GIRL FROM HIGH SCHOOL*)

Attachment Mania
(ASTON MANIA – ASTON CONVO – ALL DYNAMICS UNDERSTOOD – PERSONAL PARADIGM SHIFT – PARENTAL COMPASSION – IVY)

INFJ
(HOMELESS – DOG WHISPERER – FEELING FEELINGS – SELF SACRIFICE – DESIRE TO HELP – FRIEND PSYCHOLOGIST – PEOPLE UNDERSTANDING – SCHOOL COMFORT – *HIGH SCHOOL GIRLS* – NBC HR MEETING – DEFENSE OF WHAT'S RIGHT – DOOR SLAM – MOVING – ATTACHMENT WOUNDS – TIMES IN LIFE – FEELING – REASONING – ROOM METAPHOR – WHEN THE RULES CHANGE)

First Encounter – The "Tests"

Ivy Talk & I Saw God

I'm Crazy

THE POISONED WELL

OCD
(ATOMS…. – MOVING – CONCUSSIONS – WRITING – LIPS – STDS – NOSE – HAIR – GAY? – OCD THINGS (2s & 3s) – PRAYING – PARENTS – RITUALS – TESTS & CHECKING – CLEANLINESS – HAIR – ETC.)

Or I?

Golf/Sports
(*GOLF* ("Woody" – PCC junior thing OR The Buccaneer first? – Burlingame – PCC Junior Champ – 13 on 8) – SKIING – CARS – LACROSSE OCD – CONCUSSIONS)

Drinking
(FIRST DRINKS – HIGH SCHOOL – ESCAPE – COLLEGE – *COLLEGE FRIEND'S SUICIDE* – WEED – NYC – UNEMPLOYMENT – COVID – BIG MOMENTS (BIKE *CRASH* OCD) – AIRPORT – RELAPSES – HANGOVERS – DOCTORS – FITNESS – LOSS OF CONTROL – ANXIETY – COMPULSION – SNEAKING – SOBRIETY JOURNEY)

Psychology
(HS PHYSICS – MYSTERIES OF THE UNIVERSE – FASCINATION WITH UNIVERSE – COLLEGE PHYSICS – PSYCHOLOGY RELATION – ABNORMAL PSYCH TEST – CONTINUED EDUCATION – PSYCHOLOGIST – CODE EDITOR)

Relationship Problems
(PARENTS – GIRLS – FRIENDS – MOVE – NO FRIENDS – ALONE – COVID – GILLY – DETROIT – COVID – NAPLES)

Job Problems
(PARALYSIS – PAGE PROGRAM – MOVE – ETC.)

Ivy Details – Flawed Perspective Examined
(NO FEELINGS – FEELING ANXIETY – BUTT HURT – ADMISSION – HANDLING REJECTION – MY POV – BDAY? – PRESENTS – RECONCILIATION – STOP AT THE START – ATTACHMENT DYNAMIC)

TURNING TIDES

Momentum Builds – Multiple Sections
(WEDDING SPEECH – ADDERALL – SPIRITUALITY – SOBRIETY – EXERCISE – CODE EDITOR – SKI AWAKENING – PSYCHOLOGY – SPIRITUALITY – THE POUCH – 11:11 – TAROT – SHOOTING STARS – KIDS – OCD/ADHD DIAGNOSES – PHILLY – *HIGH SCHOOL FRIEND'S DEATH* – STUTZ – *LAST COMPANY NAME JOB* ENDING – STYLE)

BACK FROM WHICH WE CAME

After Phone Call *With Tulip*
(WHAT'S HAPPENING? – REALIZE I'M DEEP IN OCD SPIRAL WHILE ON PHONE WITH TULIP (ASK HER FOR CLARITY) – SNAP OUT OF IT – THINK OF LESSONS – THINK OF LIGHTS – THINK ABOUT ALL OTHER OCD – REALIZE FULL EXTENT OF OCD – MAKE THE CONNECTION TO EVERYTHING – etc.)

State Of Mind
(PURPOSE EPIPHANY – MEDITATE – BODY MOVEMENTS – CHAKRA ALIGNMENT – THIRD EYE CONNECTION – CONNECTION WITH THE UNIVERSE – INTUITION LINE – LOOK AT NOTES – "LET GO" – SHOOTING STARS – READY TO DIE – OCD BATTLE – LOSE STATE – IVY FEAR – IVY RETURN – OLD FEELING – "FAILED TEST" – STRUGGLE WITH LOSS – END UP GRATEFUL – WILL DEDICATE LIFE TO THIS – 2 EPS – MEDITATE – BED – TELL IVY NO PSYCHOTIC BREAK – WRITE – CONTENT – *A FRIEND* – AUNTIE – DAD – MOM…)

Integration
(ACTIVATION SHAKES – CALM/KNOWING – WRITING STOPS – FUZZY – REALIZATIONS ABOUND – WRITING PURPOSE – "OCD TESTS" (IVY/RULES) – DOOR SLAMMING LESSONS – IVY DETACHMENT ONCE AND FOR ALL – LET IT GO – ROOM CLEANSING (NEED TO DO MORE OF) – ORCHIDS – CHAKRA ACTIVATION – EVERYTHING HAPPENS FOR A REASON – BE THE WATCHER – MOOJI – *A FRIEND* – AUNTIE – BRUTUS)

GIVING THANKS

Parents
(IVY PROXY – BOUNDARIES (NEED SPACE) – "FRIENDS" – DAD PROGRESSION – MOM PROBLEMS – BAD HOUSE ENERGY – TULIP GRATITUDE – TULIP PICKUP – EVERYTHING HAPPENS FOR A REASON (WHO AND WHAT WAS SHARED) – COINCIDENCES – CHAKRA PROGRESSION – HIGHER SELF GUIDANCE – HIGHER SELF AWARENESS – MOM FIGHT – CONTEMPLATION – THE LESSONS –

Or I?

DETACHMENT – BRUTUS – MOM PHONE CALL – *A GIRL FROM HIGH SCHOOL)*

SPIRITUALITY TO ME

Misc. Thoughts
*(*UNSHARED REVELATIONS – PSYCHOLOGY/PHYSICS/SPIRITUALITY EXPLAINED – ANY RELEVANT JOURNAL ENTRIES – POEMS – THE POUCH? – WHAT'S HAPPENED SINCE – WHERE I'VE BEEN WRONG – GENERAL OBSERVATIONS – WHAT'S NEXT?*)*

Lions & Tigers & Bears

EPILOGUE

CODE EDITOR 2.0

Or I?

11-25-23 – 12-16-23

...

...

...

12-17-23

1st Writing Post Hospital

<u>Series of Events</u>

Date?

Aston call > sun at Auntie's – chakra alignment with bursts of light/different colors (red, black, bright white) – bright white chakra fully clear – back to house – to beach – yoga on beach – nirvana – was this the same night as *dinner with A Friend*?

•

Date?

Setting everything up at home (random wandering – thinking that's tuning) – going to 7-11 – shining green/red/white lights – think of lottery – back to house – then what?

•

Headstand on roof – following Universe lead – thinking of death – accept – walk on roof – experience with Venus and planets – information about everyone in my life – *warned about* parent deaths – *dinner with A Friend* – no voices afterwards – back to apartment here? – try to get in touch *with planets* again – yoga outside – painful headstands inside – can we do this somewhere else? – weed ok/Adderall ok – jump off balcony – park visions – quest through woods – Betelgeuse – run on MacArthur – meteors – 7/11 (meteor identification – lottery games – act homeless, don't get caught – wandering around looking for rocks – picking up trash – begging for money – meteors get better and better – Mom plane crash *warning* – Mom call – ice – amount of rocks in pockets – testing for meteors (charge) – get a dollar asking for 25 cents – rocks changing – give away rocks – etc.) – go to Lexus – headstands there first – headstands at Jamboree/MBUSA – under bridge headstands on rocks – journey in Back Bay (heron, quicksand, leave pants/phone) – walk of no shame – sit outside apartment – inside – shower/clean/valuable meteors – walk Fido – exorcism – TALK NOW – hospital 1 – phone uber – Hoag…

•

JOURNAL

Wow what a crazy fucking trip this has been. It's going to take a minute to unravel everything. The hallucinations and hazing I went through… I don't even know what to say about that. Certainly what the psychiatrist was saying in the hospital was very reminiscent of a lot of the things I was experiencing, but there were things there that are going to be truly hard to explain away. One of the big ones is the **HERON** and the **HEADSTAND UNDER THE BRIDGE**. Also the fact that **EVERYTHING IS HAPPENING FOR A REASON STILL**. Regardless of what I think, I was supposed to go through all of this. Ultimately I wasn't resisting at all. Yes, I was not resisting the OCD. And yes, I was completely engulfed in the hazing ritual or whatever. Check Insight Timer too because there was a period of time where I did stop meditating. However I was listening to Will Knight on repeat and doing nothing but following and watching. Think of all the painful positions and things I went through. Think of how perfect the dance choreography was. Think about how perfect it was with the glass. Surely what happened at the crystal shop was spiritual. I know it was. The way I was finding those little pieces of glass. The way my phone was directing me. All of that was real. I know it was. And so was the interaction with the planets. I hope to figure out exactly when the OCD stepped in. Sleep deprivation and Adderall definitely fucked shit up. Remember that after you first experienced enlightenment you knew that Adderall wasn't necessary anymore. You just wanted it. It will be helpful to get some non-stimulant ADHD meds. I need them. It's much harder for me to focus without them. But also this is much more necessary training too. It is very strange how everyone seemed to separate *from me* just when this was going on. And strange the change in Brutus' and everyone's closeness to me. They all

Or I?

say it was the drugs. I know I was strung out. But at the same time, I was seeing things for how they were. And there were greater forces at play. Universal forces. But here I am speaking with certainty again when I just spent 3 days in the hospital. The fact of the matter though is that it was all a perfect storm. Completely completely perfect. I'm exactly where I need to be and the only mistake will be to resist.

In thinking about things today I realized that I forgot a lot of what I have come to know meditation to be about. Part of that is that over the past week during whatever the psychotic break was and in all of that, I went full on into the yoga/breathwork type stuff more than anything else. **THE MAIN THING I FORGOT WAS THAT THE POINT IS *TO* PAY ATTENTION TO EVERYTHING EVERYWHERE ALL AT ONCE – BE THE WATCHER. THIS IS WHAT BEING THE WATCHER IS ALL ABOUT.** During the series of events that led me to the hospital, I was watching, but I was also completely following. And ultimately somewhere along the way in there the voices that I was following became more sinister and Betelgeuse-y. But ultimately all of it was my decision. I kept deciding to follow. Because I was proving myself. And prove myself I did. To me more than anyone. Because the shit that I willingly did was fucking unreal. And completely ballsy. And you really stopped giving a fuck during all of that which is the greatest gift of all.

∞

Made in United States
North Haven, CT
20 February 2025